MYTHS, STORIES, AND ORGANIZATIONS

Myths, Stories, and Organizations

Premodern Narratives for Our Times

Edited by
Yiannis Gabriel

OXFORD
UNIVERSITY PRESS

OXFORD

UNIVERSITY PRESS

Great Clarendon Street, Oxford OX2 6DP

Oxford University Press is a department of the University of Oxford.
It furthers the University's objective of excellence in research, scholarship,
and education by publishing worldwide in

Oxford New York

Auckland Bangkok Buenos Aires Cape Town Chennai
Dar es Salaam Delhi Hong Kong Istanbul Karachi Kolkata
Kuala Lumpur Madrid Melbourne Mexico City Mumbai Nairobi
São Paulo Shanghai Taipei Tokyo Toronto

Oxford is a registered trade mark of Oxford University Press
in the UK and in certain other countries

Published in the United States
by Oxford University Press Inc., New York

© Oxford University Press 2004

British Library Cataloguing in Publication Data
Data available

Library of Congress Cataloging in Publication Data
Data available

ISBN 0–19–926447–3 (hbk.)
ISBN 0–19–926448–1 (pbk.)

1 3 5 7 9 10 8 6 4 2

Typeset by Newgen Imaging Systems (P) Ltd., Chennai, India
Printed in Great Britain
on acid-free paper by
T. J. International Ltd., Padstow, Cornwall

Fugitives that we are, renegades fleeing a dry,
three-dimensional logic, why should we care for truth?
[...] We yearn to escape into infinity, into the vertigo
of the imagination. Let us become chimeras, then, and
let us satiate our thirst with the sacramental wine of
fairy-tales and of legends.

M. Karagatsis 1942, The Lost Island
(A fantastic Novella, tr. Mika
Provata)

FOREWORD: A SEMIOTIC READING OF STRONG PLOTS

Barbara Czarniawska

IN his various polemics with Richard Rorty concerning the difference between 'interpretation' and 'use' of texts, Umberto Eco (1990, 1992) suggested that there are two levels of interpretation: *semantic* and *semiotic*. A semantic interpretation is the one that looks for the meaning of the text: 'what does this text say?' A semiotic interpretation is a critical one—it wants to know how it is possible for the text to say what it does (Eco, 1990: 54–5). One could, as Eco does, call the first type of interpretation 'naïve', but this would be to introduce an unnecessary hierarchy; after all, it is often quite enough to figure out what a text says ('Trespassers will be fined') and leave it at that. It is also possible to be suspicious of critical interpretations as running the risk of overinterpretation, that is, seeing things that are not there, or as pre-empting the possibility of enjoying a text as it is. Eco is wary of overinterpretations, but points out that a critical reader, whilst seeking to understand how a text is made, can still enjoy it as text, and perhaps to enjoy it even more.   Whichever way one looks at it, it seems clear that researchers ought to be semiotic readers, and, in the media-dominated societies of today, it would be good if there were more critical readers in general.

But how does one learn to interpret critically? One possibility, says Eco, lies within the text itself. Each text creates, among other characters, its Model Author and its Model Reader. Some texts, according to Eco, explicitly require a semiotic interpretation—a semantic interpretation will simply not suffice. His example is Agatha Christie's (1926/1957) *The Murder of Roger Ackroyd*, where the narrator is the murderer who, after having been revealed, points out to the readers that they should have noticed it if they had read closely enough. So successful was Agatha Christie in her education of semiotic readers, that Pierre Bayard (2000) claimed in his *Who Killed Roger Ackroyd?* that both she and Hercule Poirot were quite mistaken as to the identity of the murderer.

There are also texts in which the Model Reader is a semantic reader, where critical reading is strongly discouraged. Corporate annual reports are such texts. This means that researchers cannot always rely on the text's intentions, and may need help in developing the art of semiotic/critical reading. The collections of texts gathered and edited by Yiannis Gabriel not only offer sheer pleasure to semantic readers, but can also offer an object lesson in critical reading.

But why have the contributors chosen to read closely myths and fairy tales rather than annual reports? Because, I would like to claim, annual reports are informed and inspired by myths and fairy tales, and not the other way around. Myths and fairy tales are retold and reused in popular culture, including the culture of management. What is more, popular culture shapes and influences everyday practices, including practices of organizing.

What is the attraction of the 'strong plots' offered by mythologies, Greek dramas, or folk tales? Those who believe in deep structures have a ready answer—traditional plots rely on archetypes that capture the essence of human psyche and destiny. For those who, like myself, believe in surface connections rather than deep archetypes, plots are strong because they have been institutionalized, repeated through the centuries, and well-rehearsed with different audiences. One should therefore speak of conventional rather than traditional plots, and of dominant rather than strong plots: they are 'strong' in a given time and place. Observe that there are many mythologies and each of them contains many myths, many Greek dramas, and a great many folk tales, of which certain are better remembered in certain times than others. Thus, first, but not most important, traditional plots are used because they belong to a common collective memory, from which they can be retrieved in order to be shared (I am evoking here Avishai Margalit's (2003) distinction between common and shared memory). Second, and most important, they are chosen, among many, on the grounds of our current concerns. Greek mythology has had periods of neglect and periods of concentrated attention, not least in Greece. The myths of Sisyphus and Oedipus, Yiannis Gabriel reminds us, were retrieved and made famous by Camus and Freud not so long ago. Consequently, the choice of the texts that are given a close reading in this book is as telling of the contemporary situation as the interpretations they contain. Third, 'strong plots' that are ubiquitous in popular culture seem to build their strength on the back of their apparent simplicity. But this simplicity is an epiphenomenon of their constant retrieval and reuse: it is popular culture that makes them simple. Going back to the original, as the interpretations in this book do, helps us to recover their initial complexity: why these texts? why now? what can we learn from re-reading them?

References

Bayard, Pierre (2000). *Who Killed Roger Ackroyd? The Mystery Behind the Agatha Christie Mystery.* London: Fourth Estate.

Christie, Agatha (1926/1957). *The Murder of Roger Ackroyd.* London: Fontana.

Eco, Umberto (1990). *The Limits of Interpretation.* Bloomington, IN: Indiana University Press.

—— (1992). *Interpretation and Overinterpretation.* Cambridge: Cambridge University Press.

Margalit, Avishai (2003). *The Ethics of Memory.* Cambridge, MA: Harvard University Press.

PREFACE

T‍HE idea for this book emerged at the 2001 EGOS (European Group of Organizational Studies) Conference in Lyon. The conference, master-minded by Roland Calori, revolved around the theme of 'The Odyssey of Organizing', and I was invited to give the opening plenary. As a lover of the Odyssey, I found this task exhilarating, but also challenging. The world of the Odyssey could not be farther apart from that of organizations. It is a world of heroes and heroines, gods and goddesses, ghosts and dragons; a world created by illiterate poets, with no rules, no regulations, no documents, no offices, and no roles. It is a world with no information storage capacities beyond indi-vidual memories. There are no markets, no cash, and no customers.

And yet, the very distance between our world of organizations and the world of the Odyssey prompted me and an unprecedented number of parti-cipants at the conference to look for similarities and points of contact. Some started thinking of Odysseus as a prototypical modern manager, using sub-terfuge, trickery, and disguise to pursue a goal, downsizing his crew as situ-ations demanded, and displaying a wide array of leadership virtues and vices. Others thought of journeys of discovery and journeys of survival, of suffering, deception, and self-deception. Some reflected on boundaries and transgres-sion. Over the three days of the conference, the Odyssey comfortably installed itself as a text animating our discussions, our disagreements, and our discoveries. The remarkable thing was how many openings the Odyssey, with its heroes and heroines, appeared to create in our engagement with today's organizations, and their dramas and adventures.

It was then that the idea occurred to me of editing a collection of essays, each one of which would use as its starting point a myth, a legend, a story, or a fable, to explore its contemporary relevance to a world of globalization, organizations, and consumerism. Each contributor would start from a short but rich text, a narrative with which they identified deeply, a text which had become part of them. They would then use this narrative as a springboard for an analysis of contemporary social and organizational realities. Such an approach may be criticized as intellectually dilettante. However, I believe that a strong theoretical justification can be provided, suggested by the Odyssey experiment at Lyon—by looking at the contemporary society through the prism of old narratives, certain features of our social reality that we take for granted emerge in sharp relief, while others are found to be embedded in societies across the ages. This seemed at the very least a very promising enter-prise, experimental to be sure, but not altogether new. One immediately thinks of Camus' use of the Sisyphus myth as the starting point for the remythologizing of secular experience without moral absolutes—Sisyphus seemed to epitomize for Camus the predicament of modern people, who must learn to live without hope, yet also without despair. Even more tellingly, one thinks of Freud's dramatic encounter with Oedipus, the narrative that was to provide the foundational myth for psychoanalysis, and one of the defining moments of human self-discovery. Subsequently, Freud was to develop other fundamental insights from his fascination with Narcissus and Moses. Such authors provide a reference point for the central idea of this book.

Numerous colleagues found this to be a worthwhile experiment and offered proposals for chapters, which I narrowed down to a manageable number. I looked for chapters which would offer stimulating but rigorous discussions, avoid esoteric or wild arguments, and would be well-written and accessible to different audiences. I also looked for a reasonable spread of narrative materials, which would draw from different mythological and folkloristic traditions. The first enthusiastic champion of the project was Roland Calori, who promised an irresistible chapter to be co-authored with his son, Paul, on the Japanese story of Rashomon, known from Kurosawa's famous film. Roland's unexpected death in July 2002 not only robbed us of a dear colleague, a brilliant mind, and a truly humane spirit, but also denied this book his much-anticipated contribution. His support and enthusiasm were vital in the early stages of the project which, for me, will always be associated with him.

The texts that have inspired the authors of this collection are varied—some are myths, some are stories, one is a children's tale. The origins of these texts also vary, from the scriptural to the folkloristic, from high art to oral tradition. What all the texts have in common is a distinct and compelling plot, a cast of recognizable characters with an ability to touch us and speak to us through the ages, and, above all, a powerful symbolic aura, one that makes them identifiable landmarks in storytelling tradition. The driving force behind this project was each author's love for their chosen narrative. It is not an exaggeration to say that the book is a true labour of love—that became quite apparent in my discussions with the authors and during the meeting in which we discussed the first drafts of the different contributions, which proved to be one of the most fecund that I have attended. I am confident that the authors' genuine enthusiasm for their text will be communicated to readers of this book and that their insights will prove of lasting and energizing quality.

The book emerges as a quilt of different panels, texts, and textures—each chapter a complete entity in its own right, yet sharing ideas and materials with others. Some of the patterns on the quilt are well-known and have become an intrinsic part of our culture—the eternal search for a paradise on earth, Prometheus and the promise of salvation by technique, and the voyage of Ulysses as a journey of (self-)discovery and (self-)exploration. Others, such as David and the Flying Dutchman, are equally well-known through their representation in immortal artistic masterpieces. Some are less well-known, and I hope that this book will bring them to a wider audience. All of them radiate with multiple meanings, puzzle us, perplex us, and eventually reward us. In these old texts, we recognize many of our experiences, worries, and discoveries. I hope that readers of this book will find something to appreciate in every panel of the tapestry, and yet come away from it with an impression, an argument, an image that is more than the sum of its parts, and a real sense of enlightenment and elation.

Beyond enjoying the inventions of the authors, however, the reader will find a very serious and concerted attempt to analyse our contemporary cultural landscapes of large organizations, imposing technologies, rampant consumption, wide-ranging anxieties, and enduring social problems, through 'readings' of old stories. This is not so unusual. Following the pioneering work of Weick (1979, 1995, 2001), Czarniawska (1997, 1998, 1999), Czarniawska-Joerges and de Montoux (1994), Boje (1994, 1995, 2001), and several contributors to this collection, we now understand very well that narrative and organizing activities, consumption and storytelling activities, and production and poetic activities do not belong to different spheres of human experience. 'Reading' a story is not so fundamentally different from 'reading' a crisis or another organizational situation. Likewise, writing or telling a narrative is not so fundamentally different from resolving a crisis or reorganizing a set of resources. The quest for meaning characterizes organizing, consuming, and producing as well as purely narrative acts. The void of meaning threatens them all.

I am also confident that readers from other disciplines will discover a lot of value in the chapters of this book. Scholars of myths and folklore will discover some fascinating new takes on old texts that turn them into vibrant expressions of contemporary concerns and desires; students in different branches of the social and political sciences will find a model for generating insights into contemporary social and psychological phenomena; humanities scholars will discover a compelling mode of argument building and argument testing. Finally, while the book is not intended for men or women of action (they usually have limited time for reading, although they may like stories), it could be that in its pages they will discover heroines and heroes with whom to identify, diverse ways of resolving crises and overcoming adversity, and some truly far-reaching ideas on how to read the times in order to maximize advantage and reduce loss.

Thanks are due to many people. First and foremost, I want to thank the contributors to this book, who placed their faith in the project, working tirelessly and with imagination and dedication, without a guarantee of publication. I also want to thank those authors whose contributions were not in the end included in the book and hope that their involvement in this project has opened certain paths for research that will be worth pursuing further. David Musson, my commissioning editor, deserves enormous credit for this project, with which he has been involved since the very start. He participated in discussions and meetings with authors, and was always prompt with friendly criticism and sympathetic and intelligent advice. I must also thank Marinda Moolman who patiently collated and prepared the final manuscript. Lastly, I must thank Mika Provata, someone who initially was going to be involved in the project as an author. Mika's work moved in a different and very imaginative direction from this project, but she remained on board, reading all the contributions and offering uniquely helpful feedback to all of us. She was also involved in the editing of the book and her polyglot skills ensured that contributions from no fewer than seven countries were sympathetically and expertly edited. Throughout the different phases of this project, Mika has been an invaluable partner, an astute reader, and a sympathetic critic, and has earned my gratitude as well as the gratitude of all the scholars who participated.

References

Boje, D. M. (1994). 'Organizational storytelling: The struggles of pre-modern, modern and postmodern organizational learning discourses'. *Management Learning*, 25(3): 433–61.

——(1995). 'Stories of the storytelling organization: A postmodern analysis of Disney as "Tamara Land"'. *Academy of Management Review*, 38(4): 997–1035.

——(2001). *Narrative Methods for Organizational and Communication Research*. London: Sage.

Czarniawska, B. (1997). *Narrating the Organization: Dramas of Institutional Identity*. Chicago: University of Chicago Press.

——(1998). *A Narrative Approach in Organizational Studies*. London: Sage.

——(1999). *Writing Management: Organization Theory as a Literary Genre*. Oxford: Oxford University Press.

Czarniawska-Joerges, B., and de Montoux, Guillet, P. (1994). *Good Novels, Better Management: Reading Realities in Fiction*. Reading, CT: Harwood Academic Press.

Weick, K. E. (1979). *The Social Psychology of Organizing*. Reading, MA: Addison-Wesley.

——(1995). *Sensemaking in Organizations*. London: Sage.

——(2001). 'Sensemaking in organizations', in K. E. Weick (ed.), *Making Sense of the Organization*. Oxford: Blackwell.

CONTENTS

III. THE TRAGIC NARRATIVES: POSTMODERNITY AND ITS DISCONTENTS

IV. THE REFLEXIVE NARRATIVES: EMOTION, IDENTITY, AND THE NATURE OF RELATIONS IN ORGANIZATIONS

LIST OF CONTRIBUTORS

Yiannis Gabriel is a Professor in Organizational Theory at Imperial College London. His main research interests are in organizational and psychoanalytic theories, narratives and storytelling, and consumer studies. He is the author of several books including *The Unmanageable Consumer, Organizations in Depth*, and *Storytelling in Organizations*. He has been Editor of the journal *Management Learning* and is Associate Editor of *Human Relations*.

Silvia Gherardi is a Professor of Sociology of Organization at the University of Trento, Italy, where she coordinates the Research Unit on Cognition, Organizational Learning, and Aesthetics (www.soc.unitn.it/rucola). She has a degree in sociology and has been trained in the sociology of organization at the Faculty of Sociology of the University of Exeter (UK). Her theoretical background is in qualitative sociology and organizational symbolism. At present, her research activities focus on gender, and workplace learning and knowing.

Peter Case is Professor of Leadership and Organization Studies, Centre for Leadership Studies, Unversity of Exeter. His academic interests centre on the study of the social and organizational impacts of information and communication technologies. His work has been published in such journals as *Organization, Journal of Management Studies, Management Learning*, and *Culture and Organization*. He is Chairperson of the *Standing Conference on Organizational Symbolism*.

Dimitris J. Kyrtatas is an Associate Professor in Ancient History at the University of Thessaly and Research Fellow at the Research Centre of Greek Society (Academy of Athens). He has a degree in economics (Thessaloniki), a PhD in sociology (Brunel), and carried out postdoctoral research at King's College, London. He is the author of *The Social Structure of the Early Christian Communities* and numerous publications on the social history of the ancient Greek world, and especially on the sociology of early Christianity.

Keith Grint is the Director of Research at the Saïd Business School and a Fellow in Organizational Behaviour, Templeton College, University of Oxford. His books include *The Sociology of Work; The Gender–Technology Relation*, (edited with Ros Gill); *Management: The Machine at Work* (with Steve Woolgar); *Leadership: Classical, Contemporary, and Critical Approaches*, (edited); *Fuzzy Management; The Arts of Leadership*; and *Work and Society*. His most recent book, *Organizational Leadership* (with John Bratton and Debra Nelson), will be published in 2004. He is currently completing a book entitled *D-Day and Leadership*.

Robert French is a writer, Reader in Organization Studies at Bristol Business School (University of the West of England), and independent organizational consultant. He has a BA in German and French (Cambridge) and an MEd (Bristol), and taught in secondary schools for some twenty years. He has co-edited two books, *Rethinking Management Education* (with Chris Grey; Sage 1996) and *Group Relations, Management, and Organization* (with Russ Vince; Oxford University Press 1999), and published in a variety of journals in the field.

Patrick Moore is a Scholar-in-Residence at Sarum College, Salisbury. He was educated at Saint Catharine's College, Cambridge, and received his PhD from the University of Leicester. He has taught in California, Cambridge, and London, and is currently teaching in the graduate programme of the Cambridge Theological Federation. He has been a Guest Fellow at Yale and has a special interest in the relationship between aesthetics and spirituality.

Donncha Kavanagh is a Senior Lecturer in Management at the National University of Ireland, Cork. He has degrees from University College Dublin, the University of Missouri, and Lancaster University. His research interests include the premodern, the history of management thought, eschatology, and the sociology of knowledge and technology. He is currently researching the translation of management technologies into higher education.

Majella O'Leary is a Lecturer in Management at the University of Exeter where she teaches change management and business ethics. Before moving to Exeter in 2002, she lectured in University College Cork for five years. Her research and publications are in the areas of knowledge and knowing in organizations, organizational storytelling and folklore and cynicism, and lies and deception in organizations.

Peter Pelzer has studied economics with an emphasis on planning and organization, and philosophy, in Wuppertal, Germany. He has spent most of his professional life working in and for banks, currently as an independent consultant. He is the author of a book exploring the contribution of postmodern philosophers and aesthetic thinking to organization theory. He is interested in understanding the processes he experiences during his projects beyond the textbook knowledge of organization and management theory.

Yvonne Guerrier is a Professor of Organization Studies and the Head of the School of Business and Social Sciences at Roehampton University of Surrey. Her research mainly focuses on the nature of work within the hospitality and tourism sectors, particularly on the interrelationships between frontline service staff and guests.

Ulrich Gehmann has an educational background in the classics, as well as having studied biology and business administration. He has worked as a manager in the chemical industry and in a worldwide active consultancy company, where he has focused on enterprise restructuring, institutional development, and interministerial cooperation, mostly in the former Soviet Union and Eastern European countries. He is currently leading a research project with focuses on the self-dynamics of social systems.

Diana Winstanley is a Senior Lecturer in Management and Personal Development, and the Deputy Director of the full-time MBA at Imperial College Business School; she has written four books and more than thirty articles on management, many concerned with issues of management succession and development.

Heather Höpfl is a Professor of Organizational Psychology at Essex University. She has held posts in the R&D department of an engineering company, at a convent grammar school, and as the tour manager for a repertory company. Her research is post-structuralist and she has published on aspects of performance, gender, and the body. Recent books include *Casting the Other* (with Barbara Czarniawska) and *Interpreting the Maternal Organisation* (with Monika Kostera). She is the co-editor of *Culture and Organization*, a former Chair of SCOS, and a Fellow of the British Academy of Management.

David Sims is a Professor of Organizational Behaviour, Cass Business School, City University. His research interests are in agenda forming, problem construction, and the relationship between managerial living, thinking, learning, and storying. He has an academic background in operational research and organizational behaviour, and has been a consultant in organizations in the oil, power, computer, publishing, airline, hotel, and engineering industries, as well as in the public sector.

Tony Watson is a sociologist and a Professor of Organizational and Managerial Behaviour at Nottingham Trent University. He is intrigued by the ways in which the personal lives and biographies of organizational actors connect with their organizational (and especially 'strategic management') lives. This theme was present in his ethnography *In Search of Management* (1994 and 2001), plays an important part (along with storytelling) in his *Organising and Managing Work* (2002), and is at the heart of his current research work on smaller organizations and the lives of the people who create and shape them.

Introduction

Yiannis Gabriel

AMONG the many stories I remember telling my children there was one that was guaranteed to generate unparalleled mirth and hilarity. The story from Aesop's fables relates how the frogs, annoyed with the anarchy in which they lived, asked Zeus to give them a king, with an excited frogs'/ children's chorus of 'Give us a king, give us a ruler'. Seeing that they were simple creatures, Zeus dropped a log in the pond where they lived. The frogs were initially impressed by the splash that the log made. They then started climbing on the log but, before long, they were disappointed that the log did nothing—it did not speak, it did not move, it did not rule. So they sent a second deputation to Zeus with a request for a new king, a 'real king' this time. Zeus got impatient with the frogs' nagging and sent them a water-snake; their new leader very soon had eaten up all the frogs (Adapted from Aesop 1998: 53). The sad end of the frogs never diminished the delight earned by their demise.

Later in our family's history, one of the parents unwisely invoked that final and most ridiculous of parental utterances to justify a command—'I am the leader of this house'—whereupon they received the deserved and triumphant children's chorus: 'We don't have a leader in this house, *we are not like those frogs!*'. The laughter has stayed with me ever since, along with the deep impression of the power with which a story that is over twenty-five centuries old can influence the delicate balance of family politics and is able to write itself into a contemporary narrative. Thus Aesop's story becomes part of a family narrative, which itself becomes part of the argument of this introduction.

Stories travel and stories stay. Stories cross boundaries and frontiers, settle in different places, and then migrate to or colonize other places. They resurface in different spaces at different times, preserving their ability to entertain, to enlighten, and to bewitch. It is in this sense that we can reasonably talk of a narrative tradition, a long lineage of storytellers and their narratives, of themes, plots, characters, motives, adventures, and predicaments, which endlessly return in new guises with new twists. This is the tradition that appeared to have reached the end of its life (along with folk songs, proverbs, recipes, herbal remedies, and many other folkloristic entities) as modernity, with its massive narratives with forged concepts, ideas, and theories, seemed to sweep away the delicate arts of storytelling and story listening. And yet, in a curious twist, this is the tradition that has triumphantly re-emerged in our times, as people's thirst for meaning and identity seems to call upon narratives and stories to provide them with what science, in its majestic objectivity, appears singularly unable to do. It is to stories, the ones we invent ourselves and the ones others offer us, that we now routinely turn in order to make sense of different events we experience.

We live surrounded, suffused, and saturated by stories and narratives, some of which we create ourselves in our conversations and in the texts we author. The broadcast and print media function as mass-production manufacturers of stories, having achieved a major logical contrivance, that of fishing for the story even as they proclaim themselves to be tracking down the fact. Advertising, the entertainment and film industries, the whole cultural megastructure feeding consumption and consumerism are assiduous story generators and disseminators. In parallel to them, however, individuals constantly create, test, and live through their own stories. It is through such stories that people seek to make sense of events, personal and social, to turn inchoate, senseless experiences into experiences infused with meaning and significance. It would be fair to say that we are now very sensitive to the narrative webs that surround us and run through us—what Boje (2001) calls an 'antenarrative' space, a space from which a narrative or a story is likely to spring through the act of people who decide to 'take an ante', that is, go in search of the narrative that is looming in this space.

Academics too are now taking a keen interest in stories and narratives.[1] Long tarnished as mere hearsay, opinion, or invention, stories, with all their inaccuracies, exaggerations, omissions, and liberties, are now seen as providing vital clues not into what happened, but what people experience, or even into what they want to believe as having actually happened. Furthermore, academics are becoming increasingly aware of how stories, embedded in a kind of knowledge we now label 'narrative knowledge', frequently provide

---

[1] As often happens, the appropriation of concepts like texts, narratives, and stories by discourses that had previously been oblivious to their existence (such as organization studies and medicine or policy studies) has led to definitional difficulties and debates as to their precise meanings and boundaries. It seems to me that premature definitions tend to destroy possibilities and foreclose exploration. On the other hand, excessive definitional laxness, where 'text', 'narrative', and 'story' are used almost interchangeably, inhibits communication and understanding. For the purposes of clarity, I therefore suggest that stories are particular types of narratives and that narratives are particular types of texts, all of which may feature in discourses. What makes narratives different from other texts is a clear time sequence and what makes stories different from other narratives is plot. Different authors have offered different interesting definitions of stories (see Polkinghorne 1988; Czarniawska 1998, 1999; Boje 2001). If pushed, my own preferred definition is: 'Stories are narratives with plots and characters, generating emotion in narrator and audience, through a poetic elaboration of symbolic material. This material may be a product of fantasy or experience, including an experience of earlier narratives. Story plots entail conflicts, predicaments, trials, and crises, which call for choices, decisions, actions, and interactions, whose actual outcomes are often at odds with the characters' intentions and purposes' (quoted from Gabriel 2000: 239).

guides or recipes for action (Czarniawska-Joerges 1995; Orr 1996; Czarniawska 1997, 1999; Chia 1998; Tsoukas 1998; Weick 2001*b*; Gabriel 2002). Where we imagined that technically qualified people acted on the basis of expert, generalizable, scientific knowledge, we now discover that they often act on hunches based on recognitions of patterns furnished by stories. Researchers have also become aware that stories and narratives do not merely offer accounts of politics, but can also act as political interventions, challenging dominant discourses, subverting them, or questioning them. Stories set agendas, express emotions, and fashion ways of thinking. In these and other ways, they are no longer seen purely as effects of a 'superstructure', mere by-products of core social and political processes, but very much as parts of these core processes (e.g. Mumby 1987; Watson 1994; Gabriel 1995). Similar developments in psychology have led to an appreciation of stories for the ways we construct our identities, revising them and renegotiating them whenever necessary. It is no longer common to view people as having given or fixed identities which then enter the plots of distinct stories; instead the identities are themselves seen as reflexively built on top of core narratives and stories—the search and even the struggle for a story itself becomes part of a person's story (Rappaport 1993; McAdams 1996). In all these ways, as the human sciences are going through the 'linguistic turn', stories have woven themselves conceptually into many contemporary academic discourses, revealing what was previously opaque.

The study of organizations has somewhat belatedly taken an interest in the stories and storytelling that goes on in and about organizations. This is not altogether surprising. Unlike pubs and cafés, dinner tables and chat show studios, organizations do not appear to be natural storytelling milieus. For one reason, people are too busy working, manipulating materials, information, and other people, to allow the delicate, time-consuming processes of storytelling and story listening to take root. Furthermore, at least the official spaces of organizations appear dominated by facts, information, rational explanations, and theories of all kinds, in short texts in which precision, rationality, and literalness hold sway over fantasy, emotion, and poetry. It would seem that the antenarrative spaces in organizations are far less rich than those of other social contexts.

And yet, in the last fifteen years or so, we have become aware that organizations are far from story-free spaces (Boje 1991; Gabriel 1991*a,b*, 2000; Hansen and Kahnweiler 1993; Boyce 1996; Weick 2001*a*). On the one hand, we have realized that there are official organizational stories, stories reproduced in organizational rituals, advertisements, websites, and official publications, which express some of the desirable qualities that at least those managing and leading the organization would wish to see associated with them. These may include narratives of great achievements, of missions successfully accomplished, of crises successfully overcome, of dedicated employees, effective managers, and heroic leaders.

In addition to such narratives, however, and often in direct opposition to them, we have become aware of a wide range of stories existing outside the managed terrains of organization. Many of these stories emerge as people compare notes and trade experiences and tips in quasi-gift relations. There are times when such stories build on official organizational stories, develop them, and qualify them. More often, however, such stories remain stubbornly indifferent to the official stories, or alternatively, explicitly challenge, ridicule, or subvert official organizational texts, celebrate resistance and recalcitrance, castigate injustices and hypocrisies, and extol comradeship and solidarity. Such stories express a wide range of emotions, including anger, bitterness, pride, hope, nostalgia, fear, anxiety, shame, guilt, happiness, and love, and capture powerfully some of the diverse experiences of organizational members, enabling them to make sense of these experiences, and even to endure them when they are hard or brutalizing. They also vent desires (for success, retribution, or mere survival) through fantasies and fictions. Stories like these do not belong to the managed terrains of organization, but they are part of an unmanaged organization, where they may surface from time to time and collide with, avoid, or merge with each other. In this unmanaged organization, desire takes precedence over actuality, emotion over rationality, and fantasy over literal fact (Gabriel 1995).

It now seems curious that these stories went virtually unnoticed for so long in mainstream organizational theory (though not in ethnographic accounts of workplace relations). We are currently witnessing something of a reversal, whereby researchers seem to encounter stories and narratives in almost every organizational nook and cranny, in addition to the official self-presentations of organizations. Numerous diverse aspects of organizational functioning are currently being approached through the prism of storytelling. These include cognitive as well as emotional processes (such as organizational learning, memory, and emotional labour), a wide range of social and political phenomena (such as bullying, whistle-blowing, and resistance), a variety of discursive practices (including the construction of professional expertise and career narratives and the construction of gender and sexuality), as well as numerous managerial and leadership practices (such as strategy and planning, envisioning, and goal setting). It would be fair to say that there is scarcely an area of qualitative organization research in which stories and storytelling have not been used as part of the methodology.

Another important development in the area of organizational storytelling in recent years has been its embracement by management gurus and consultants as a form of strategic intervention in the running and management of organizations. Whether in managing change, overcoming resistances, or disseminating a particular amalgam of corporate values, managers are now encouraged to use storytelling (along with other textual and narrative devices, such as metaphors, mnemonics, images, acronyms, etc.) as a crucial part of their communication arsenal (Denning 2000; Simmons 2002). It has long been recognized that stories can be effective and memorable devices in the management of meaning and motivation for the sake of action. Educators, philosophers, and religious leaders in the past have relied on them to drive home their message and promote the moral education of their followers, due to their memorable and emotional qualities. Good stories 'resonate' in ways that bullet lists, opinions, exhortations, and even theories rarely do.

This 'performative' use of stories has been criticized by management theorists, who argue that in this way they become instruments of emotional manipulation and control. A militant anti-performative way of thinking is currently challenging the knee-jerk adoption of any insightful or original idea by some entrepreneurial management guru and its banalization and prostitution into a managerial gizmo or panacea (Lyotard 1984; Fournier and Grey 2000). This critical discourse is suspicious of attempts to use spin and 'rhetoric' to obfuscate, seduce, and persuade and has made considerable contributions in articulating subtle, discursive forms of social and organizational controls. Militant anti-performativity is critical of any organizational theory, idea, or concept that directly or indirectly (usually via the laptop of a consultant) finds its way into a managerial repertoire of words or actions.

There is undoubted merit in criticizing the corruption of a theory, a method, or an idea in the interest of its convenient 'application'. Yet, as is well-known, bricolage does not make a distinction between proper and corrupt uses, and there is evidence that many managers operate more as bricoleurs than as 'professionals' applying scientific theories (Linstead and Grafton-Small 1990; Weick 2001a; Gabriel 2002). It is certainly vital to expose and criticize applications that are exploitative, deceitful, or dishonest. This, however, should not, in my view, tarnish indiscriminately all performative approaches to stories, that is, all approaches that aim to make use of them in the effective management of organizations. If stories can be used to reduce the numbers of air accidents (e.g. by offering memorable guidelines of what not to do in moments of crisis), increase the efficiency of hospitals or universities enabling them to offer better and cheaper services to their constituents, enhance the morale of a beaten or depressed workforce (without creating false hopes or wishful delusions), improve understanding among different pressurized departments, or even enhance the moral education of managers, this is all to the good, or, at any rate, a valid area of investigation.

Of one thing, however, there can be little doubt—where a crass performativity is allowed to take over, the result tends to be highly contrived and therefore ineffectual stories. This is exactly what happens when preachers or pedagogues create stories with the explicit purpose of instilling a particular moral with no sensitivity to the needs of the narrative or the needs of the people to whom the narratives are addressed—the stories simply fall flat, they fail to captivate, to 'resonate'. In this respect, stories are just like other textual devices, including metaphors, similes, and even theories—they can easily be reduced to slogans, clichés, and platitudes, whereby instead of helping create meaning and understanding, they become black holes into which meaning disappears. Alternatively, such contrived stories spawn counter-stories of deceit, duplicity, or comeuppance. It therefore seems important to me to recognize that many stories have a performative function and it would be unreasonable to exclude managerial or organizational stories from these. What can rightfully be criticized is the banalization of stories in the interest of a purported performative function that never materializes.

Interest in organizational narratives and stories, whether theoretical, practical, or performative, has undoubtedly re-awakened academic attention to folklore and mythology, to say nothing of disciplines like philology, linguistics, and semiotics that have studied plots, characters, symbolism, and other narrative phenomena. Organizations are now regarded as possessing certain folkloristic and even mythological qualities, such as proverbs, recipes, rituals, ceremonies, myths, and legends. Some discussion has been devoted to the issue of whether organizational stories should be approached as myths or, alternatively, as folk tales. Undoubtedly, they possess certain characters, such as heroes, fools, tricksters, and so forth, as well as plot elements, such as accidents, deceptions, mistakes, punishments, coincidences, and conflicts, which can also be found in ancient myths. Some theorists have detected mythological archetypes in organizational stories (Mitroff and Kilman 1976; Allaire and Firsirotu 1984; Schwartz 1985; M. L. Bowles 1989, 1997; Moxnes 1998). Others have argued that organizational stories are more similar to folk tales than to myths. Stories do not have the larger-than-life heroic presence of mythical heroes, nor the sacral qualities of myths. They rarely have the complexities and ambiguities of mythical plots, nor do they resonate at the different emotional level that myths do. By contrast, many organizational stories have the pithy and earthy qualities of folkloristic stories, like those of the Grimm brothers; their characters are the ordinary 'John' or 'Jane' (or 'Prince' and 'Princess') with whom individuals can all readily identify, and their point, whether to entertain or warn, to persuade or to earn sympathy, is a lot more straightforward than that of myths. These theorists prefer to speak of organizational folklore, akin to the folklore of truck drivers, bodybuilders, or computer hackers, rather than organizational mythology (Turner 1986; Gabriel 2000).

However, whether we view organizations as having mythologies or folklore, their study has brought them closer to the narrative tradition, which has inspired the contributions in this book. Some of the authors have chosen mainstream mythological texts with towering heroes, like Prometheus and David, or gods, like Phoebus Apollo and Pallas Athena. Others have drawn inspiration from folkloristic sources, such as the Gaberlunzie girl of Scottish folklore or children's tales, such as the velveteen rabbit. They are all part of the narrative tradition; they are all texts with plots and characters, full of meaning and capable of stirring emotions. In every case, the story cannot be left half-told; it demands to be completed, and when completed, it leaves a mark. Each author must also face the plurality of variants in which these stories exist. This adds to the richness of the interpretations offered and the connections with our times and concerns. Some of the authors have used narrative tradition to illuminate the large tableaux of modernity, its culture and politics, as well as its anxieties and discontents. Others have used the narrative tradition as the vantage point from which to paint miniatures of intimate lives of our times, personal experiences and meanings, and delicate constructions of identity. What every author achieves is a novel and relevant interpretation of his or her chosen narrative, and a new variant of the story, since, as Levi-Strauss has convincingly shown us, interpretations become variants in their own right. Freud's Oedipus and Camus' Sisyphus are now legitimate and inescapable variants of the old texts. I am convinced that readers of this book will follow the authors in discovering new stories in old texts; a new Flying Dutchman, a new Ulysses, and a new Hercules.

In this sense, then, the book is not only inspired by the narrative tradition, but also seeks to make a contribution to this tradition. Inevitably, each author must walk a tightrope between two discourses, the discourse of the storyteller and the discourse of the interpreter, the theorist and the analyst; a difficult but not impossible task. I am especially keen that the book should not be regarded as an enterprise of exporting the narrative tradition to the organizational theory outpost, but as part of a wider circulation of ideas across borders and boundaries. During the early stages of development of the discourse on organizational stories and narratives, much of the traffic of ideas was one-way—organizational theorists drew from a wide range of discourses and traditions, while their own discourses remained relatively bound to those interested in organizations, scholars, managers, and consultants. This is now beginning to change. Some highly inventive theories and ideas on narratives and stories are currently originating in the realm of organizational theory and beginning to be recognized by other discourses and disciplines. One of the purposes of this volume is to introduce some of these ideas to a wider audience, to people who love and study stories and narratives, even if they are not especially interested in their organizational variants. As the chapters that follow suggest, their insights can find extrapolations and applications in wider areas of the social and human sciences and cultural studies. Stories travel and stories stay...

References

Aesop (1998). *The Complete Fables (with an Introduction by Robert Temple)* (O. Temple and R. Temple, trans.). Harmondsworth: Penguin.

Allaire, Y. and Firsirotu, M. E. (1984). 'Theories of organizational culture'. *Organization Studies*, 5(3): 193–226.

Boje, D. M. (1991). 'The storytelling organization: A study of story performance in an office-supply firm'. *Administrative Science Quarterly*, 36: 106–26.
——(2001). *Narrative Methods for Organizational and Communication Research*. London: Sage.
Bowles, M. L. (1997). 'The myth of management: Direction and failure in contemporary organizations'. *Human Relations*, 50: 779–803.
——(1989). 'Myth, meaning and work organization'. *Organization Studies*, 10(3): 405–21.
Boyce, M. E. (1996). 'Organizational story and storytelling: A critical review'. *Journal of Organizational Change Management*, 9(5): 5–26.
Chia, R. (1998). 'From complexity science to complex thinking: Organization as simple location'. *Organization*, 5(3): 341–69.
Czarniawska, B. (1997). *Narrating the Organization: Dramas of Institutional Identity*. Chicago: University of Chicago Press.
——(1998). *A Narrative Approach in Organizational Studies*. London: Sage.
——(1999). *Writing Management: Organization Theory as a Literary Genre*. Oxford: Oxford University Press.
Czarniawska-Joerges, B. (1995). 'Narration or science? Collapsing the division in organization studies'. *Organization*, 2(1): 11–33.
Denning, S. (2000). *The Springboard: How Storytelling Ignites Action in Knowledge-era Organizations*. London: Butterworth-Heinemann.
Fournier, V. and Grey, C. (2000). 'At the critical moment: Conditions and prospects for critical management studies'. *Human Relations*, 53(1): 7–32.
Gabriel, Y. (1991a). 'On organizational stories and myths: Why it is easier to slay a dragon than to kill a myth'. *International Sociology*, 6(4): 427–42.
——(1991b). 'Turning facts into stories and stories into facts: A hermeneutic exploration of organizational folklore'. *Human Relations*, 44(8): 857–75.
——(1995). 'The unmanaged organization: Stories, fantasies and subjectivity'. *Organization Studies*, 16(3): 477–501.
——(2000). *Storytelling in Organizations: Facts, Fictions, Fantasies*. Oxford: Oxford University Press.
——(2002). 'Essai: On paragrammatic uses of organizational theory: A provocation'. *Organization Studies*, 23(1): 133–51.
Hansen, C. D. and Kahnweiler, W. M. (1993). 'Storytelling: An instrument for understanding the dynamics of corporate relationships'. *Human Relations*, 46(12): 1391–409.
Linstead, S. A. and Grafton-Small, R. (1990). 'Organizational bricolage', in B. A. Turner (ed.), *Organizational Symbolism*. Berlin: De Gruyter, pp. 291–309.
Lyotard, J. (1984). *The Postmodern Condition: A Report on Knowledge*. Manchester: Manchester University Press.
McAdams, D. P. (1996). 'Personality, modernity, and the storied self: A contemporary framework for studying persons'. *Psychological Inquiry*, 7: 295–321.
Mitroff, I. I. and Kilman, R. H. (1976). 'On organization stories: An approach to the design and analysis of organizations through myths and stories', in R. H. Kilman, L. R. Pondy, and D. Slevin (eds.), *The Management of Organization Design*. New York: New Holland.
Moxnes, P. (1998). 'Fantasies and fairy tales in groups and organizations: Bion's basic assumptions and the deep roles'. *European Journal of Work and Organizational Psychology*, 7(3): 283–98.

Mumby, D. K. (1987). 'The political function of narrative in organizations'. *Communication Monographs*, 54 (June): 113–27.

Orr, J. E. (1996). *Talking About Machines: An Ethnography of a Modern Job*. Ithaca, NY: ILR Press/Cornell.

Polkinghorne, D. E. (1988). *Narrative Knowing and the Human Sciences*. Albany: State University of New York Press.

Rappaport, J. (1993). 'Narrative studies, personal stories, and identity transformation in the help context'. *Journal of Applied Behavioral Science*, 29: 239–56.

Schwartz, H. S. (1985). 'The usefulness of myth and the myth of usefulness: A dilemma for the applied organizational scientist'. *Journal of Management*, 11(1): 31–42.

Simmons, A. (2002). *The Story Factor: Inspiration, Influence, and Persuasion Through the Art of Storytelling*. London: Perseus.

Tsoukas, H. (1998). 'Forms of knowledge and forms of life in organized contexts', in R. C. H. Chia (ed.), *In the Realm of Organization: Essays for Robert Cooper*. London: Routledge.

Turner, B. A. (1986). 'Sociological aspects of organizational symbolism'. *Organization Studies*, 7(2): 101–15.

Watson, T. J. (1994). *In Search of Management: Culture, Chaos and Control in Managerial Work*. London: Routledge.

Weick, K. E. (2001a). 'Improvisation as a mindset for organizational analysis', in K. E. Weick (ed.), *Making Sense of the Organizations*. Oxford: Blackwell, pp. 284–304.

——(2001b). 'Organizational culture as a source of high reliability', in K. E. Weick (ed.), *Making Sense of the Organizations*. Oxford: Blackwell, pp. 330–4.

I

THE KNOWLEDGE NARRATIVES: EXPERIENCE, LEARNING, AND TRUTH

Introduction

THE high school that I attended together with Dimitris Kyrtatas, another contributor to this book and a childhood friend of mine, regularly invited eminent people to address the school assembly. Many of these people were foreign visitors to Greece who enjoyed this opportunity to try out a story or an idea before a very different kind of audience. Indeed, many of the narratives told by these speakers left me with deep memories, partly because they were culturally quite out of step from the views that I was used to. I distinctly remember an elderly American gentleman spending the best part of an hour discussing in English the meaning of the expression 'Thank you for the experience'. Accustomed as I was to thinking that knowledge came primarily from books, second, from wise people, and third, from extremely profound moments of abstract reflection, I was rather surprised to hear a vindication of knowledge as the product of ordinary, everyday, mundane experience. The Americans, the speaker had sought to argue, believe that all experience is good, since all experience, even unpleasant or hard experience, can be a source of learning and the basis of knowledge. The speaker hardly convinced me, yet his idea stayed with me, like an annoying thorn embedded in my flesh, which from time to time made its presence felt. What I could not bring myself to acknowledge was that experience was a quintessential part of learning and could not be superseded as a source of knowledge by abstract reasoning, reading, or talking. After all, Pythagoras had not discovered his theorem from experience; and even the great Archimedes had not discovered his principle merely by lying in a warm bathtub like thousands of others like him. No; knowledge, I believed, came firmly from a superior type of enterprise, for which the words 'science' and 'philosophy' worked extremely well.

As I reflected on the chapters that make up this anthology, four of them clearly seemed to stem from texts that are instantly recognizable as knowledge narratives, dealing with the nature of truth and its relation to learning and experience. This prompted the periodic resurfacing of that thorny idea, summed up in 'Thank you for the experience'. A line runs through these four chapters, one that at the same time extols experience as a source of knowledge, yet cautions against the possible deceptions and self-deceptions to which our experiences can also lead.

My own chapter (Chapter 1) stems from a certain dissatisfaction with the conceptualizations of stories in current academic writing, that have become rather too comfortable. Starting with a story from Pliny, I try to demonstrate how easily we become seduced by the text, oblivious to its tensions and contradictions. Seduction is of course the enemy of criticism, since the object is imagined as being free from any possible blemish. My argument is that, while to appreciate a story we must become loyal fellow-travellers to the storyteller, as researchers, we must examine the tensions in a story, not only as text but also as a representation of reality. Stories, I argue, can be vehicles of self-enlightenment and emancipation, allowing people to discover a voice and construct an identity. But they can also lapse into hegemonic discourses, becoming instruments of domination and obfuscation. More generally, my chapter addresses what I view as a core discursive clash of our times—the clash between the authority of the expert, based on impersonal generalizations and the claim to objectivity, and the authority of experience, residing in the person who has experienced events at first hand, and can engage with their diverse meanings. I argue for a rapprochement between the two approaches, whereby the expert seriously engages with the voice of experience without raising it above criticism.

Silvia Gherardi's contribution (Chapter 2) was inspired directly by the 2001 EGOS Conference in Lyon, on the Odyssey of Organizing. She draws her inspiration from Dante's radical reinvention of Odysseus as Ulysses, a man whose travels beyond the pillars of Hercules are driven by a passion for knowledge, a passion that is fuelled by the transgressive quality of the enterprise. Knowledge in organizations, argues Gherardi, is all too frequently reduced to its performative impersonation, the instrument for solving problems and gaining competitive advantage. Instead, she tries to vindicate a truly libidinal variant of knowledge, one that is fuelled by desire to find out about what is forbidden and out of bounds. And this includes a knowledge of inner as well as outer worlds.

Her argument must surely find eloquent illustrations not only in the activities of whistle-blowers, researchers, and others who seek to discover the ugly and secret side of organizations, but also those entrepreneurs and innovators who deliberately pursue paths that are counter-intuitive or even strewn with the skeletons of those who tried them in the past. It must also resonate with academics who sometimes see themselves as fuelled by an intellectual curiosity to pursue avenues of study that seem taboo or forbidden, and who delight in stirring up occasional storms in the tranquil seas of normal science (Kuhn 1970). Gherardi's argument recalls Freud's identification of an epistemological drive, a child's thirst for knowledge arising from an interest in things sexual, such as the anatomical distinction of the sexes or the origin of children, things that are out of bounds and yet endlessly fascinating (Freud 1905/1977, 1908/1977, 1926/1977). Where Gherardi's argument seeks to go beyond Freud's is in her insistence that the knowledge that is fuelled by passion involves experience of actually venturing beyond those Pillars of Hercules, rather than merely finding out about them through books or hearsay. Thus knowledge is intertwined with experience in two distinct ways—first, as a scientific mastery that seeks out experience in Odyssey-like adventures that are both transgressive and libidinally engrossing; and second, as a narrative knowledge, a stock of stories and narratives, that results from such experiences. Without a trace of irony, one can envisage Ulysses' brine-covered crew turning to him and saying 'Thank you for the experience'—how many managers could claim the same compliment?

An old Buddhist tale of the blind people and the elephant from the *Pali Canon* is Peter Case's (Chapter 3) point of departure for a journey that brings together two fields of experience in his own life, which had earlier stayed separate—as a scholar of organizations and as a practising Buddhist. The story of the blind people, who cannot get a full understanding of an elephant because they each touch a different part of it, has been used before by eminent theorists of organization as an allegory for the multifaceted nature of organizations and for the difficulties, if not the impossibility, of ever arriving at an integrated understanding of them. Case's skilful retelling of the story offers a remarkable reinterpretation of its message, leaving us with a sense of surprise at not having seen this message before. It is clear, in other words, that the story when told as a perspectivist allegory loses a deeper meaning, one that seeks to highlight the vanity and folly of arguing about things over which we only have limited knowledge. In Case's rendering, the story acts as a warning against embracing views with fanaticism, which leads to violence and suffering, as if humans did not already have enough suffering to put up with.

Case offers two illustrations drawn from academic life. The first is the well-known academic hoax perpetrated by Alan Sokal, an academic prank in which Gherardi would instantly recognize the transgressive delights of knowledge in stirring up the waters of complacency, and the so-called 'paradigm wars' that afflicted organizational theory following the drawing of two lines in the sand by Burrell and Morgan (Burrell and Morgan 1979) in their justly famous *Sociological Paradigms and Organizational Analysis*. What Case discovers in these examples is how easily people, including academics, become attached to views in support of which they find themselves perpetrating mental and verbal violence on those who hold contrary views. Case's argument recalls the Trojan War, sparked off by an argument over an apple and concluded through a hoax horse. If Gherardi's chapter undoubtedly high-lights the erotic in knowledge, Case's underlines how closely the pursuit of knowledge is intermingled with the vicissitudes of warfare and death—not only are wars fought over beliefs that are espoused as incontrovertible knowl-edge, but knowledge is mobilized to inflict maximum damage on those who do not share such beliefs.

Like Gherardi, Kyrtatas (Chapter 4) starts with a story linking knowledge with transgression—what greater transgression can there be than the one of Adam and Eve tasting from the forbidden tree of knowledge? Like Gherardi, Kyrtatas explores the implications of boundaries and borders, in his case the boundary of paradise from which humans have forever been banned, guarded as it is by winged creatures with a fiery sword. Yet, what is inaccessible may still be sought, as we learn from the story of the monk Macarius, an ascetic reincarnation of Odysseus, who, driven by hunger, intuition, and curiosity, sets out to discover a paradise on earth and discovers it in the middle of the Egyptian desert: an oasis with strange fruit and magnificent fountains, peopled by holy men. Macarius' knowledge of paradise could not have been sounder—it is based on experience, he saw paradise with his own eyes. On his return, he reports his discovery to his fellow-ascetics who gently dismiss his claims as the product of hallucination induced by hunger and thirst. In con-trast to Case's blind people, they are content to allow him to live with his experience, which they neither ridicule nor seek to deny. The holy book makes clear that there can be no paradise on earth—this settles the issue, but if Macarius believes that he discovered such a place, so be it.

Visions of paradise, Kyrtatas argues, are not restricted to ascetics and vision-aries. Earthly paradises have now become common escape destinations for overworked Westerners, whether they come in the form of tropical islands or indeed those resorts, casinos, cruise-ships, and shopping malls that Ritzer (Ritzer 1999) has described as cathedrals of consumption. Disneyland with its walled boundaries, vigilant guards, and invisible technical props stands as the epitome of such an earthly paradise, where dreams come true and fantasies are real. How interesting then that those plastic dragons and staged safaris come to symbolize a new type of adventure, a simulated adventure where the acknowledged artificiality of the sets enhance rather than diminish the sense of discovery and fun. (Baudrillard 1983; Campbell 1989) Thank you for the experience, Mr Disney!

References

Baudrillard, J. (1983). *Simulations*. New York: Semiotext(e).
Burrell, G. and Morgan, G. (1979). *Sociological Paradigms and Organizational Analysis*. London: Heinemann.

Campbell, C. (1989). *The Romantic Ethic and the Spirit of Modern Consumerism*. London: Macmillan.

Freud, S. (1905/1977). 'Three essays on the theory of sexuality', in *On Sexuality* (Vol. 7). Harmondsworth: Pelican Freud Library, pp. 33–169.

——(1908/1977). 'On the sexual theories of children', in *On Sexuality* (Vol. 7). Harmondsworth: Pelican Freud Library, pp. 183–204.

——(1926/1977). 'Some psychical consequences of the anatomical distinctions between the sexes', in *On Sexuality* (Vol. 7). Harmondsworth: Pelican Freud Library, pp. 323–44.

Kuhn, T. (1970). *The Structure of Scientific Revolutions* (2nd edn.). Chicago: Chicago University Press.

Ritzer, G. (1999). *Enchanting a Disenchanted World: Revolutionizing the Means of Consumption*. Thousand Oaks, CA: Pine Forge Press.

ONE

The Narrative Veil: Truth and Untruths in Storytelling

Yiannis Gabriel

It is said that an ancient Greek painter was challenged by a younger rival to a painting contest. The younger man produced a painting of grapes so realistic that it attracted the attention of nearby birds that mistook them for real. Confident of victory, he invited his rival to reveal his own painting, hiding under a veil. The older man asked him to lift the veil himself, whereupon the young man realized that the veil was the painting. He at once acknowledged the superiority of his rival.

THIS is a story recalled from memory and written down immediately following a jogging session. It is a story that I had heard or read in childhood; it had been stored in some recess of my mind, from which it was awakened by the task at hand. What particularly triggered off the memory of the story was the idea of the artistic possibility of perfect representation.

Perfect representation was an ideal for Greek art—and hence, perfect imitation or mimesis. According to this view, the perfect painting is one that is so perfect that one does not realize it is a painting. Note then how the perfect representation, the perfect mimesis, is also a perfect deception, since it conceals its own standing as representation. Hence the closer it gets to the truth, the more it deceives. This is the paradox of verisimilitude, the veil of deception.

I found this an enjoyable, even a profound story. It seduced me before I had time to finish my jog. Seduction elevates any text and any object above criticism, above interrogation. But in addition to seducing me, the story intrigued me and perplexed me. It seemed to resurface in my consciousness, prompting a number of questions. One line of interrogation is forensic—note how the story started with 'It is said'. Who said it? Did this incident actually happen or was it merely an invention? Does this matter at all?

Before we seek to settle these questions, let us interrogate the story psycho-logically. Keeping the question of whether the incident actually happened in suspense, let us question the motives of the characters. For the sake of the argument, let us call the older painter Parrhasios and the younger Zeuxis. Zeuxis painted some grapes trying to make them look real and felt that he had succeeded brilliantly by deceiving the birds. He did not intend to deceive the birds but the fact that he did offered a measure of his success. Parrhasios, on the other hand, painted a veil. What makes one choose a veil as the subject of a painting? Of course, we can never enter the mind of Parrhasios, but we can be sure that the painter of veils, unlike the painter of grapes, never has deception far from his mind. What if he chose to paint the veil with the expressed intention to deceive, indeed to lie. What if the very point of the painting was to deceive?

Let us keep probing, adopting now the stance of an authenticator of art. What if the veil itself is not the only painting on the canvas, but a cover for another image or images lying beneath it? Imagine for a moment that before Parrhasios painted the veil, on that same canvas he or indeed someone else had painted a portrait so powerful that those who cast eyes on it died on the spot. What if the veil was actually covering such a dreadful image behind it? This would amount to a double deception, since not only did it pass itself for real but it masked the dreadful image behind it, an image that is thereafter consigned to oblivion, unless some future generation equipped with X-rays could discern it on the canvas. What then if we, the viewers, are so fascinated by the veil that we fail to probe what lies behind it, even once we realize that we have been victims of deception? What if we suspect that there is another image behind the veil, which we steadfastly refuse to investigate? Can we be said to be doing our job properly as social scientists?

Let us keep interrogating the story. What if our fascination with the veil has already led us to forget the grapes. The grapes in the story, so realistically painted, deceived the birds, but have they deceived us too? Has anyone ever seen birds go for a set of painted grapes or even a perfect photograph of them? Do birds ever attack the numerous mouthwatering images of fruit on advert-isers' roadside posters or on the sides of supermarket lorries? Is it plausible then that they went for Zeuxis's painting? Did the author of the story then deceive us with a story whose plausibility is thin? Or did we suspend our dis-belief as a condition for understanding and appreciating the story?

And what about me? Am I too in the process of deceiving you, the reader? Did I recall the story from memory as I was jogging, or did I find it by putting a few well-chosen words in the search facility Google (try 'painter, grapes, birds' and you will find a remarkably similar story surface on your computer screen)? And even granting that I recalled the story, did I recall the names of the painters and the other details of the story?

Such questions begin to undermine our confidence in the story being itself a representation of some truth. What if the story itself is deceiving us? Are we perhaps even dumber than those birds that mistook the painted grapes for real by mistaking the story for reality? Furthermore, if the story deceived us so easily, in what ways have we colluded with the deception—just like audiences of a 'magic show' may collude with the wiles of the magician? What makes us so susceptible to such deceptions? Surely the birds had no reason to wish to be deceived by the grapes—but could it be that, when listening to stories, watching a play, or observing a work of art, we actively desire to be deceived?

This chapter grows out of a feeling that, over the past ten years or so, the concept of story has become distinctly too comfortable. Ideas that once seemed crisp and provocative (e.g. 'we are all storytelling animals', 'stories are repositories of knowledge', etc.) have assumed the standing of unquestioned truths, almost 'facts', in Latour's view. Moreover, I have come to view some of the current 'controversies', notably over performance versus text or over the precise definition of a story, as diversions from more problematic aspects of the use of stories in organizational research. The purpose here is to reproblematize the idea of story, to recover some of its recalcitrant and even dangerous qualities once more. In particular, I would like to temper some of the current enthusiasm with stories displayed by critical researchers, by pointing out that stories can not only be vehicles of contestation and opposition but also of oppression, easily slipping into hegemonic discourses; furthermore, that they can not only be vehicles to enlightenment and understanding but also to dissimulation and lying; and finally, that they do not obliterate or deny the existence of facts but allow facts to be reinterpreted and embellished—this makes stories particularly dangerous devices in the hands of image-makers, hoaxers, spin doctors, and fantasists.

Stories in and out of organizations are privileged among other discursive devices by a unique combination of two qualities, those of having a plot at the same time as claiming to represent reality. Stories not only purport to relate to facts that happened, but also to discover in these facts a plot or a meaning, by claiming that facts do not merely happen but that they happen in accordance with the requirements of a plot. In short, stories are not 'just fictions' (although some, like 'jokes', may be fictions) nor are they mere chronologies or reports of events as they happened. Instead, they represent poetic elaborations of narrative material, aiming to communicate *facts as experience*, not facts as information (Benjamin 1968). This accords the storyteller a unique narrative privilege, *poetic licence*, which enables him or her to maintain an allegiance to the effectiveness of the story, even as he or she claims to be representing the truth.

Poetic licence is a vital feature of the storyteller's unique *voice;* it forms part of a *psychological contract* between the storyteller and his or her audience, which allows a storyteller to twist the material for effect, to exaggerate, to omit, to draw connections where none are apparent, to silence events that interfere with the storyline, to embellish, to elaborate, to display emotion, to comment, to interpret, even as he or she claims to be representing reality.

All of these poetic interventions are justified in the name of experience. I shall refer to this psychological contract as a *narrative contract*. Different types of narrative, such as historical accounts, chronicles, jokes, myths, film, novel, and opera, involve different types of narrative contracts between authors and their audiences or readers. In this chapter, I shall focus mostly on the narrative contract between storyteller and listener, and, later, between memoir-writer and reader.

Poetic licence enables the storyteller to buy the audience's suspension of critical judgement in exchange for pulling off a story that is at once *meaningful* and *verisimilar*. The story is a poetic elaboration on events, one that accords with the needs of the teller and the audience, and one that requires considerable ingenuity on the part of the narrator. Storytellers must walk a tricky tightrope across two potentially undermining questions—the 'so what?' question and the 'did it really?' question. The 'so what?' question indicates that the plot is failing to carry meaning, while the 'did it really?' indicates that the plot fails to carry verisimilitude. Treading this tightrope between two questions that threaten the narrative contract is one feature that sets the storyteller apart from narrators of other narratives, such as chronicles, reports, myths, and films.

Such moulding of events allows the storyteller considerable latitude in constructing plots and deploying poetic tropes in creating a narrative (Gabriel 2000). Does this amount to falsification? Undoubtedly, if the criterion of truth is the accuracy of reporting. If, however, the criterion of truth is something different, then it may be that distortions, omissions, and exaggerations serve a deeper truth. What may such a deeper truth be? The answer often given to this question is that *the truth of the story lies not in its accurate depiction of facts but in its meaning* (e.g. see Reason and Hawkins 1988). Poetic licence and all the falsifications that it justifies aim at generating a deeper truth, one that gives us greater insight into a situation than the literal truth. 'Let us create a fiction that is truer than truth', says one of the characters in Pirandello's *Six Characters in Search of an Author*. But is it possible for fiction to be truer than reality? The argument that goes back to Aristotle (1963) claims that reality as represented by the work of art is more true and more profound than that represented by the historian or the chronicler—instead of imitating mere superficial appearance, it represents the essence, the general. A literal untruth, according to this view, may be closer to the true nature of things than a literal truth that remains at the superficial and the mundane. Where literal representation accurately imitates the veil, art and poetry (including storytelling) reach out towards what is hidden from sight, the enduring. They thus reveal a deeper truth, a truth that pertains to the general rather than the specific. Seen in this light, Zeuxis, by actually reproducing the image of grapes, may have failed to convey a deeper truth about them.

I have long found this view that the truth of a story lies in its meaning rather than in its accuracy compelling. I have now developed serious doubts and have come to regard it as a comforting but inadequate rhetorical gesture where proper argument is called for. Could it be that a story deceives us precisely because its meaning rings true? Could it be that the more authentic a story seems, the more reason we have to approach it with caution? This would seem to be the case with two recent imbroglios involving memoirs, par excellence the literary genre that voices experience. Both achieved great success by combining the qualities of authenticity and verisimilitude that marked them as expressions of people who had experienced extraordinary events. In *I, Rigoberta Menchú* (Menchú and Burgos-Debray 1984), a Guatemalan Indian woman (later honoured with the Nobel Peace Prize) painted a torrid account of the brutality inflicted on her family and her village by wealthy landowners and the government in trying to drive them off their land. Subsequently, David Stoll (Stoll 1999), an American anthropologist sympathetic to the plight of Guatemalan Indians, challenged substantial parts of Menchú's narrative. With the help of interviews with numerous villagers, Stoll offered convincing evidence (both narrative and factual) that some of the reported atrocities had not actually happened to Menchú's own family and that many of her claims were inaccurate (not least her claim to have been illiterate or that her father was a landless peasant). On the basis of this evidence, Stoll challenged Menchú's contention that the Mayan Indians had been enthusiastic recruits by the *focista* guerrillas. Instead he makes a very convincing argument that they were caught between two armies, both of which bullied and brutalized them. Even more devastating was the discovery that *Fragments: Memories of a Wartime Childhood*, an award-winning Holocaust memoir written by Binjamin Wilkomirski (Wilkomirski 1996), was a fake, its author being neither a Jew nor a Holocaust survivor (Peskin 2000; Suleiman 2000; Maechler 2001). Both of these memoirs represent unspeakable suffering told by the presumed victims and generate powerful emotions in the reader—compassion for the victims as well as admiration for their courage and outrage against the oppressor. However, when we learn that the events could not have taken place as told, we feel that the authors have abused our trust, exceeding the limits of poetic licence to present fictions as facts.

Some have defended Menchú and Wilkomirski on similar grounds. Israel Gutman, for example, the director of the revered Yad Vashem and a Holocaust survivor, defended Wilkomirski on the grounds that 'Wilkomirski has written a story which he has experienced deeply; that's for sure... He is not a fake. He is someone who lives this story very deeply in his soul. The pain is authentic' (Finkelstein 2000). Others have argued that Menchú and Wilkomirski speak not just for themselves but with a collective voice, on behalf of a whole class of disempowered and silenced victims. 'If you take each of the events (Wilkomirski) describes, they seem to be the sum of experience of all survivors' (Maechler 2001). Some indeed have seen this as a perfectly legitimate defence, refusing to acknowledge any difference between factual truth and a presumed symbolic truth (Binford 2001; Gledhill 2001). The mere contestation of testimonies like Menchú's and Wilkomirski's, according to such defendants, amounts to a denial of every survivor's experience, a virtual blasphemy. 'I was there, not you', exclaimed Wilkomirski to his detractors, implying that no historical research, not even by distinguished scholars like Raoul Hilberg and Yehuda Bauer, could cast any doubt on his testimony. Historical scholarship cannot match, at this level, the authority of personal experience.

Yet, in spite of attempts to defend the authenticity of the voice of experience (with all its inexactitudes, artifices, and partialities), it seems incontestable to me that incidents like the above (and numerous less well-publicized others) alert us to the possibility of grave breaches of the psychological contract between author and reader. In each case, knowingly or unknowingly, the authors have exceeded the prerogatives of poetic licence and ventured into the field of misrepresentation. If we hesitate to refer to Menchú and Wilkomirski as hoaxers, it is because their deception is, by all accounts, a self-deception as much as a deception of others. Yet, their narrative acquires a different hue once certain facts about them have come to light. For many, the fundamental credibility of such narratives has been broken. Verisimilitude has given way to dissimulation. The narrative veil has slipped to allow us to catch a glimpse of the storyteller as deceiver. The narrator is no longer a creditable one and having proven untrustworthy once, the narrator remains so forever—his or her narrative damaged beyond repair. This in itself generates a new type of literary narrative, the literary exposé, which has emerged as the antithesis of the memoir, establishing its own psychological contracts between authors and their audiences. Others may take a less extreme view—they may, for instance, seek to understand why a very strong identification with the experience of someone else may come to be felt as a self-experience.

What is true of literary memoirs is also true of stories. We can no longer believe that the 'truth of stories lies in their meaning, not in their accuracy', since the meaning of stories is radically different, depending on whether the facts reported were experienced at first hand or not. The trauma experienced by individuals like Wilkomirski may be real, but the meaning of the trauma is different, depending on whether they actually experienced the brutality at first hand or whether they sought to recreate it by imagining it. The argument here is identical to the issue that has long made psychoanalysis a target for criticism, namely that what matters is the experience of trauma, not whether the events causing the trauma actually happened or not (see Crews 1995; Forrester 1997; Gabriel 1999). While the experience of trauma may be very similar in the cases of individuals who were brutalized by their parents and those who imagined themselves brutalized by their parents, I would contend that the meaning of the trauma is very different.

What we learn from the Wilkomirski and Menchú affairs is that once the facts have been successfully challenged the credibility of the storyteller has been corrupted and the narrative contract lies in tatters. To the two questions feared by every storyteller, 'so what?' and 'did it *really* happen?', we must now add a third one: 'who are you to speak with authority?' Once the authority of personal eyewitness experience has been supplanted, the story becomes absorbed in a new narrative, a narrative of deceit, delusion, or manipulation. Poetic licence then must be seen as part of a very complex contract between the storyteller and the audience, which entails the granting of the audience of attention, a temporary suspension of disbelief, a temporary curbing of criticism and inquiry, in exchange for delivering a narrative which makes sense (verisimilitude), yields pleasure or consolation (entertainment or catharsis), but sustains numerous hidden assumptions about legitimate and non-legitimate forms of representation. For a storyteller to say 'I witnessed it with my own eyes' may be legitimate distortion for effect in some instances or entirely fraudulent in others. Poetic truth, therefore, becomes a product of this narrative contract, which continuously defines legitimate and non-legitimate deviations from the facts, legitimate and non-legitimate forms of representation (Veyne 1988).

Stories and Narratives in Organizations

Interest in organizational storytelling is relatively recent, though scholars seem to be making up for lost time. Once it was acknowledged that a narrative does not have to be factually accurate in order to be of use, a whole range of opportunities opened up for the study of organizational stories. Stories could reveal how people make sense of organizational events or fail to do so; they can give useful insights into organizational politics and culture, where they reveal hidden agendas, taboos, and lacunae; very often they can disclose not what happened, but something equally important: what people believe or want to believe happened. There is now a profusion of 'narratological' analyses of virtually any organizational phenomenon, ranging from management of change to leadership, to group behaviour, and to modalities of management control (e.g. see Boje 1991, 1994, 1995; Buskirk and McGrath 1992; Hansen and Kahnweiler 1993; Gabriel 1995, 2000; Clark and Salaman 1996; Hatch 1996; Czarniawska 1999).

What can be said of stories and narratives in organizations, which does not apply to stories and narratives in general? In the first place, I would contend that stories in organizations have to compete with other sense-making devices that find a very hospitable environment there. A person or a group seeking to understand an action or an event may very well resort to purely rationalistic explanations which do not require a supportive cast of characters, chronology, or plot. 'Why did the travel agency lay off a thousand people? Because, in the light of the current crisis facing the tourist industry, the organization was facing bankruptcy and it had to reduce costs.' This may not be an explanation that possibly makes sense to those thousand people or their families, but it makes perfectly good sense to numerous others. In addition, many actions and events in organizations can be understood in terms of bureaucratic rules and procedures from which they emanate. 'Why was X fired by organization Y? Because he was found guilty of gross professional misconduct and, according to the organization's disciplinary code, he was summarily dismissed.' This type of rationalistic and legalistic explanation may not exhaust the sense-making requirements of outsiders and often of insiders, but it would be wrong to dismiss them as either infrequent or inadequate—they perform their functions very well much of the time in organizations.

If stories and narratives as sense-making devices are far from hegemonic in organizations, they are even more severely contested as means of communication. Here organizations mobilize formidable resources that prima facie stand in the way of narratives and include rule books and manuals, recipe books and reports, instructions and orders conveyed by word of mouth, paper and electronic means, circulars, and so forth. Undoubtedly, these frequently invite narrative support or qualification (for a good discussion see Tsoukas 1998). 'What is the story?' is usually an invitation to offer a narrative elaboration on what appears factual and definitive. Yet, on innumerable occasions instructions are followed, procedures are adhered to, and information is assimilated without a call for such narrative elaborations. Even where symbolic elaborations are called for to reinforce or to contest rationalistic or legalistic explanations or to support other information, they are not limited to stories and narratives. Various non-narrative linguistic devices can do so, for instance metaphors, labels, and platitudes (Czarniawska-Joerges and Joerges 1990).

There are additional qualities to organizations that inhibit narratives. Organizational controls on time, movement, space, and on what people are allowed to say often inhibit the delicate and time-consuming narrative process. Many people work in organizations where they have little time for storytelling (as tellers or listeners) or where the emphasis on factual accuracy is such that storytelling is severely impaired. Even when stories do emerge, they frequently have to compete with official narratives and reports, frequently being silenced in a din of information and data. Numerous people simply do not have the time, the inclination, or indeed the skill to tell stories. Many narratives are fragmented, cursory, or incomplete—they are hardly narratives at all, only embryonic narrative fragments that may be regarded as 'proto-stories', but contain hardly any plot or characters. To all these difficulties, we must add a generalized narrative deskilling, a feature of modernity that was commented upon by Walter Benjamin (Benjamin 1968); while late modernity has rediscovered narratives in a wide variety of contexts and media, including journalism, advertising, political and other commentary, memoirs, and so forth, it can scarcely be said to represent a storytelling culture in the way that traditional cultures were (Gabriel 2000).

All in all then, organizations are not storytelling communities—communities where stories represent the only or even the main currency for sense-making and communication. Of course, stories and narratives do exist in organizations in different measures. The importance of stories and narratives in organizations lies precisely in their ability to create symbolic spaces where the hegemony of facts, information, and technical rationality can be challenged or sidestepped. This is the domain of the *unmanaged organization*, that dimension of organizational life where fantasies and emotions can find expressions in often irrational symbolic constructions. Emotional truths, half-truths, and wishful fantasies inhabit this domain, which evades or sidesteps organizational controls, and allows individuals and groups to seek pleasure and meaning in stories, gossip, jokes, graffiti, cartoons, and so forth. (Gabriel 1995)

Stories, Narratives, and the Rise of Experience as a Source of Authoritative Knowledge

Twenty years ago, it was not uncommon for researchers to complain that narratives and stories were not taken seriously in organizational, or more generally in social, research. One still hears such complaints though they are far less justified. The climate of opinion has changed. While some research on organizations has remained indifferent to them, scholars have increasingly turned to narratives and stories for a wide range of organizational studies, including strategy, power and politics, emotion and rationality, ethics and morality, management learning and practice, aesthetics and identity, as well as the more predictable ones such as sense-making, communication, and culture. As was suggested earlier, much of this work has challenged the standard platform of organizational theory and has sought to reconceptualize organizations as narrative spaces, where discourse is, if not hegemonic and constituting, at least constitutive of what organizations stand for.

Numerous benefits have accrued. We have now become infinitely more alert to the role of language in shaping perceptions and understanding, in discursive forms of control that operate in a subtle and often invisible manner, as well as discursive forms of opposition and contestation. We have been able to observe and study emotions and fantasies operating in organizations and note that far from being extra add-ons, they are vital in many aspects of organizational life. We have realized that much knowledge and information in organizations is disseminated and transformed through narrative processes. Our understanding of leadership and management has turned increasingly on the discursive resources deployed, which are every bit as important as material and human resources. Numerous aspects of organizational functioning which were either invisible or opaque have gradually come into view. All this is to the good.

A few years ago, during what could be referred to as the high-noon of post-modern scholarship if not of postmodernity, there was a tendency to celebrate the plasticity of facts and their ability to accommodate a virtual infinity of interpretations and symbolic constructions. Baudrillard's mischievous proclamation of the 1991 Gulf War as a virtual war, conducted on television monitors for the benefit of television viewers, could be seen as a turning point in postmodern denial of the facticity of the material world. Following the events of 11 September 2001, I have encountered few social scientists willing to argue for the non-existence or irrelevance of facts or celebrating the infinity of interpretations and symbolic constructions. Instead, there is a reawakening to the recalcitrance of facts. Thousands of people dying, whether in New York, Afghanistan, Iraq, or Africa, are no virtual deaths, irrespective of whether the dead are symbolically constructed as victims, martyrs, heroes, or collateral damage. Facts are recalcitrant—they cannot be modified at will, although they may be contested, interpreted, or explained. It is a fact that Wilkomirski was not a concentration camp inmate, just as it is a fact that Rigoberta did not witness the execution-by-burning of one of her brothers, even if both of these individuals insist that they 'experienced' these events with total conviction.

If the facticity of facts cannot be denied, the ability of people to 'experience' them in many and diverse ways can also not be denied. It is to the standing of experience as a source of authoritative knowledge that we shall now turn.

Who Can Speak with Authority?

Who Can Speak with Authority on Behalf of Another Person or a Group?

Over centuries of human development, various sources of authority were proffered—the authority of the prophet with his or her personal line to the divine, the authority of tradition that Burke sought to reclaim, the authority of the artist, the intellectual, or the outsider who can speak his or her mind with parrhesia. Modernity undoubtedly elevated the authority of the expert, the specialist, the scientist above others, though in late modernity, with the rise of the mass media, the pundit may be seen as the scientist's brother and popularizer. Yet, our earlier discussion suggests that in late modernity the authority of specialist expertise, the core feature of Plato's political philosophy, is certainly facing a challenge from the authority of experience, the person who lived and witnessed events at first hand. It will not have escaped the reader's attention that this is especially so when the experience is one of suffering and oppression; articulating such an experience enables the subject to discover a voice, akin to the confessional, that allows him or her to turn shame and sorrow into defiance and pride—the acknowledgement of victimhood becomes a celebration of survival.

We owe to Foucault the assertive linkage of knowledge and power, knowledge not merely being a tool or an instrument of power but being enmeshed with it. What is defined as knowledge is inextricably linked to the operation of power relations in both an oppressive and an exploitative fashion. Foucault also alerted us to a type of discourse, the confessional discourse, whose power agenda is not merely the humiliation or purification of the subject, but the definition of a domain of experience as a domain of surveillance and control:

The confessional is a ritual of discourse in which the speaking subject is also the subject of the statement; it is also a ritual which unfolds within a power relationship, for one does not confess without the presence (or virtual presence) of a partner who is not simply the interlocutor but the authority who requires the confession, prescribes and appreciates it, and intervenes in order to judge, punish, forgive, console and reconcile... A ritual which exonerates, redeems and purifies him. (Foucault 1978: 61)

More recently, we have witnessed the emergence of a different type of confessional discourse, the discourse that seeks to inoculate experience from criticism, safeguarding it from the assault of objectivity, the fact and the scientist. *'Thou shalt not deny my experience; thou shalt not silence my voice!'* This approach asserts the *primacy of experience* over other ways of establishing truth, and in the view of Eagleton (1996: 67) is 'one of the commonest forms of postmodernist dogma,... the intuitive appeal to "experience", which is absolute because it cannot be gainsaid'. A result of this has been an argument, implicit or explicit, that *only* he or she who has lived through a certain experience can speak authoritatively about it—thus, only black people can speak authoritatively about race, only women about gender minoritization, only gay people about sexual marginalization, and only black women about the combined effects of racism and sexism. In this way, in a generally contested environment where most fragments of discourse are criticized, undermined, and subverted, stories of personal experience offer a shelter from criticism, an oasis of trust, an island of tranquility, where a person can speak with uncontestable authority and expect, if not being respected, at the very least being believed.

Why is personal experience coming to be privileged as a source of knowledge? It would seem that, in late modernity, science is undergoing a decline in authority not unlike that experienced by religion and tradition as sources of knowledge in earlier times. Science has undoubtedly been guilty of long disregarding the voice of personal experience. In fields as diverse as medicine, architecture, history, and engineering, to say nothing of the social and psychological sciences, the voice of experience was lost in the midst of the authoritative proclamations of the experts. This is changing now. It may be more broadly connected with what has been described as a therapeutic culture, or even the 'Oprahization' of culture, that is, the increasing hegemony of an incontestable confessional discourse, which enables the victim to become a survivor through the magic of finding a voice. When the knowledge of experts is routinely devalued (and often for excellent reasons), knowledge from introspection, divination, or faith are virtually dismissed, and facts become infinitely accommodating of diverse interpretations and spin, we are left with knowledge and truth from authentic personal experience, and the different voices that it takes (art, story, memoir, reminiscence), which assumes pride of place. Far from storytelling then being overwhelmed by other scientific narratives and texts as some theorists of modernity imagined (Benedict 1931; Benjamin 1968), storytelling enables people to discover a voice through which they can validate their experience, communicate it, debate it, and share it with other people. It is as fellow-sufferers and fellow-survivors that people can now speak with authority on behalf of their fellow-people, a substantial reversal from the lofty, if arrogant, humanism and universalism of science. How can a man understand the experience of a woman, let alone speak, as Tolstoy, Ibsen, or Freud presumed to do, on behalf of women?

The authority of experience as a source of knowledge should not be seen as a unique invention of late modernity. As Gherardi eloquently illustrates (Chapter 2, this volume), knowledge from direct exploration, from the transgressive venture into the forbidden and unknown, lies behind Dante's reinvention of the voyage of Odysseus, not as an endurance and ordeal, but as enlightenment and pleasure. What is novel to the current elevation of experience as a source of knowledge is precisely the pre-Dante experience of suffering and victimization. It is in this regard that experience has gained over the knowledge of the detached and objective expert. People suffering from asthma, tinitus, or a whole range of 'syndromes' are as likely to seek recourse to support groups of fellow-sufferers than to the authority of the expert. Even when the authority of the expert is sought, his or her prescriptions, medications, and interventions are likely to be put through the filter of experience.

Our discussion suggests that if science can no longer be trusted to speak on behalf of people and groups to whose voices it is deaf, neither can the voice of experience be elevated to unquestioned and unquestionable authority. As Moore and Muller (1999: 199) have argued:

The reduction of knowledge to the single plane of experience through the rejection of 'depth analysis' and its epistemology (that allows for and requires a separate and autonomous non-mundane language of theory) produces differences of identity alone, but differences that are, in essence, all the same. The postmodern proclamation that there is only 'surface' echoes the earlier phenomenological claim that science is simply another species of commonsense—an everyday accomplishment of members of the science community or form of life... The world is viewed [as] a patchwork of incommensurable and exclusive voices or standpoints. Through the process of sub-division, increasingly more particularized identity categories come into being, each claiming the unique specificity of its distinctive experience and the knowledge authorized by it.

Where does this leave us? Undoubtedly, experience as a source of authoritative knowledge is here to stay. There is much to learn from direct experience and science can no longer disregard it or take automatic precedence. Equally, however, knowledge from experience cannot be accepted without interrogation, verification, and criticism. While Descartes' rationalism has lost much of its appeal in our time, we would do well to remember his warning about the 'deceiver, supremely powerful, supremely intelligent who purposely always deceives me' (Meditation 2) and approach experience with a healthy dose of scepticism. Our experience can often deceive us, and, in our self-deception, may deploy it to deceive others. Desire, whose whims can lead us to passionate knowledge (Gherardi), can just as easily surface as wishful thinking and self-deceitful misknowledge.

Instead of accepting all voices of experience as equally valid and equally worthy of attention, I would argue that it is the job of researchers to interrogate experiences, seeking to examine not only their origins, but also those blind spots, illusions, and self-deceptions that crucially and legitimately make them up. Far from being an unqualified source of knowledge, experience must be treated with the same scepticism and suspicion with which we approach all other sources of authoritative knowledge. Joining the postmodern choirs of ever smaller voices does little credit to academic research. Disentangling these voices, understanding them, comparing them, privileging those that deserve to be privileged and silencing those that deserve to be silenced, questioning them, testing them, and qualifying them—these seem to me to be essential judging qualities that mark research into storytelling and narratives as something different from the acts of storytelling and narration themselves. Deception, blind-spots, wishful thinking, the desire to please or to manipulate an audience, lapses of memory, confusion, and other factors may help mould a story or a narrative. It is the researcher's task not merely to celebrate the story or the narrative, not to use it to seduce and deceive his or her peers, but to use it as a vehicle for accessing deeper truths than the truths of undigested personal experience.

Conclusion

It is time to return to our story. It may be difficult to withstand the seduction of the veil of Parrhasios, that miraculous *trompe l'oeil* which deceives as it reaches for perfection. It may also be difficult to withstand the various narrative seductions that give us solace and pleasure; and it would be wrong to do so, for we would lose much in the process. But it would be equally wrong, adopting the stance of an objective scientist, to put the canvas under the microscope in the hope of discovering in the microlayers of paint the cause of our deception. Presenting a variety of birds with different images of grapes in the hope of establishing the possibility of perfect deception may be a temptation for the scientist in some of us, though this too would disappoint and hinder our understanding.

No, engaging with the story means engaging with ourselves, questioning ourselves as we experience the narrative, and acknowledging our desire to be tempted, to be seduced, and even to be deceived. Those landscapes that we must revisit with new eyes, as Proust must surely have realized, lie within us as much as beyond the Pillars of Hercules. Engaging with the story also means engaging with the storyteller, his or her motives, fantasies, and desires. Finally, it means not losing sight of certain facts, contestable, problematic, sometimes unknowable and often unknown, upon which the meaning of a story vitally depends.

References

Aristotle (1963). *The Poetics*. London: Dent.

Benedict, R. (1931). 'Folklore', in *The Encyclopaedia of the Social Sciences* (Vol. VI). New York: Longman.

Benjamin, W. (1968). 'The storyteller: Reflections on the works of Nikolai Leskov', in H. Arendt (ed.), *Walter Benjamin: Illuminations*. London: Jonathan Cape.

Binford, L. (2001). 'Empowered speech: Social fields, testimonio, and the Stoll–Menchú debate'. *Identities—Global Studies in Culture and Power*, 8(1): 105–33.

Boje, D. M. (1991). 'The storytelling organization: A study of story performance in an office-supply firm'. *Administrative Science Quarterly*, 36: 106–26.

——(1994). 'Organizational storytelling: The struggles of pre-modern, modern and postmodern organizational learning discourses'. *Management Learning*, 25(3): 433–61.

——(1995). 'Stories of the storytelling organization: A postmodern analysis of Disney as "Tamara Land" '. *Academy of Management Review*, 38(4): 997–1035.

Buskirk, W. and McGrath, D. (1992). 'Organizational stories as a window on affect in organization'. *Journal of Organizational Change Management*, 5(2): 9–23.

Clark, T. and Salaman, G. (1996). 'Telling Tales: Management consultancy as the art of storytelling', in D. Grant and C. Oswick (eds.), *Metaphor and Organizations*. London: Sage, pp. 166–84.

Crews, F. (1995). *The Memory wars: Freud's Legacy in Dispute*. New York: New York Review of Books.

Czarniawska, B. (1999). *Writing Management: Organization Theory as a Literary Genre*. Oxford: Oxford University Press.

Czarniawska-Joerges, B. and Joerges, B. (1990). 'Linguistic artifacts at service of organizational control', in P. Gagliardi (ed.), *Symbols and Artifacts: Views of the Corporate Lanscape*. Berlin: Walter de Gruyter.

Eagleton, T. (1996). *The Illusions of Postmodernism*. Oxford: Blackwell.

Finkelstein, N. G. (2000). *The Holocaust Industry: Reflections on the Exploitation of Jewish Suffering*. London: Verso.

Forrester, J. (1997). *Dispatches from the Freud Wars*. Cambridge, MA: Harvard University Press.

Foucault, M. (1978). *The History of Sexuality: An Introduction* (Vol 1). Harmondsworth: Penguin.

Gabriel, Y. (1995). 'The unmanaged organization: Stories, fantasies and subjectivity'. *Organization Studies*, 16(3): 477–501.

——(1999). *Organizations in Depth: The Psychoanalysis of Organizations*. London: Sage.

——(2000). *Storytelling in Organizations: Facts, Fictions, Fantasies*. Oxford: Oxford University Press.

Gledhill, J. (2001). 'Deromanticizing subalterns or recolonializing anthropology? Denial of indigenous agency and reproduction of northern hegemony in the work of David Stoll'. *Identities—Global Studies in Culture and Power*, 8(1): 135–61.

Hansen, C. D. and Kahnweiler, W. M. (1993). 'Storytelling: An instrument for understanding the dynamics of corporate relationships'. *Human Relations*, 46(12): 1391–409.

Hatch, M. J. (1996). 'The role of the researcher: An analysis of narrative position in organization theory'. *Journal of Manangement Inquiry*, 5(4): 359–74.

Maechler, S. (2001). *The Wilkomirski Affair*. Basingstoke: Picador.

Menchú, R. and Burgos-Debray, E. (1984). *I, Rigoberta Menchú: An Indian Woman in Guatemala* (E. Burgos-Debray, trans.). London: Verso.

Moore, R. and Muller, J. (1999). 'The discourse of "voice" and the problem of knowledge and identity in the sociology of education'. *British Journal of Sociology of Education*, 20(2): 189–206.

Peskin, H. (2000). 'Memory and media: "Cases" of Rigoberta Menchú and Binjamin Wilkomirski'. *Society*, 38(1): 39–46.

Reason, P. and Hawkins, P. (1988). 'Storytelling as inquiry', in P. Reason (ed.), *Human Inquiry in Action: Developments in New Paradigm Research*. London: Sage, pp. 71–101.

Stoll, D. (1999). 'Rigoberta Menchú and the story of all poor Guatemalans'. Oxford: Westview Press.

Suleiman, S. R. (2000). 'Problems of memory and factuality in recent Holocaust memoirs: Wilkomirski/Wiesel'. *Poetics Today*, 21(3): 543–59.

Tsoukas, H. (1998). 'Forms of knowledge and forms of life in organized contexts', in R. C. H. Chia (ed.), *In the Realm of Organization: Essays for Robert Cooper*. London: Routledge.

Veyne, P. (1988). *Did the Greeks Believe in their Myths?* (P. Wissing, trans.). Chicago: University of Chicago Press.

Wilkomirski, B. (1996). *Fragments: Memories of a Wartime Childhood*. New York: Random House.

TWO

Knowing as Desire: Dante's Ulysses at the End of the Known World

Silvia Gherardi

Introduction

WHY do people and their organizations seek out knowledge? Most of the usual explanations emphasize the instrumental use of knowledge: we need knowledge in order to solve problems, gain competitive advantages, exploit innovation commercially, or contribute to the well-being of future generations. Alongside the practical necessity and purposefulness of knowledge gathering, however, there is another incentive that is perhaps undervalued in organization studies: the search for knowledge that is driven by a love of knowledge for its own sake. Are not people and organizations motivated also by knowledge as an end in itself? This is what I intend to argue in this chapter. The essential premise of organizational studies has been, and largely still is, the instrumental role of knowledge in the solving of problems, or to use Lyotard's term, its *performativity* (Lyotard 1984). According to Lyotard, the ancient principle that the acquisition of knowledge is inseparable from the formation of the spirit and the personality is lapsing into disuse in post-industrial society and postmodern cultures. This is because knowledge is considered to be like any other commodity: it is produced in order to be sold and consumed, so that it may then be valorized in a new type of production. The impact of technological changes on knowledge has primarily affected research and the transmission of knowledge. Knowledge has become the driving force of production; it has altered the composition of the active populations of the more developed countries; and it is the main constraint on the growth of the developing countries. Knowledge is already one of the main commodities at stake in the competition sustained by the legitimizing power of technical and scientific knowledge. Scientific knowledge provides false evidence, Lyotard argues, because it does not comprise the whole of knowledge.

Yet, in organization studies, analyses of organizing as a narrative activity (Czarniawska 1997), of the aesthetic knowledge of organizational life (Strati 1999), and of the emotional dimension of storytelling (Gabriel *et al.* 2000), have made it possible to look at knowledge in organizations and in organizing practices in a broader sense, accepting Lyotard's warning that scientific knowledge has always existed in a relationship of tension and competition with subjective and narrative knowledge (Lyotard 1984).

Myth is the fundamental form of narrative knowledge. The code that allows knowledge to be derived from the observation and interpretation of reality, is transmitted through the medium of myth. In organization studies, the symbolic approach to organizations (Alvesson and Berg 1992; Strati 1998) has treated myth as a form of knowledge that does not convey factual knowledge as much as it transmits a *forma mentis*: a cognitive grid used to interpret experience, and which subsequently conditions the way people, as well as work communities, perceive internal and external reality. Myth, the knowledge embodied in stories and traditions, connects us to the past and future humanity, thereby situating practical knowledge within the stock of knowledge that is our collective heritage. A broader view, which sees knowing as a socio-cultural phenomenon in organizations, helps us explore a less intentional, less instrumental, and therefore more reflexive aspect of knowledge.

I have argued elsewhere, in connection with learning in organizations and practical knowledge, that we can explore knowing not only as problem-driven but also as 'knowing in the face of mystery' (Gherardi 1999). The concept of mystery encourages us to see ourselves as integrally connected to others, as co-constructors of developing narratives of life, which become entangled with our sense of being (Goodall 1991). Knowing in the face of mystery also conveys the idea that acquiring knowledge is not only an active process, but a passive one as well: its control point may be external to individuals. Activity, domination, rationality, instrumentality, and masculinity are some of the symbolic meanings associated with problem-driven knowing; while passivity, subjugation, emotionality, creativity, and femininity can be associated with mystery-driven knowing and its heuristics.

According to Polanyi (1958: 127–8), learning in a passive mode (and learning how to learn) is like teaching a person to surrender himself or herself to works of art: 'this is neither to observe nor to handle them, but to live in them. Thus the satisfaction of gaining intellectual control over the external world is linked to a satisfaction of gaining control over ourselves' (Polanyi 1958: 196). As in the arts, which are the best example of human non-instrumental activity, we commit ourselves to knowledge for its own sake. We engage in art and in knowing for the love of creation; both forms of activity may be seen as an endeavour without a specific purpose. The Greek term for this 'doing' as an end in itself is *poiesis*. The pursuit of an end for its own sake is an endeavour without a specific purpose. It does not claim to be useful; nor does it claim to contribute to some undertaking or resolve some problem. We engage in art for the love of creation; we engage in a new experience for the love of adventure; we breach the boundaries between the known and the unknown in order to satisfy a desire for transgression.

Is 'knowing' in organizations some sort of *poiesis*? Brown (1977: 7) argues that the critical concepts associated with literary texts—that is, poetics—provide a privileged vocabulary for the aesthetic consideration of forms. I propose to consider the poetic art of organizing, and the organizational process, equally as activities for their own sake: in short, as poetics. Poetry gives embodied form to feelings and to intangible objects of desire.

In what follows, I shall provide an example of how mythic knowledge may be used in order to explore an organizational issue: that of the role of desire in practical knowledge. To do so, I shall refer to the literary motif of the 'journey into the unknown' and to one of the greatest of all travellers: Dante's Ulysses.

Ulysses, Desire, and Transgression

A figure of discourse, as Barthes (Barthes 1977) points out, is a *topos* offered to the reader so that he or she may take possession of it, add something to it, remove what he or she does not need, and pass it on to others. I shall offer the *topos* of the 'journey into the unknown', drawing parallels with commonly occurring organizational situations, in order to elicit in the reader the shared experience that myth is able to create between writer and reader. Mythic knowledge, in fact, operates by establishing social bonds among persons, generations, and different contexts of use. Homer's *Odyssey* represents one of the earliest forms of such knowledge sharing, through the medium of myth and narrative. Over time, it has come to stand as a timeless reflection on humanity's voyage into the unknown. The men and women who work in organizations share, in my opinion, much more with Odysseus than appears at first sight. The thirst for knowing is what attracts humanity to the unknown, to discovery, to exploration, and to creativity. Obscurity and mystery provide the incentive for the realization of knowledge. The thirst for knowing was the force behind every vicissitude that beset Odysseus and his crew.

Odysseus is the hero who 'roamed far and wide, and saw the towns of many people, and knew their minds' (*Odyssey* I.2–3). He is the one who saw, and who knows because he saw. This representation of Odysseus illustrates a relationship with the world that is central to Greek culture: that sight is a privileged way of knowing. To see and to know are the same thing.

The Greek hero 'who roamed far and wide' is also the one who suffered on his return journey; he is an unhappy traveller, a traveller despite himself.

The sea is everywhere, but it is an object of hate that drags the sailors to perils and death. The Greek hero would never have been able to pronounce the words of adventure, and of the desire to see and to know, that C. P. Cavafy (1975) puts in the mouth of Odysseus. In fact, as Leed (1992) and Hartog (1996) argue, the voyage motif in the classical world represented pain and punishment, the expiation of guilt and the desire to return. The *Odyssey* tells of a voyage decreed by the gods, and is a narrative of male power. The old English term 'travail' is derived from the French, which in turn comes from the Latin *tripalium/tripaliare*—to torture with a three-pronged stick.[2] It carries the meaning of pain, and the verbs 'to fare' and 'to fear' have the same etymological root. In the centuries that followed, and especially during the Renaissance, the voyage became valued as a moment of discovery, exploration, and personal transformation. Van Gennep (1909) stresses how the voyage is a sphere of global metaphors, where all kinds of transitions and transformations are expressed.

Dante's treatment of the journey of Odysseus presages the change that takes place regarding the very meaning of travelling. In fact, a new narrative of Odysseus emerges through Dante's text: his Ulysses is the modern hero who thirsts for knowledge, and who is punished both as a pagan and also as a modern man who was too curious and wished to see too much. In the words of the poet George Seferis (1966), the shipwreck of bodies and of minds narrated by Dante is like a deep and indelible scar, reminding us of the disappearance of the antique world.

Dante's myth of Ulysses represents humanity in search of knowledge. For Dante, the thirst for knowledge is what makes humanity human. It is a desiring process, a journey whose meaning lies in the very act of travelling itself, and not merely in reaching the destination.

Dante recounts that Ulysses and his companions were old and slow when they came to the narrow passage where Hercules had set up landmarks to signal that no man should venture beyond them. On their right, they had just left Seville, and on their left, they had already passed Ceuta. This was the moment when Ulysses said:

> O brothers, who through a hundred thousand dangers have
> reached the west,
> to this so brief vigil of our senses that remains to us, choose
> not to deny experience,
> following the sun, of the world that has no people.
> Consider your origin: you were not made to live as brutes, but
> to pursue virtue and knowledge.
>
> (Dante Alighieri, *Inferno*, XXVI: 112–20)

---

[2] I would like to thank the reviewers for their suggestion of the precise etymology of the English term.

In what follows, I shall examine the rhetorical devices used by Ulysses in order to persuade his companions to do what he wanted: to push forward into the unknown, and transgress the limits of legitimate knowledge that the Pillars of Hercules represented for the humanity of his time. My intention is to elicit the reader's mythic knowledge in order to invite reflection on the presence of desire in knowing practices.

> O brothers, who through a hundred thousand dangers have
> reached the west

Ulysses wished to awaken in his companions passion, and a desire for knowledge. To do so, he appealed to their identity and to the pride that accompanies a collective identity. He accorded them the status of 'experts': they were men who had persisted onwards through a thousand perils, and their survival testified to their skill as mariners, and to their worth as companions. Ulysses' exhortation emphasizes that their achievement was not the outcome of luck, but the result of mastery over specific expertise. The sailors had 'made their own way'; they had subjected events to their will, endowing their voyage with sense and direction. They were men who had voluntarily undertaken a voyage to the west. Ulysses was therefore appealing to their expert knowledge, to their identity as 'masters', whose right to such a title had been proven by their survival and their victory over adversity. His description of these men as brothers was therefore confirmed by the skill they had demonstrated in mastering difficult situations, and by their ability to give deliberate direction to what they did and to what they knew. They resembled Ulysses, because they were joined to him by comradeship and because he shared a bond of brotherhood—of deep trust—with them. They were like Ulysses, and he was like them; together they reciprocally mirrored the same, mutually shared attributes.

Mirroring in the other is a moment of fulfilment, a lull in the quest. Pleasure resides in moments of reciprocal mirroring, which are moments of fulfilled desire. The collective celebration of skills and achievements within a community of practitioners not only contributes to the creation of a communal memory (Orr 1993), but also constitutes a ritual that satisfies a desire for reciprocal mirroring.

In order to classify, in organizational terms, what Ulysses accomplished through the discursive act of 'exhortation', I would like to call that act the 'transmission of passion in a community of practitioners'. The undertaking of long voyages westwards across the Mediterranean was certainly not a widespread social practice in Ulysses' time; it constitutes, therefore, a unique 'adventure', rather than a regular 'activity'; however, it enables us, nonetheless, to see how the *topos* of a passion for adventure may provide insight into the transmission of passion in daily organizing. Work groups and all forms of professional communities with a relatively stable structure of social and organizational relations, which give rise, in turn, to shared practices for more or less extended periods of time, share, by the same token, a practical form of knowledge that is not merely instrumental; they display not only mastery of these shared practices, but also a passion, a feeling that denotes emotional and aesthetic understanding. Passion about what one does, and about doing it well, is a sentiment that pertains to a community of practitioners and anchors its identity. However, if this sentiment is not kept alive, celebrated, and relived in memory and stories, if it is not transmitted to novices, it will fade into routine, into passionless activity. Transmitting passion for a profession, occupation, or skill, for the mastery of practical situations, is an organizational practice for managing expert, tacit, and collective knowledge. It has to do with knowledge management.

The knowledge of the expert consists of mastery over canonical and non-canonical practices—over a body of knowledge acquired through social and cognitive learning processes. But it also consists of passion, shared experience, collective identity (and the pride that accompanies it), pleasure and fulfilment, as well as their opposites, pain and frustration (Himanen 2001). Inherent in the practice of mentoring—as a relation between two people for the purposes of learning and development—'is the notion of desire: the desire to learn, to support, to challenge, to achieve, to understand, to influence, to manipulate, to dominate, and the desire of physical attraction' (Megginson and Garvey 2001: 7). Learning, development, and mastery are logical, emotional, and social achievements; they are situated in a personal and collective knowing trajectory relating not only to the conscious level, but also to the deeper, psychoanalytic one (Antonacopoulou and Gabriel 2001).

Knowledge does not consist solely of a set of denotative statements. It also comprises the ideas of knowing how to act, live, and listen. It therefore concerns a competence which goes beyond the determination and application of the criterion of truth alone, in order to include also those of efficiency (technical qualification), justice and/or happiness (ethical wisdom), sonorous or chromatic beauty (auditory, visual sensitivity), etc. Thus understood, knowledge coincides with an extensive 'formation' of competencies. It is the unitary form embodied in a subject made up of different kinds of capabilities (Lyotard 1984).

The story is the pre-eminent form of this knowledge, and the narrative obeys certain rules that establish its pragmatics. Folk stories, for example, as Lyotard argues, recount positive or negative formations—or, in other words, the successes or failures of heroic endeavours; these successes or failures legitimize, in turn, particular social institutions (this is the social function of myths), or they represent positive or negative models of integration in consolidated institutions.

As a result, when knowledge is reduced to mere instrumentality, what is lost is knowledge as a desire that takes us far from the realm where necessity, structuring, and cognition are expressions of mental activity; instead, we are brought closer to pleasure, play, and aesthetic knowledge. In studying the circulation and transmission of expert knowledge, one should investigate the transmission of passion within the LUDIC spaces of work, and the expression of passions in the formation of professional identity.

> To this so brief vigil of our senses that remains to us, choose
> not to deny experience...

As Ulysses exhorts his comrades, he reminds them of the finitude of life and of the time that separates them from the end of sensory experience.

What is the purpose of insisting here that the human condition is dominated by the certitude of its end? This sense of time—of the *hic et nunc*—emerges in relation to the span of an entire lifetime. While enhancing our awareness of the dramatic force of the 'here-and-now', this also casts doubt over the possibilities and the boundaries of the human will. As finite beings, do Ulysses' mariners follow a script that has been written for them by fate or previous experience, or do they have the power to decide their own futures? Ulysses' reference to 'this so brief vigil' suggests that whatever the answer that might be given to the question, the 'here-and-now' is decisive, and that in the recognition of decisive moments time becomes absolute, because past and future implode into the present. Contrary to the claims of an analytic thought that projects desire onto the desired object and its absence, the time of desire is not, in fact, the future. It depends, rather, on the recognition of an absolute time, which establishes the urgency and absoluteness of desire in the 'here-and-now'.

Therefore, regardless of whether Ulysses' mariners have come to live that moment through the inertia of history, or as a consequence of their endeavour to find a route westwards, or whether they are by nature volitional beings able to control their destinies, they are, nonetheless, faced with the drama of choice in the 'here-and-now'. In organizational terms, Ulysses directs a well-established social practice, which holds that 'great decisions' become 'great' by virtue of a social ritual that dramatizes the present, builds tension towards the highest pitch of uncertainty, and foreshadows the moment of relief that comes with the resolution of doubt and the suspension of the will. Yet what is it that suspends the mariners' will and establishes their desire as an absolute value? The answer is the forbidden experience of passing beyond the Pillars of Hercules. Nevertheless, Ulysses is not urging the mariners to action. He rather emphasizes the experiential meaning that such action would hold for them. Experience is dense with significance, and it is this that differentiates it from mere events. An event becomes an experience when it is imbued with a particular meaning that locates it temporally and meaningfully in the flux of events.

Ulysses' exhortation kindles the mariners' desire for knowledge because it is expressed in a negative form, and because it endows the present with absolute value. Ulysses is not urging his men to engage in a hazardous experience, to throw themselves headlong into something which may prove fatal—as, in fact, it subsequently did. He exhorts them instead not to deny themselves the chance of engaging in experience. He invites them to let themselves desire, dare, and be protagonists.

It is common knowledge that experience enriches; that it contains lessons for those able and willing to learn. Much has been written on learning from experience, and also on how experiences can be artificially multiplied by increasing the power to appropriate knowledge. Thus, knowledge learned through experience becomes endowed with a distinctiveness that abstract and decontextualized knowledge does not possess. Experience derives from 'experiencing', namely from knowing through the senses, knowing through suffering, knowing through the creative act of appropriating a contextually produced meaning. Acquiring knowledge through experience enhances the creative nature of learning.

However, once the positive character of experience has been affirmed, what meaning can there be left in the double negation of not denying oneself? There are experiences that lie beyond a prescribed limit; such that we may decide to ignore or to forgo.

Ulysses' mariners were volitional beings able to choose whether or not to respect such limits, whether or not to deny themselves the experience of eating the forbidden fruit of knowledge. An invitation not to deny oneself the experience is an exhortation to abandon oneself to the desire of knowing what lies beyond a limit imposed from within or from without. Desire is transgressive. It subverts the social order, whether external or internalized. To generate new knowledge, to experience unknown situations, is to go beyond a certain threshold and venture into the unknown and the forbidden.

Exploring the unknown, therefore, entails going beyond the threshold that separates the known from the unfamiliar. At the same time, a desire to explore the unknown affects the structure of temporality: the force of desire works, above all, through the negation of the present. The feeling of transgression is inherent in the message: at this specific moment, that thing is possible.

The time of desire is an absolute time, in which one looks towards the unknown and feels the allure of forbidden experience; this brings us to the theme of the gratuitous nature of negation: it is a desire to know and to transgress boundaries not for functional reasons, but rather for expressive, poetic ones.

The literature on knowledge management and on knowing has insisted on pure knowledge as consisting the whole sphere of learning; it is obsessed with codifying and structuring knowledge, and with making tacit knowledge explicit. This implicit guiding principle leads to an undervaluation of the fact that the most fruitful knowledge-management processes are those that involve the generation of knowledge through discovery, play, and invention. These are the processes that abandon the safe havens of knowledge in order to explore the obscure region of non-knowledge. A poetic interest with knowledge-generative processes requires that attention be paid to the gratuitous nature and purposelessness of the desire to know.

Experience, Following the Sun, of the World that has no People

The Pillars of Hercules marked the boundary of the known world for the ancients. Beyond them lay an unpopulated, or at least unknown, world, forbidden to humans. Crossing the Pillars of Hercules was thus to disobey the gods, because beyond them was the end of the known world. Ulysses was therefore firing his men with the desire to know the unknown, and this desire for knowledge then became a transgressive force. Bataille (1962: 72) reminds us that a ban exists only in order to be transgressed. In fact, the very nature of a ban is grounded not in reason, but in sensibility. Desire is transgressive because it evades reason and obeys, instead, the impulses and the passions. Yet it is not always blind. The desire drawing us to the unknown is a force that does not respect the limits of the known world. It therefore transgresses in the twofold sense of going beyond and of disobeying. It is a force that flouts conventions, which does not believe in common sense, and which appeals to direct experience as a source of knowledge. Venturing into the unknown is therefore a transgressive experience, for the realm of the 'known' is sustained by the institutions that preserve what is recognized as knowledge. These institutions and shared beliefs defend what a community deems worthy of being believed and transmitted, on the grounds that it has been subjected to the socio-historical norms of knowledge validation. By contrast, the unknown is deemed as being potentially dangerous and contaminated by false beliefs and magical thought.

The relation between knowledge and transgression has been largely ignored by organizational literature, which endorses the control, and therefore the codification, of knowledge in restricted and presumably unequivocal settings, much more than it is willing to sanction the infringement of rules and non-canonical practices, or the underground knowledge that circulates in every community of practitioners, and is the source of discovery, invention, and new knowledge.

The organizational dilemma between exploitation (of already acquired knowledge) and exploration (of new knowledge) has been analysed in relation to the economic consequences of their respective strategic orientations (March 1996). The dilemma has been less studied at the symbolic level. Exploratory behaviour does not recognize boundaries, which it regards as mutable. It arrogates to the explorer the right to recognize or to otherwise assess the correctness of what is taken to be commonsensical, or assumed to be scientifically valid. It is therefore a knowledge that can only be discovered by disobeying the institutions.

The relation between the generation of knowledge and boundary crossing has been recognized in studies on innovation (Robertson *et al.* 1996) and scientific discovery (Bijker *et al.* 1987). Experience has a logic that is unlike that of conventional logic, argues Bourdieu (1994: 140), and experts or specialists on the subject have highly complex systems of classification, which are never constituted as such, and which can only be so constituted with great effort. This is the problem that arises in the construction of systems of expertise, and with respect to artificial intelligence or knowledge management. The relationship between experts and the givens of their activity is not a calculated act, as utilitarianism would have it, but a *habitus*,[3] a combination of practical reason and a specific form of libido. What makes people compete in the scientific arena is different from what makes them compete in the economic one. There are as many forms of libido as there are social domains. Knowledge management literature asserts the instrumentality of knowledge as an economic *nomos*. Ulysses proposed instead a libido of *poiesis*, a *nomos* where knowledge is the realization of our inherent humanity.

Consider Your Origin: You were not Made to Live as Brutes, but to Pursue Virtue and Knowledge

With these words, Ulysses completes his definition of what distinguishes humans as human, and what makes human life worth living. It is the search for knowledge that differentiates human beings from animals. By exhorting his men to remember their true nature and their origin (the word *semenza*—seed/germ—denotes both the seed as nucleus and original unit, as well as its place in a line of descent), Ulysses rounds off the definition of their identity that he had begun by calling them experts, volitional beings, and masters of their destiny. By now appealing to their most profound and existential humanity, he transposes them from the plane of necessity to that of freedom. In so doing, he justifies the search for knowledge for its own sake, and implicitly asserts the superiority of the force that attracts humanity to the unknown, as compared to the impulse for instrumental reason. The desire for knowledge for its own sake is not a desire directed at a single object, but rather a force, a tension, an orientation aimed towards the future. This is a form of knowledge (knowing) which is not directed at the object (known object), but is instead a knowing relating to an interior experience or a sentiment (Bataille 1934).

---

[3] Sociologists have usually relied on habits, dispositions, routines, customs, and traditions in order to account for the reproduction of practices. In particular, Bourdieu's (1992) *habitus* maintains that the actors' sense of the game sustains human activity and is inscribed in the body as a system of sense perception and taste. Giddens, to the contrary (Giddens 1984), claims that practical consciousness alone determines routine actions. The social character of habits can be better understood as the mode of engagement of people acting strategically in ordinary situations. For a discussion of the notion of *habitus*, see Héran (1987).

Ulysses defines the ultimate purpose of human existence as the pursuit of virtue and knowledge. He thus introduces an element that flanks the desire for knowledge as a force driving human beings beyond the confines of what is known—thus appearing perhaps to contradict his own exhortation to transgress. Yet the concept of virtue relates to a dimension of subjective responsibility that gainsays the common belief that there is no human (populated) world beyond the Pillars of Hercules; it also clashes with the prohibition against crossing that threshold imposed by the gods. This is therefore not a matter of reprehensible disobedience. Ulysses' emphasis on an ethical dimension reinforces the central tenets of his argument: that it is the desire for knowledge that makes humanity human, and that the pursuit of knowledge is virtuous because it is an ethical imperative stronger than the dictates of institutions, whether religious (the gods) or social (the institutionalized belief in an unpopulated world).

Virtue and knowledge are also present in the concept of compassion used by Peter Frost to invite organizational scholars to build notions of empathy, of concern for the inhabitants of the world they study (Frost 1999). Paying attention to compassion opens up the way for research into the emotions as well as the intellect. To act with compassion requires a certain degree of courage in inventing new practices that have within them empathy and love and a readiness to connect with others. In Frost's words, 'compassion counts as a connection to the human spirit and to the human condition. In organizations there is suffering and pain, as there is joy and fulfilment' (1999: 131). Concepts like virtue, compassion, and empathy are not only dispositions or feelings, but also competencies, which, if not used, are lost. And we may now wonder whether Ulysses was a compassionate leader—who exhorted his crew to follow their inner nature—or an egoist who was only interested in his own desire to transgress boundaries.

It is worth noting that in Dante's account, Ulysses and his crew perished as they passed beyond the Pillars of Hercules. Contrary to the Greek and Latin traditions, in which Odysseus'/Ulysses' adventures concluded at Ithaca, accounts appeared during the Middle Ages of a second voyage by Odysseus away from Ithaca.[4] Dante therefore transposed these later accounts onto the original story of Odysseus. The relevant canto in the *Inferno* demonstrates his admiration for the Greek hero and the implicit parallelism between the 'journey of knowledge' undertaken by Dante through the nether regions of life and Ulysses' 'journey of knowledge'. While Dante's journey is guided by

---

[4] I am indebted to Attila Bruni for drawing my attention to this detail and for providing me with bibliographical material. Dante located Ulysses in the *Inferno* among the fraudulent counsellors because he was guilty of various deceptions: he 'unmasked' Achilles (who had disguised himself as a woman and gone into hiding), forcing him to take part in the war in which he lost his life; he stole the statue of Minerva at Troy which protected the Trojans; he devised the deception of the Trojan Horse and won the war by deceit.

Virgil, Ulysses' voyage is a 'pagan' journey where the limits of knowledge are natural limits, and where the Pillars of Hercules perform the same signifying function as the annotation '*hic sunt leones*' on medieval maps.

Ulysses and Dante activate semiotically the same discursive categories: the journey of knowledge, knowing as an adventure into the unknown, the desire for knowledge. As a recognizable discursive *topos*, Ulysses may give rise to various associations in organizational life. My intention here is to examine an issue that I believe has been neglected in studies concerning the sharing of knowledge and the role of power. What is it that induces people in organizations and communities of practitioners to embark upon a 'journey of knowledge'? How and where do knowledge-generation, innovation, and exploration originate?

A rationalist reply would be that the need to solve problems and to reduce uncertainty stimulates people to act or react. A motivationist reply would be that the sense of belonging, the need for recognition, the growth of collective identities provide the incentive for personal and collective investment. I believe that both replies fail to take account of the fact that organizations in so-called knowledge societies consider personal involvement in work as essential, and that research in business organizations is increasingly common and economically important. It is therefore experience-based knowing, practical reasoning, and a poetic understanding of knowledge-generating activities and of the individuals and work groups which engage in them, that provide an answer of specific interest to organizations. Yet there is a lack of theoretical models with which to explore the way that desire, pleasure, and mystery animate a quest for knowledge among organizational practices. The above commentary on Ulysses' speech has focused on the desire for knowledge as a pervasive feature of organizational activities. I shall now systematize the elements that have emerged in a detailed framework.

Desiring/Knowing: Concluding Remarks

Discussions of desire in organizational studies show that desire is significant in a number of ways to the proper understanding of organizational life. Gabriel, Fineman, and Sims emphasize the usefulness of desire in providing an explanation for human motivation, which differs from those based on need, and incorporates instead 'a social and psycho-sexual dimension' (Gabriel *et al.* 2000: 293–4). Desire differs from need, and also from instinct, by virtue of its meaning, fantasy, imagination, and value, which render it 'culturally constituted'. The importance of culture, thrown into relief mainly by sociology, is matched by the connection between desire and pleasure, emphasized by depth psychologists, and by the discourse on 'things sexual as against things unsexual' proposed by Michel Foucault and discourse theorists.

Strati argues that 'luckily, no precise definition of desire has been formulated. Nor has it been possible to assess its exact influence on human action' (Strati 2001: 3), despite the efforts of a large segment of the human sciences, including the philosophy of the mind (Schueler 1995). Hence, the concept of desire is ambiguous and imprecise, and cannot explain the motives for social action. And yet, it provides us with a rare opportunity to refer action to the inner complexity of the human personality, beginning with—in my view—its ability to develop aesthetic knowledge and to construct symbolic systems.

Several authors (Lyotard 1984; Bruner 1986; MacIntyre 1990) have juxtaposed the dispassionate and paradigmatic form of knowledge with another: that of narrative knowledge. We only know the world through the accounts that others and we give of it; and, according to ethnomethodologists, when we recount the world, we create social bonds and the social world itself. We generate narratives in order to make sense of experience and to convince ourselves and others of its meaning, not only in cognitive terms but in emotional and motivational ones as well. Rhetoric is a discursive practice intended to motivate, to arouse desire, to persuade, to create objects of desire, and to relate language to action and identity. Work practices are not mediated by linguistic artefacts, such as meanings, beliefs, or schemata; it is discursive practices that create reality in the form of 'objects of desire', 'objects of knowledge'. Those who investigate discursive practices at work and in organizing should pay attention to the transformative capacity of language and—as I have argued in this chapter—to the covert but linguistically expressed action of the power of desire. Language does not create meaning alone; it also fascinates, enthrals, seduces, and produces pleasure, terror, horror, contempt, emotion, and therefore passionate knowledge. Besides the dimensions of logos and ethos, also pathos acquires citizenship in organization studies (Gagliardi 1996; Frost 1999).

Another form of passionate knowledge is aesthetic knowledge. According to Strati (1999: 2), aesthetics in organizational life 'concern[...] a form of human knowledge, and specifically the knowledge yielded by the perceptive faculties of learning, sight, touch, smell and taste, and by the capacity for aesthetic judgement'. In organizational practices, aesthetic judgements and the expression of emotions are subject to social negotiation, definition, and redefinition, which shape the identity of the community of practitioners and define its boundaries. In aesthetic knowledge, 'feeling', understanding, and knowing are intermeshed, and they merge into their 'use and wont' within the organization (Strati 1999: 92).

Knowing through experience, therefore, has a logic which differs from that of formal logic (Bourdieu 1994), and in order to understand it, we must break with the intellectualist tradition of the *cogito* and venture into the realm of desire as intentionality, as a form of libidic investment. Practical reason expresses a passionate knowledge, which holds the narrative, emotional, affective, and aesthetic dimensions of work practices together.

I have used the story of Ulysses—the *topos* of the journey into the unknown—in order to show how narrative knowledge works. By appropriating the myth, the reader may insert himself or herself in a narrative of the desire for knowledge that began many years ago, but which can be re-enacted in many other stories where he or she is the protagonist. As Marcel Proust wrote, 'the voyage of discovery lies not in finding new landscapes, but in having new eyes'. I have developed the notion of knowing in relation with the union of knowing and desiring expressed in narrative knowing and through rhetoric.

Ulysses and his crew have at least two features in common with a contemporary project group working together: they possess both a myth that operates through the *topos* of the journey of knowledge, and a shared practice that operates through the sharing of a repertoire of knowledge about the world and about the place of that community in the world.

This is, then, the thesis of this article: to claim that organization scholars can reasonably examine desiring practices as one of the elements that explain how and why social practices are transformed, and with them the communities that perform them. I have developed my argument on the basis of the following assumptions.

Desire is not merely a profound and individual impulse that dominates the private sphere and life outside the workplace. It is socially constructed and operates through the social dynamics of organizing and knowing. Hence, not only are 'organizing' and 'knowing' social processes, but the endeavour to 'organize' and 'know' has been conceptualized as 'desiring'. I have therefore proposed that desire should be viewed from the standpoint of a sociology of verbs and not of nouns (Law 1999), so that it is conceived as a desiring practice which underlies other practices in a community (working, learning, knowing, etc.).

Desire and knowledge can be investigated as regards both their objective relationships with the objects of desire and knowledge, and their poetic dimension as ends in themselves—as forces that drive the formation of the objects of knowledge, and as technological objects, or as material or non-material artefacts.

Desire can therefore be conceptualized as a form of narrative knowledge, which acquires form through the rhetorical and discursive devices that create social bonds among people, between them and the world that they jointly face, and between them and the instruments that they use in order to know that world. Narrative knowledge creates social bonds and expresses them in a celebratory, ritual, and fantastic form. Narrative creates identities, it stabilizes a corpus of traditional knowledge, it preserves the distinctive skills of the group, and it expresses the mastery of situations at both the instrumental and symbolic levels. The *habitus* of a group is therefore founded on the narrative modality of knowing and transmitting knowledge.

Habitus can therefore be better represented as an active process of knowledge generation, oriented to values (to use a Weberian category) rather than to a static set of custom-based norms. In its social and dynamic form, the *habitus* is a form of life that expresses the logic of what is desirable or non-desirable, as well as the style and taste that have formed within social practices. The *habitus* entails a demarcation not only between good and bad practices but also between beautiful and ugly practices, and between socially desirable and undesirable ones.

The objects of knowledge, like the objects of desire, are both material and non-material. In order to evade the Cartesian tradition that separates the mind from the body, the sensible world from the world of ideas, one may think in terms of epistemic practices rather than of epistemic objects (as opposed to technical objects). In this case, situated epistemic practices are those that momentarily define the epistemic objects that are transformed by the practices themselves. Passing through the Pillars of Hercules was an epistemic object for Ulysses and his crew, an object formed within a desiring/knowing practice. Every material object is simultaneously an epistemic object and an object of desire. Every object acquires the status of an object within an objectifying practice of separation between the force of desire and its aim. The objects of knowledge/desire are emerging objects that are transformed in the process of knowing and desiring. They are social objects that convey further knowledge and further desire by acting as their intermediaries.

This chapter has ambitiously sought to elicit mythic knowledge in the reader in order to answer a philosophical question that has never been resolved: what is it that drives the human quest for knowledge? The question is still unanswered, and it will remain so, but it has been revived here in order to direct the attention of organization scholars to the question of whether it is solely the necessity and instrumentality of knowledge that characterize the 'knowledge-based practices' of organizations and our society. My answer is that the examination of desire as a force that drives a search for knowledge reveals a recent practice in organization studies as well, and sheds light on the role of pleasure, fantasy, and the imagination in the generation of practical knowledge and of knowledge management.

To paraphrase Foucault, the inextricability of power/knowledge is flanked by that of desire/knowledge. Foucault says that power not only represses but also liberates; it is strong because it produces effects at the level of desire and also at the level of knowledge (Foucault 1980: 59).

References

Alighieri, Dante (1970). *The Divine Comedy* (Charles S. Singleton, trans. with commentary). London: Routledge & Kegan Paul.

Alvesson, Mats and Berg, Peer Olof (1992). *Corporate Culture and Organizational Symbolism*. Berlin: De Gruyter.

Antonacopoulou, Elena and Gabriel, Yiannis (2001). 'Emotion, learning and organizational change: Towards an integration of psychoanalytic and other perspectives'. *Journal of Organizational Change Management*, 14(5): 435–51.

Barthes, Roland (1977). *A Lover's Discourse: Fragments*. London: Penguin Books.

Bataille, Georges (1934). *L'Expérience Intérieure*. Paris: Gallimard.

——(1962). *'L' Erotisme'*, Editions du Munuit, Paris.

Bijker, Wiebe, Hughes, Thomas, and Pinch, Trevor (eds.) (1987). *The Social
Construction of Technological Systems*. Cambridge, MA: MIT Press.

Bourdieu, Pierre (1992). *The Logic of Practice*. Cambridge: Polity Press.

——(1994). *Raisons Pratiques. Sur la Théorie de l'Action*. Paris: Ed. du Seuil.

Brown, Richard (1977). *A Poetic for Sociology*. Cambridge: Cambridge University
Press.

Bruner, Jerome (1986). *Actual Minds, Possible Worlds*. Cambridge, MA: Harvard
University Press.

Cavafy, Constantine P. (1975). *Collected Poems* (Edmund Keeley and Philip
Sherrard, trans.). Princeton: Princeton University Press.

Czarniawska, Barbara (1997). *Narrating the Organization: Dramas of Institutional
Identity*. Chicago: University of Chicago Press.

Foucault, Michel (1980). *Power/Knowledge*. New York: Harvester Wheatsheaf.

Frost, Peter (1999). 'Why compassion counts!'. *Journal of Management Inquiry*, 8(2):
127–33.

Gabriel, Yiannis, Fineman, Stephen, Sims, David (2000). *Organizing and
Organizations*. London: Sage (1st edn. 1993).

Gagliardi, Pasquale (1996). 'Exploring the aesthetic side of organizational life', in
S.R. Clegg, C. Hardy, and W.R. Nord (eds.), *Handbook of Organization Studies*.
London: Sage, pp. 565–80.

Gennep, Arnold Van (1909). *Les Rites de Passage*. Paris: Nourry

Gherardi, Silvia (1999). 'Learning as problem-driven or learning in the face of mystery?' *Organization Studies*, 20: 101–24.

Giddens, Antony (1984). *The Constitution of Society*. Berkeley: University of
California Press.

Goodall, H. L. (1991). *Living in the Rock 'N Roll Mystery: Reading Context, Self and
Others as Clues*. Carbondale, IL: Southern Illinois University Press.

Hartog, François (1996). *Mémoire d'Ulysse. Récits sur la Frontière en Grèce Ancienne*.
Paris: Gallimard.

Hèran, François (1987). 'La second nature de l' habitus. Tradition philosophique et
sens commun dans le language sociologique'. *Revue Française de Sociologie*,
XXXVIII: 385–416.

Himanen, Pekka (2001). *The Hacker Ethic and the Spirit of Information Age*. New York:
Random House.

Law, John (1999). 'After ANT: Complexity, naming and topology', in J. Law and
J. Hassard (eds.), *Actor Network Theory and After*. Oxford: Blackwell, pp. 1–14.

Leed, Eric (1992). *The Mind of the Traveller. From Gilgamesh to Global Tourism*. Basic
Books.

Lyotard, Jean Francois (1984). *The Postmodern Condition*. Manchester UK:
Manchester University Press.

MacIntyre, Alasdair (1990). *After Virtue*. London: Duckworth Press.

March, James G. (1996). 'Exploration and exploitation in organizational learning',
in M. Cohen and L. Sproull (eds.), *Organizational Learning*. Thousand Oaks, CA:
Sage, pp. 101–23.

Megginson, David and Garvey, Bob (2001). 'Odysseus, Telemachus and Mentor: Stumbling into, searching for and signposting the road to desire'. Paper presented at the 17th EGOS Colloquium, Lyon, 5–7 July.

Orr, J. (1993). 'Sharing knowledge, celebrating identity: War stories and community memory among service technicians', in D. S. Middleton and D. Edwards (eds.), *Collective Remembering: Memory in Society*. Beverly Hills, CA: Sage, pp. 169–89.

Polanyi, Michel (1958). *Personal knowledge*. London: Routledge.

Robertson, M., Swan, J., and Newell, S. (1996). 'The role of network in the diffusion of technological innovation'. *Journal of Management Studies*, 33(3): 335–61.

Schueler, G. F. (1995). *Desire. Its Role in Practical Reason and the Explanation of Action*. Cambridge, MA: MIT Press.

Seferis, George (1966). *On the Greek Style* (Rex Warner and Th. D. Frangopoulos, trans.). London: Bodley Head.

Strati, Antonio (1998). 'Organizational symbolism as a social construction: A perspective from the sociology of knowledge'. *Human Relations*, 51(11): 1379–402.

——(1999). *Organization and Aesthetics*. London: Sage.

——(2001). 'Aesthetics, tacit knowledge and symbolic understanding: Going beyond the pillars of cognitivism in organization studies'. Paper presented at the 17th EGOS Colloquium, The Odyssey of Organizing, Lyon, 5–7 July.

THREE

The Blind People and the Elephant

Peter Case[5]

Introduction: A Subjective Subtext

A COMMON convention in scholarly writing is, of course, to suppress the voice of the first person the better to convince the reader of the objectivity and impersonality of the knowledge represented. It is still widely accepted (certainly in the field of organizational studies) that the excoriation of the personal or human voice from social scientific accounts produces better, more credible knowledge. Adoption of the third person perspective in narrative thus leaves the object of rational study uncontaminated by the messy irrationality of the subject (Nagel 1986; Gergen 1994; Case 2003). However, dualistic premises that seek to enshrine strict demarcations between subject and object, rational and irrational, self and other, and so forth appear increasingly unstable in the light of the sustained poststructural critique being pursued across the humanities and social sciences. With specific regard to organizational theory, a growing body of literature seeks to use narrative research and reporting methods as a means of challenging positivist orthodoxy and rehumanizing accounts of organizational life (Czarniawska 1997a,b, 1999; Gabriel 2000; Boje 2001). In taking seriously arguments that seek, as it were, to re-enchant the disenchanted texts of organizational science, I endeavour from the outset of this chapter to tell a *personal* story reflecting a process of inquiry prompted by the narrative theme of this volume.

The present chapter marks a confluence of ideas flowing from two sources that I have, until very recently, elected to keep quite separate: (1) a long and

[5] A version of this work was presented at the Subaltern Story-Telling Seminar, 28–29 June 2002, Unversity College Cork, Ireland. I would like to thank my colleagues Yiannis Gabriel, Donncha Kavanagh, and Peter Pelzer for their detailed comments on the earlier drafts of the chapter. Their generous help and encouragement is greatly appreciated. Jim Vuylsteke offered helpful assistance with Pali reference material. My thanks also go to the other contributors to this volume who, along with David Musson of OUP, offered valuable feedback on the text of this chapter.

abiding interest in what might be characterized as the social theory of organizations; and (2) the practice and study of Buddhism, which I have been pursuing for the best part of two decades. In my life as a student of organization writing primarily for other students of organization, I have been wary of the danger of discussing topics that might seem unnecessarily esoteric or irrelevant to my intended readership. It is all too easy for discussions in which one has some personal investment to cross the line of self-indulgence. I also have a low regard for the intellectual laxity, narcissism, and fuzzy-minded New Age eclecticism that marks much of the current literature espousing a concern for 'spirituality in organizations'. The prospect of addressing a readership interested in both narrative tradition *and* organization, however, changes the picture considerably.

My aim in this chapter is to contribute to the growing body of work in the field of organizational studies that draws inspiration from various schools of narrative scholarship. To this end, I offer a genealogical account of a story that is used by well-known organizational theorists to characterize the multifaceted nature of their subject matter. I highlight two key moments in the history of organizational theory where the fable of the 'blind people and the elephant' appears, and seek to identify one of its possible sources within Theravadin Buddhist scripture. This brief genealogy is followed by an exegesis of the 'born blind' discourse within which the fable appears. I suggest that a richer and more informed reading of the 'blind people and elephant' tale from the position I develop is helpful in understanding the nature of academic attachment to views. Examples based on the 'Sokal Affair' and the 'paradigm wars' of organizational theory illustrate how the moral of the story might meaningfully apply to contemporary academic debates.

Perspectives on Organizations

At least we are all blind men (*sic*). We fumble about that elephant that we call "the organization" and dutifully report on the warts, trunks, knees and tails, each of us reporting confidently that we have found the nature of the beast. But it is worse than that, for we are not even looking at the same beast. The zoological garden of organizational theorists is crowded with a bewildering variety of specimens. Only after I talk with you for some time do you learn that I was talking about a large industrial firm, publicly held, when I kept saying that organizations are this or that, while you were disputing me, thinking about a small privately held one, or a union, or a government agency, or a church, or a voluntary agency, or whatever. (Perrow 1974: 11)

Thus begins Charles Perrow's essay 'Perspectives on Organizations', in which he uses (without reference) what appears to be an apocryphal story of 'blind men' fumbling for elephants as an allegory through which to introduce, illustrate, and discuss competing dimensions of organizational theory. The metaphor returns later in Perrow's (1974: 13, 22) essay as a vehicle for invoking both complexity and perspectivism in the reporting of organizational research.[6] Perrow's discussion of perspectivism, however, seems constantly to be grappling with or fighting off the spectre of complete relativism with regard to knowledge of organizations. Despite the seeming hopelessness of the task, Perrow nonetheless holds out the implicit possibility that some time off in the future, when all the pieces have been assembled, an overall picture of the 'organizational beast' will emerge. As he puts it,

In a sense, organizational theory is in the Neanderthal stage of progressively breaking down large questions for which there are no answers, into specific ones where there might be some answer. But it does this in terms of shifting peaks of interest. That is to say, no one is going to be able to "put it all together" for a long time to come (p. 20).

Social scientific knowledge of organizations is a cumulative enterprise that, although resistant to consensual understanding and interpretation in its 'early stages', given sufficient time and application is destined to yield to the progressive march of systematic inquiry. Viewed some thirty years on amidst the debris of sustained assaults on structuralist thinking, Perrow's guarded optimism may seem rather quaint. However, as we shall see when I discuss briefly the 'paradigm incommensurability' debate in organizational studies, similar epistemological outlooks still persist.

Even at the time of publication, Perrow's account of the progressive ambitions of organizational theory did not go unchallenged. In a formal response, Silverman (1974: 60) anticipates elements of the paradigm incommensurability debate by posing some reflexive problems for Perrow from an ethnomethodological perspective:

Have we now, in Perrow's words... "*come any closer to the reality of organizations*"? You may recall that his argument was that we cannot "*feel the whole of the beast*" because we are all feeling for different things ("*playing at different fantasies*", as he puts it). This conjures up a picture of a beast ("*the reality of organizations*") with certain characteristics which are distorted each time we study them because of the different perspectives we bring. But, then, how are we to locate distortion? Doesn't it imply that we know the "*whole of the beast*" already, when all we can do is feel our different things?

Silverman's challenge to the ontological assumptions of Perrow's perspectivism is well taken, although, in light of his subsequent advocacy and pursuit of

---

[6] This perspectivism is also mirrored in the opening chapter of Perrow (1970). Barbara Czarniawska has drawn my attention to an article by Waldo (1961), 'Organization theory: An elephantine problem', in which reference is made by organizational theorists to 'the fable of the blind men (*sic*) describing an elephant' (p. 216) more than a decade before Perrow's invocation. This story has evidently resonated with selected contributors to the field of organizational theory since its modern inception.

incremental and cumulative forms of social scientific knowledge through the formal programme of Conversation Analysis (Silverman 1993), these historical remarks contain no little irony. Whereas the Silverman of today is eager to attract for sociology the scientific kudos that goes along with investing in the myth of knowledge closure, the Silverman of the 1970s was evidently happier with the troubling uncertainties of relativity with regard to social scientific interpretation and representation.[7]

A decade after the appearance of Perrow's essay, Gareth Morgan published a best-selling book on organization theory entitled *Images of Organization*. Morgan (1986) amplifies and unashamedly celebrates the perspectivism spoken of by Perrow by proposing a series of metaphors—organizations as machines, organisms, brains, cultures, political systems, psychic prisons, and so forth— through which organized social worlds may be represented, analysed, and interpreted. Although Morgan makes reference to some of Perrow's work, there is no explicit mention of the essay in which the 'blind people and the elephant' story appears. It is interesting, then, that in the concluding chapter of *Images* Morgan includes a section entitled 'On elephants and organizations'. Here is how Morgan renders the tale:

At first sight, much of what I have tried to say has a great deal in common with the old Indian tale of the six blind men and the elephant. The first man feels a tusk, claiming the animal to be like a spear. The second, feeling the elephant's side, proclaims that it is more like a wall. Feeling a leg, the third describes it as a tree; and a fourth, feeling the elephant's trunk, is inclined to think it like a snake. The fifth, who has seized the elephant's ear, thinks it remarkably like a fan; and the sixth, grabbing the tail, says it is much more like a rope...There can be little doubt that, as with the blind men, our actual experiences of organizations are often different and hence we make sense of our experiences in different ways. Thus a person in a dingy factory may find obvious credibility in the idea that organizations are instruments of domination, while a manager in a comfortable office may be more enthusiastic about understanding the organization as a kind of organism faced with the problem of survival, or as a pattern of culture and subculture. (Morgan 1986: 340–1)

Morgan goes on to identify two ways in which the parallels between the 'Indian tale' (unlike Perrow he makes nods in the direction at least of a

---

[7] For my part, I cannot resist bringing a psychoanalytic perspective to bear on this exchange between Silverman and Perrow. In their respective ways both men may be seen to be struggling with the shadow side of their rationalistic sense-making activities. Consider how ripe the language is with psychoanalytic suggestion: 'fumbling' in the dark in order to 'feel' a way towards some unknown and potentially unknowable 'beast', contending with real or apparent 'distortion' of its characteristics, not to mention the implicit male autoeroticism and homoeroticism of feeling 'our different things'. The accounts seem, at the very least, libidinously charged and might lead a Freudian to infer a form of existential confrontation with Thanatos expressed subliminally through Eros. Or, more immanently, can we read into Silverman's remarks a suggestion that organizational theory is often something of a male masturbatory enterprise? But perhaps I am overstepping the interpretative mark...

geographical source) and organizational analysis break down. In the first place, he points out that the reader understands the story of the 'blind men' from the vantage of a sighted person. In the same way that Silverman objects to Perrow's cumulative model of organizational knowledge, Morgan points out that organizational analysts can *never* hope to enjoy such omniscience; that our understanding is always destined to be representational and thereby inevitably partial. We have to live with an inherent level of uncertainty in any form of organizational analysis. As he asserts, 'we are *all* blind men and women groping to understand the nature of the beast' (p. 341, original emphasis). I should note in passing the striking resemblance between Morgan's phraseology and that of Perrow, 'At least we are all blind men. We fumble about that elephant that we call "the organization"...' (Perrow 1974: 11). The parallels speak to a remarkable degree of coincidence between the two authors' choice of expression and interpretation of the *moral* of the tale.

The second divergence between understanding organizations and the message of the Indian fable, according to Morgan, is that 'the very same aspect of organization can be many different things at the same time' (Morgan 1986: 341). Morgan seems here to be making an ontological point. The Indian story draws its moral force from the fact that we understand the concept of 'elephant' as a meaningful, discrete, and coherent category, whereas social organizations continually resist closed categorization. In his words:

...different ideas about organization do not stem just from the fact that like the blind men we are grasping different aspects of the beast, but because different dimensions are always intertwined. For example, a bureaucratic organization is simultaneously machinelike, a cultural and political phenomenon, an expression of unconscious preoccupations and concerns, an unfolded aspect of a deeper logic of social change, and so on. It *is* all these things at one and the same time. (Morgan 1986: 341, original emphasis)

In order to be sustained, Morgan's claims about the multiple ontology of organization require a form of underlying metaphysics; that is, the various *real* perspectives on organization—mechanical, cultural, political, and so forth—must logically be founded on an ultimately unknowable reality. Whereas the proliferation of metaphors in Morgan's scheme might be taken as a move towards relativism with regard to organizational interpretation, he steps back from this position and instead uses the fable to assert a relatively sophisticated form of *realism*. Aligning himself implicitly, as it were, with the doctrine expressed in W. I. Thomas' famous dictum, 'if men (*sic*) define situations as real, they are real in their consequences', Morgan seems to be suggesting that although we can never know the *ding an sich* upon which our readings are based, those readings and representations are nonetheless *real*.

We have thus far seen how two prominent organizational theorists have used versions of the same elephant and blind people narrative to make certain epistemological points about the nature of organizational research, analysis, and representation. Perrow believes that organizational theory, being interest based and subject to fashion, is at an early stage of its development, and at present offers a set of mutually exclusive perspectives that, nonetheless, hold out the promise of one day being integrated into a coherent body of knowledge. The parallel between organizational theory and the story breaks down not because we cannot know in principle the elephant/organization in its entirety but because we have to recognize that we theorists and analysts are talking about different elephants/organizations. Once we sort out the confusion that results from this fundamental misunderstanding through more effective research and dialogue, we might be able to communicate more meaningfully across perspectives. Morgan, however, takes the story as a point of departure for developing a reasonably sophisticated realist epistemology of organization. We will never enjoy the privilege of knowing the elephant in its entirety even though it may be there as a metaphysical entity. What we *can* know is that the various metaphorical readings and interpretations that are simultaneously made of that entity are real enough and will be acted upon.

While the fable is obviously powerful enough to spark the imaginations of these two significant organizational theorists, I want to draw on much earlier source material to suggest some interpretative possibilities that go beyond their application. Neither Perrow nor Morgan mentions the scriptural origins of the elephant story which, in fact, may be traced at least as far back as c.580 BC (Woodward 1974) where it appears in a discourse delivered by Gotama Buddha. It may well be that the story has an even longer legacy, possibly originating in Vedic traditions that predate Buddhism, but I have been unable to verify this or track down any earlier source materials. Whatever its ultimate genesis, however, the version of this narrative as it appears in the *Pali Canon* is significant, insofar as scholars generally consider the discourses it contains to be the earliest record of what the Buddha taught. When considering this source material, one is also struck by the philosophical sophistication it exhibits, albeit deriving from a tradition that is very different from the classical Greek heritage of our own. Close reading of the scriptural text leads one to revisit and question some of the coarser assumptions made about the tale by Perrow and Morgan.

'Born Blind': A Scriptural Version of the Story

What, then, does the ancient discourse actually say, what is its purpose and in what context is the fable of the 'blind people and the elephant' invoked by the Buddha? I shall draw on two translations of the narrative into English from Pali[8] (Woodward 1948: 81–3; Ireland 1997: 86–9) to construct my version of the tale. My choice of translation is based partly on personal poetic preference and partly on my own (limited) knowledge of Pali and judgement as to the appropriateness of the rendering. All Buddhist *suttas* (the Pali word for 'discourse'—Sanskrit *Sutra*) begin with the statement 'Thus have I heard', as the teachings were, and still are, passed along by oral recitation. *Suttas* are recited in Pali by groups of monks and nuns who systematically memorize various parts of the substantial Canon (which numbers over forty volumes in English translation) and periodically rehearse them to ensure that integrity is being maintained. The Canon has been preserved and transmitted in this fashion for some 2500 years. The story we are interested in appears amongst a short selection of discourses known as the *Udána*—'Verses of Uplift' or 'Inspired Utterances of the Buddha'—so called because each discourse ends with a four line poetic verse. The title of the relevant section of the discourse concerned in Pali is *jaccandha* (*jāti*+*tya*+*andha*), meaning 'blind from birth' or 'born blind'. The elephant fable occurs in the first of these three interrelated passages that deal with sets of philosophical positions that are at odds with the Buddha's own teaching regarding *attachment to views*.

It recounts how a group of monks staying at a monastery near the town of Sāvatthi in north-west India go on a begging round for food and encounter en route a variety of 'wanderers of various sects', 'recluses', and 'brahmins'. At the time of the Buddha (sixth century BCE) it was the case that Indian society broadly sanctioned individuals who wished formally to renounce worldly pursuits in order to pursue spiritual or philosophical truths. Local communities considered it karmically meritorious to offer material support by way of food and requisites to those who elected to take up the religious life. In order to qualify for alms of this sort a would-be recluse was merely required to abandon all worldly possessions, shave his or her head, and wear a saffron robe to signify the change of social status. Monks belonging to the Buddha's order thus intermingled with wanderers who, rather like the Greek sophists, engaged in conversations and discussions on matters of philosophy, mysticism, and natural lore. In this instance the monks overhear recluses rehearsing various views: 'the world is eternal; only this is true, any other view is false', 'the world is finite...the world is infinite...the life-principle and the body are the same...the life-principle and the body are different...the self exists beyond death...the self does not exist beyond death...the self both

---

[8] Pali is an Indo-Aryan language closely related to Sanskrit and now, rather like classical Latin in Europe, extinct as a spoken language except for its use in religious chanting, scholarly discussion, and recitation of Canonical teachings. It is widely held that Magadhan, the language most likely spoken by the Buddha, was a Pali vernacular. Pali does not have an exclusive script (largely because the Buddha's teachings were orally transmitted) but has been written in scripts that adopted the Buddhist religion, notably Sinhalese, Thai, Burmese, Lao, and Cambodian. More recently, nineteenth-century western scholars also undertook the task of rendering Pali into Latin script.

exists and does not exist beyond death . . . the self neither exists nor does not exist beyond death;[9] only this is true, any other view is false'. As a result of adhering to these contradictory views the wanderers are described as being 'by nature quarrelsome, wrangling and disputatious' and destined to live 'wounding one another with weapons of the tongue' (Woodward 1948: 81). On hearing about the quarrelsome goings on from his monks, the Buddha asserts:

The wanderers of other sects, bikkhus [monks], are blind, unseeing. They do not know what is beneficial, they do not know what is harmful. They do not know what is Dhamma,[10] they do not know what is not Dhamma, they are quarrelsome . . . saying: "Dhamma is like this! . . . Dhamma is like that!". (Ireland 1997: 87)

This is the background context against which the Buddha invokes the blind people and elephant fable. To illustrate how attachment to views invariably results in partiality, disputation, and anguish, he recalls a historical event in which a local *rājah* (warrior king) set up a rather bizarre and, to our sensibilities, cruel human experiment. The story within the story, as it were, tells of how this *rājah* ordered an attendant to gather together all the blind people in the town of Sāvatthi and presented them with an elephant: 'To some of the blind people he presented the head . . . to some . . . an ear . . . a tusk . . . the trunk . . . the body . . . the foot . . . the hindquarters . . . the tail . . . the tuft at the end of the tail, saying, "This is an elephant"' (Ireland 1997: 87). This having been done, the *rājah* asked each person, in turn, to describe the animal. Those blind people who had been shown the head said it was 'like a water jar', those who felt the ear described it as 'just like a winnowing basket', the tusk was suggestive of 'a ploughshare', the trunk 'a plough pole', the body 'a storeroom',

---

[9] With regard to views of self, the discourse makes use of a form of logic unfamiliar to western philosophy but well documented in Buddhist literature. Buddhist logic permits propositions of the form: p, not-p, both p *and* not-p, neither p *nor* not-p. These logical relations reflect more fully, one might argue, the range of ordinary language use that sometimes does (p or not-p) and sometimes does not exclude the 'middle' (both p and not-p) and also facilitates talk about metaphysical possibilities (neither p nor not-p). See Bodhi (1978).

[10] The word *Dhamma* is one of the most semantically complex Pali words, which is why translators often leave it untranslated. Literally meaning 'bearer', it has been rendered variously as meaning 'law', 'doctrine', 'norm', 'justice', and 'righteousness'. In other contexts it can refer, in plural, to 'qualities', 'things' or 'phenomena'. A more general way of interpreting *Dhamma* is as a doctrine of ethics and meditative investigation that leads to the development of experiential (i.e. non-intellectual) insight and wisdom. This meaning of *Dhamma* is summarized in the Buddha's Four Noble Truths: the truth of suffering (*dukkha*), the truth of the conditioned arising of suffering based on craving (*tanhā*), the truth of the cessation of suffering (i.e. *nibbāna* or Sanskrit *Nirvāna*, the ultimate goal of Buddhist meditation practice), and the truth of the Eightfold Path (*magga*) leading to the cessation of suffering. Put more simply in the context of this discourse, *Dhamma* could be taken as denoting a pathway to the Truth, with a capital 'T' (although 'truth' is more properly a translation of *sacca*).

the foot 'a post', the hindquarters 'a pestle', the tail 'a mortar' and the tuft at the end of the tail was taken to be 'just like a broom'.[11]

Saying 'An elephant is like this, an elephant is not like that! An elephant is not like this, an elephant is like that!' they fought each other with their fists. And the king was delighted (with the spectacle). (Ireland 1997: 88)

The premodern (or, strictly speaking, should I say non-modern?) world was not without its own Stanley Milgrams, it seems. Having related the story, the Buddha draws a moral parallel between this blatant example of how attachment to a view based on partial knowledge leads to violence and suffering, and the more rarefied and privileged world (then as now) of intellectual and philosophical views. Whereas intellectual debate seldom degenerates into physical violence, it does often lead to violent verbal exchanges, mutual antagonisms, and ill feeling. Reflecting on the relationship between mental volition, words, and actions, the Buddha concludes the discourse with the following verse:

> Some recluses and brahmins, so called,
> Are deeply attached to their own views;
> People who see only one side of things
> Engage in quarrels and disputes.
>
> (Ireland 1997: 89)[12]

In my view, there seems to be a cross-cultural and timeless aspect to the contents of this discourse which, given the fact that it was uttered some 2,500 years ago in a context geographically and culturally remote, is perhaps suggestive of the universality of the *human effects* of attachment to view as characterized by the Buddha.[13] Indeed, we do not have to look far for illustrations of collective behaviour from our own civilization which readily bear out the moral of this story. Without wishing to labour the point overly, let me outline two instances of the manner in which intellectual partisanship leads to vitriolic exchanges and the creation of bad blood within and between

[11] The scriptural version of the story thus involves nine blind persons and not six as in Morgan's rendition. This suggests that either they derive ultimately from different sources or the story has become 'corrupted' in the retelling.

[12] Whereas Ireland's translation here is literally in line with the Pali prose, Woodward's earlier version is more liberal in its attempt to emulate in English the rhyme and rhythm of the original: '*Oh how they cling and wrangle, some who claim | Of brahmin and recluse the honoured name! | For, quarrelling, each to his view they cling. | Such folk see only one side of a thing.* (Woodward 1974: 83).

[13] I am aware of the potentially contentious nature of this claim. One is obliged to take into account the fact that a contemporary reading of Buddhist texts does not occur in a historical vacuum. 'Buddhism' as understood in Europe and the United States is a complex historical construction based, in part, on nineteenth-century Romantic ideals concerning the 'wholeness of vision' and 'timeless wisdom' of the East (Batchelor 1994) and reflects later forms of 'Orientalism' that implicate Buddhist scholarship firmly within a colonial nexus (Said 1978). In an earlier and more extensive version of this chapter I attempted to address such issues (Case 2002), but for reasons of brevity have omitted the detailed arguments from this version of the text.

academic communities. Although some readers may be familiar with the examples I invoke, my hope is that they will be apprehended differently when interpreted in the light of the 'born blind' discourse as just rendered.

The Moral of the Story: Two Contemporary Examples

Early in 1996 Alan Sokal published a paper in the American journal *Social Text* in which he speculated theoretically on how developments in quantum mechanics might inform a new and progressive postmodern politics (Sokal 1996*a*). On the day of publication, the same author published another article, this time in *Lingua Franca*, exposing the *Social Text* essay as a hoax and deriding its editors for being so readily duped (Sokal 1996*b*). Troubled by the 'apparent decline in the standards of intellectual rigor in certain precincts of the American academic humanities' (Sokal 1996*b*: 62), Sokal gleefully set about unmasking all the spurious and unfounded claims he had made in the original text. His work had slipped through the editorial net, he claimed, simply because it aligned with the kind of poststructural ideological dogma that editors of *Social Text* wanted to believe. Their prejudices had blinded them to the blatantly false scientific statements made in the article. Interestingly enough, Sokal's initial article appeared in a special issue of *Social Text* dedicated to the so called 'science wars' that, by the time of publication, had been raging for some years within US academic circles.

Sokal's timing was perfect. The debacle that resulted from his hoax essay led to a renewed drawing up of battle lines reminiscent of the great divide spoken of in C. P. Snow's essay, *The Two Cultures* (Snow 1963). Natural scientists and their philosophical apologists were seen to confront a loose coalition of broadly Left-leaning sociologists of science, poststructural philosophers, and feminist theorists in a frenzy of heated exchanges in journals and newspaper articles.[14] The 'science warriors' argued vigorously in favour of the possibility of pursuing objective knowledge through incremental, painstaking, and meticulous experimental methods that they claimed had a proven track record in enabling accurate prediction and facilitating powerful manipulation of the natural world. Academics from the humanities and social sciences who traduced this orthodox scientific worldview risked reopening doors to forms of anti-rationalism that modern science had striven so hard to close forever. Rejecting scientific method, it was feared, would leave the way clear for such

[14] Comprehensive details of the multitude of resulting debates (with full references) are available from Alan Sokal's own website: www.physics.nyu.edu/faculty/sokal.html (consulted 14 June 2002). A list of 'downloadable' papers include, amongst many others, the response from the editors of *Social Text* to Sokal's hoax essay, together with the latter's rejoinder.

epistemological untouchables as astrology, witchcraft, occultism, alchemy, and mysticism to reassert themselves and challenge for parity with scientifically established approaches to knowledge acquisition.

Critics of the modern scientific enterprise, on the other hand, contended that its knowledge base was inescapably a result of (unacknowledged) macro and micro socio-political processes; that it developed historically in intimate relation with the military–industrial complexes of capitalism; that science was largely if not exclusively the province of white middle-class males; that it correspondingly instituted and privileged masculine forms of knowledge; and so on. Modernity faced a major crisis, claimed these critical voices, which demanded radically new ways of thinking in order to address the multiple socio-political inequities generated by an imperialistic western scientific orthodoxy. Whatever else Sokal's Trojan Horse ploy did, it lit the blue touch paper on a highly combustible cultural mixture and resulted in much 'wounding of each other with weapons of the tongue', as the Buddha characterized it.

My second illustration comes from the world of organizational theory and concerns the emergence and persistence of what has been aptly termed a 'paradigm war' (Aldrich 1988; Jackson and Carter 1993). The publication of Burrell and Morgan's (1979) book, *Sociological Analysis and Organizational Paradigms*, effectively did for the worlds of organizational theory and organizational sociology what Sokal's essay did for the various protagonists in the 'science wars' debate. Unlike Sokal, however, it was not so much deception and hoax that set the wheels of debate in motion as much as Burrell and Morgan's contentious appropriation and application of the Kuhnian concept of 'paradigm'. With respect to social theory, they took paradigm to refer to a relatively discrete cluster of intellectual and investigative practices (i.e. a worldview) that marked out the respective space of 'legitimate' explanation and enquiry for a given social scientific community. Burrell and Morgan sought to categorize sociological approaches along two axes according to the implicit or explicit social scientific assumptions they adhered to and thus produced a map of the theoretical terrain. Their analysis resulted in the identification of four mutually exclusive and, as they argued, fundamentally incommensurate paradigms, namely radical humanism, radical structuralism, interpretative sociology, and functionalist sociology. Most importantly, for my illustrative purposes, Burrell and Morgan claimed that *translation* between paradigms was not possible; that working within one paradigm inexorably precluded meaningful exchange with others from a competing paradigm.

The book attracted sustained and sometimes sharp criticism from the outset, which is perhaps unsurprising given the scope of its ambitions and the groundbreaking ideas it introduced. This is not the place to rehearse in detail the nature of the various critiques that have been mounted, but I do want to note that Burrell and Morgan's claim about the incommensurability of sociological paradigms succeeded in antagonizing a good many orthodox organizational theorists (see Hinings *et al.* 1988) who had formerly felt secure in what they took to be the practice of 'normal organization science'. By introducing relativity into the equation, Burrell and Morgan had upset the positivists' party and they were less than happy. Their vocal objections, particularly Donaldson (1985), set the stage for the development of rules of intellectual engagement by a variety of scholars who appeared more than willing to identify themselves as mutual adversaries within the resulting 'debate'. As Burrell (1996: 648) himself was later to note:

What Burrell and Morgan's book may have succeeded in doing was to highlight the breakdown of the field of organization theory into warring encampments...

And war duly broke out in its aftermath. After almost a decade of skir-mishes and verbal spats following publication of *Sociological Paradigms and Organizational Analysis*, the journal *Organization Studies* saw fit, in 1988, to devote a special issue to 'Current Trends' in which debates over paradigm incommensurability featured prominently. It included, for example, a sympo-sium (Hinings *et al.* 1988) that centred around Donaldson's (1985) rebuttal of his 'critics', Burrell and Morgan being foremost amongst them in the latter's eyes. Scholars on both sides of the divide have made determined, but ulti-mately unsuccessful, efforts to resolve differences or to 'win' the debate out-right with a killer punch. Various tactics include, *inter alia*: (1) suggesting a pluralist strategy of steering a middle course between structural determinism and cognitive realism through the medium of practical discourse (Reed 1985); (2) settling the fight between rival paradigms through empirical testing and theoretical synthesis (Donaldson 1987, 1988, 1995, 1996); (3) reasserting par-adigm incommensurability as a defence against 'scientistic authoritarianism' (Jackson and Carter 1991); (4) overcoming paradigm closure by acknowledg-ing the necessary interpenetration of subjectivism and objectivism in social theory and recognizing the need to collapse the dualism for the practical purposes of instigating socially desirable organizational change (Willmott 1990, 1993*a, b*); (5) development or assertion of a bureaucratically determined 'consensus' around the measurement of organizational concepts (McKinley and Mone 1998); and (6) producing a synthetic 'constructivist' model of objec-tivity in organizational theory (McKinley 2002). Far from winning, resolving, or dissolving the dispute, however, these contributions have served merely to perpetuate the cycle of antagonism. During the 1990s as organizational theory introspected (belatedly) on the implications of postmodernism and poststruc-turalism, the paradigm war was reinvented anew (e.g. see contributions to Hassard and Parker 1993). Indeed, the paradigm war continues to motivate scholarly debate in organizational theory, as testified by its explicit and implicit mention in various contributions to the recent volume by Westwood and Clegg (2003). I also must confess to having added fuel to the fire in that very forum (Case 2003).

To describe the academic exchanges that I have drawn on as science *wars* or paradigm *wars* is in no way intended to trivialize the physical violence and horrors of actual wars. It should, however, be appreciated that violence need not always be physical. Indeed, mental and verbal violence—acts of rage against the other—are an invariable precursor to physical conflict of any form. As the literary critic and social theorist Kenneth Burke (1974, 1968) continually maintained, there can be no war without words. And while, according to Labinger and Collins (2001), we may have moved from 'war' to 'conversation' with respect to the science wars and Sokal affair, many of the contributions to both debates—'science wars' and 'paradigm wars'—remain staunchly bellicose in tone.

Summary

My point of departure for this chapter was the appearance of the 'blind people and elephant' fable in the work of two prominent organizational theorists. I attempted to explain how Charles Perrow and Gareth Morgan independently, and separated by over a decade, appropriated the story to make various points about perspectivism in organizational analysis. Perrow imagined that coming to an integral understanding of the elephant/organization was likely to be a difficult and elusive task but that one should not rule out the future possibility, in principle, of arriving at some kind of consensus agreement about the nature of organizations and their study. For his part, Morgan used the tale to illustrate his conception of a relatively sophisticated realism with respect to perspectives on organization. According to Morgan's scheme, the elephant/organization takes on a metaphysical and ultimately unknowable quality, whereas the interpretations we make of it (using whatever metaphor best suits our purposes) are real insofar as we believe in and act upon them. By introducing the reader to a much earlier scriptural source (and possible origin?) of the elephant fable, I tried to show that both Perrow's and Morgan's versions and interpretations of the story were, ironically enough, *at best partial* by comparison.

Understanding the role of the story within a broader Buddhist philosophical context it became clear that perspectivism is only one, albeit important, facet of the tale. Of greater importance from a Buddhist standpoint is the fact that *attachment* to views and opinions based on partial understanding is a potential precursor to acts of mental, verbal, and physical violence. That the story illustrates how attachment of this kind results in conflict is a point which neither Perrow nor Morgan are able to develop given their 'incomplete' rendition of the story (as compared to the scriptural material I draw on). To illustrate how the moral of the story might be played out with respect to contemporary social scientific debates, I explored how the Sokal Affair helped intensify the science wars and discussed how the field of organizational theory has been continually engaged in a set of paradigm wars for the past couple of decades.

Concluding Remarks

By way of conclusion I would like to explore two issues that arise from the preceding discussion: first, the question of what space my narrative voice occupies in relation to the fable and, second, why shifting the emphasis in interpreting the story from perspectivism to *attachment* to views is so important from a Buddhist standpoint. Concerning the status of my own narrative voice, I am certainly *not* trying to make a foundational claim about my account of the discourse. My interpretation is inherently subjective, reflects my own conditioned sensibilities and is, to that extent, partial. How could it be otherwise? Whatever *rhetorical force* my arguments possess, however, derive from a claim that neither Perrow nor Morgan make reference to the scriptural source of the story they invoke and are thus unable to develop the possibilities it suggests. Am I 'othering' Perrow and Morgan by using their texts as intellectual foils through which to point out partialities and inadequacies in *their* interpretations? The answer has to be yes, but I contend that this is an inescapable feature of scholarly critique. For an argument to have any analytical purchase or utility in the social sciences it will inevitably entail making recourse to 'othering' processes, that is, it will necessitate textual 'victimization' of some form. These are inescapable imperatives of the identity work we do through representational acts. As long as we occupy a dualistic universe of signs and significations we are condemned to create, implicate, and value-judge others as we perform and express our 'self'.

As I argue above, the 'born blind' discourse revolves centrally around the issue of attachment to various forms of views, which begs the question: what is wrong with such attachment? The science wars and paradigm wars, for example, could be argued to constitute sites of dispute over values—ontological, epistemological, ethical, and aesthetical—that are eminently worth warring over. To understand the difference between a view that is being *grasped at* and one that is not goes directly to the heart of Buddhist philosophy and practice. Some appreciation of the hierarchical nature of truth that Buddhism espouses is necessary in order to explain the subtle distinction being drawn. Buddhism identifies three levels of truth corresponding to three levels of reality: (1) conventional truths (*vohāra-sacca*) that relate to consensus reality as socially conditioned and constructed; (2) so called 'ultimate' truths pertaining to ultimate reality (*pararmattha-dhammā*), which reduce human experience to constituent phenomenological events and processes of consciousness; and (3) *nibbāna* or Nirvāna (Sanskrit), which refers to an intuitive experience of truth and reality that transcends duality and representation. To break free from subjective attachments, Buddhist seekers train themselves in techniques of meditative observation in order gradually to move from a conventional apprehension of reality to direct experiences of the 'ultimate' (i.e. phenomenological) constitution of consciousness, and finally to a fully transcendent freedom from subjective attachment and suffering through the realization of *nibbāna*.

Problems occur when one tries to speak about the experience of truth/reality levels (2) and (3) in terms of the dualistically constrained representations of level (1). Indeed, attempts to do so frequently result in enlightened teachers making recourse to paradoxical statements and self-contradictions (a hallmark of mystical discourse generally). When the Buddha speaks of attachment to views in the 'born blind' discourse, he is inveighing against the pain and anguish that stem from mental inflexibility and grasping after false certainties. He urges people to recognize the limitations of dualistic intellect—through seeking direct experience of realities (2) and (3)—and thus to become more open and adaptable in the face of the challenges presented by life. To give up *attachment* to a view, however, is not at all the same as relinquishing that *view*. Neither does letting go of attachment necessitate the abandonment of intellectual discrimination and judgement. Paradoxically, it is possible to express views and opinions in conventional terms, sometimes in what might appear to be an impassioned fashion (as the Buddha often did), without there being the least vestige of attachment present. Just how this is possible is literally *im*possible to describe.

Accordingly, the 'born blind' discourse should not be taken as a manifesto for political conservativism, quietism, or the abandonment of critique. On the other hand, it is a manifesto for the giving up of *attachment* to views, fixity, and dogma that originate in the processes of identification. It is also a manifesto for the careful cultivation of non-harming and non-violence with respect to one's *immediate sphere of action and influence*.

As the Buddha once observed:

In this world . . . substance is seen in what is insubstantial. [Sentient creatures] are tied to their psychophysical beings and so they think that there is some substance, some reality in them. But whatever be the phenomenon through which they think of seeking their self identity, it turns out to be transitory. It becomes false, for what lasts for a moment is deceptive. The state that is not deceptive is *Nibbāna* . . . With this insight into reality their hunger ends: cessation, total calm. (Saddhatissa 1994: 89)

In the parlance of the 'born blind' discourse, what following Buddhist teaching entails is moving beyond the telling or retelling of a story *from any perspective*—be it that of a *rājah*, 'blind people', the Buddha, or an organizational theorist—and seeking, instead, to *know directly* what it would be like, metaphorically speaking, to experience being the elephant. And, to paraphrase Wittgenstein (1953/2001: 190), 'if an elephant could talk, we could not understand'.[15]

---

[15] The original reads, 'If a lion could talk, we could not understand him'.

References

Aldrich, H. (1988). 'Paradigm warriors: Donaldson versus the critics of organization theory'. *Organization Studies*, 9(1): 19–24.

Batchelor, S. (1994). *The Awakening of the West: The Encounter of Buddhism and
Western Culture*. London: HarperCollins.

Bodhi, B. (1978). *The Discourse on the All-embracing Net of Views*. Kandy, Sri Lanka:
Buddhist Publication Society.

Boje, D. (2001). *Narrative Methods for Organizational and Communication Research*.
London: Sage.

Burke, K. (1974). *The Philosophy of Literary Form*. Berkley: University of California
Press.

——(1968). *Language as Symbolic Action*. London: University of California Press.

Burrell, G. (1996). 'Normal science, paradigms, metaphors, discourses and genealo-
gies of analysis', in S. R. Clegg, C. Hardy, and W. R. Nord (eds.), *Handbook of
Organization Studies*. London: Sage, pp. 642–58.

—— and Morgan, G. (1979). *Sociological Paradigms and Organizational Analysis*.
London: Heinemann.

Case, P. (2002). 'Blindness and sight, ignorance and understanding: An ancient
Buddhist fable speaks to contemporary issues in organizational studies'. Paper
presented at the Subaltern Story-Telling Seminar, University College Cork,
Ireland, 28–29 June.

——(2003). 'Confession of a counter-modernist: Pursuing subjective authenticity
in organizational research', in R. Westwood and S. Clegg (eds.), *Debating
Organization*. Oxford: Blackwell.

Czarniawska, Barbara (1997*a*). *A Narrative Approach to Organization Studies*.
London: Sage.

——(1997*b*). *Narrating the Organization: Dramas of Institutional Identity*. Chicago:
University of Chicago Press.

——(1999). *Writing Organization*. Oxford: Oxford University Press.

Donaldson, L. (1985). *In Defence of Organization Theory: A Reply to the Critics*.
Cambridge: Cambridge University Press.

——(1987). 'Strategy and structural adjustment to regain fit and performance: In
defence of contingency theory'. *Journal of Management Studies*, 24(1): 1–24.

——(1988). 'In successful defence of organization theory: A routing of the critics',
Organization Studies, 9(1): 28–32.

——(1995). 'Contingency theory', in D. S. Pugh (ed.), *History of Management
Thought* (Vol. IX). Aldershot: Dartmouth Press.

——(1996). *For Positivist Organization Theory: Proving the Hard Core*. London: Sage.

Gabriel, Y. (2000). *Storytelling in Organizations: Facts, Fictions, and Fantasies*. Oxford:
Oxford University Press.

Gergen, Kenneth (1994). 'The mechanical self and the rhetoric of objectivity', in
A. Megill (ed.), *Rethinking Objectivity*. London: Duke University Press, pp. 265–87.

Hassard, J. and Parker, M. (eds.) (1993). *Postmodernism and Organizations*. London:
Sage.

Hinings, B., Clegg, S. R., Child, J., Aldrich, H., Karpik, L., and Donaldson, L. (1988).
'Offence and defence in organization studies: A symposium'. *Organization Studies*,
9(1): 1–32.

Ireland, J. D. (1997). *The Udāna and the Itivuttaka*. Kandy, Sri Lanka: Buddhist
Publication Society.

Jackson, N. and Carter, P. (1991). 'In defence of paradigm incommensurability'. *Organization Studies*, 12(1): 109–27.

——(1993). ' "Paradigm wars": A response to Hugh Willmott'. *Organization Studies*, 14(5): 721–5.

Labinger, J. and Collins, H. (eds.) (2001). *The One Culture? A Conversation About Science*. London: Chicago University Press.

McKinley, W. (2002). 'From subjectivity to objectivity: A constructivist account of objectivity in organization theory', in R. Westwood and S. Clegg (eds.), *Debating Organization*. Oxford: Blackwell.

McKinley, W. and Mone, M. (1998). 'The re-construction of organization studies: Wrestling with incommensurability'. *Organization*, 5(2): 169–89.

Morgan, G. (1986). *Images of Organization*. London: Sage.

Nagel, T. (1986). *The View from Nowhere*. Oxford: Oxford University Press; *Organization Studies*, 9(1) (Special Issue: Current Trends).

Perrow, C. (1970). *Organizational Analysis: A Sociological View*. London: Tavistock.

——(1974). 'Perspectives on organizations', in C. Perrow, M. Albrow, and D. Silverman (eds.), *Perspectives on Organizations*. Milton Keynes: Open University Press.

Reed, M. (1985). *Redirections in Organizational Analysis*. London: Tavistock.

Saddhatissa, H. (1994). *The Sutta-Nipāta*. Richmond: Curzon Press.

Said, E. (1978). *Orientalism*. Harmondsworth: Penguin.

Serres, M. (1982). *The Pararsite* (Lawrence R. Schehr, trans.). Baltimore, MD: John Hopkins University Press.

Silverman, D. (1974). 'Producing organized sense', in C. Perrow, M. Albrow, and D. Silverman (eds.), *Perspectives on Organizations*. Milton Keynes: Open University Press.

——(1993). *Interpreting Qualitative Data: Methods for Analysing Talk, Text and Interaction*. London: Sage.

Snow, C. P. (1963). *The Two Cultures: And a Second Look*. Cambridge: Cambridge University Press.

Sokal, A. (1996a). 'Transgressing the boundaries: Toward a transformative hermeneutics of quantum gravity'. *Social Text*, 46/47: 217–52.

——(1996b). 'A physicist experiments with cultural studies'. *Lingua Franca*, May/June: 62–4.

Waldo, D. (1961). 'Organization theory: An elephantine problem'. *Public Administration Review*, 21: 210–25.

Westwood, R. and Clegg, S. (eds.) (2003). *Debating Organization: Point–Counterpoint in Organization Studies*. Oxford: Blackwell.

Willmott, H. (1990). 'Beyond paradigmatic closure in organizational enquiry', in J. Hassard and D. Pym (eds.), *The Theory and Philosophy of Organizations*. London: Routledge, pp. 44–60.

——(1993a). 'Breaking the paradigm mentality'. *Organization Studies*, 14(5): 681–719.

——(1993b). 'Paradigm gridlock: A reply'. *Organization Studies*, 14(5): 727–30.

Wittgenstein, L. (1953/2001). *Philosophical Investigations*. Oxford: Blackwell.

Woodward, F. L. (1948). *The Minor Anthologies of the Pali Canon Part II*. London: Oxford University Press.

——(1974). *Some Sayings of the Buddha According to the Pali Canon*. London: Oxford University Press.

FOUR

Paradise in Heaven and on Earth: Western Ideas of Perfect (Non)-Organization

Dimitris J. Kyrtatas

As every careful reader of the Book of Genesis realizes, there are inconsistencies in the story told regarding the origin of humanity. Actually, it may be reasonably assumed that the account, as it now stands, developed out of two independent traditions or two distinct mentalities. According to one, human beings were the ultimate product of creation. Heaven and earth as well as every kind of living creature were already in their place awaiting them. Having at the very end of creation made man and woman in his own image, God blessed them, saying: 'Be fruitful, multiply, fill the earth and subdue it. Be masters of the fish of the sea, the birds of Heaven and all the living creatures that move on earth'. Furthermore, he provided them with 'all the seed-bearing plants everywhere on the surface of the earth, and all the trees with seed-bearing fruit' to be their food (Genesis 1:28–9).[16]

A few verses later, however, having first created man (though not yet woman), God planted a garden in Eden. Every kind of tree grew within this garden, enticing to look at and good to eat. Two particular trees were planted in its middle: the tree of life and the tree of the knowledge of good and evil. The garden was watered by a river flowing from Eden and branching into four streams. Man was settled in this garden to cultivate and to take care of it. He was only forbidden to eat the fruits of the tree of knowledge of good and evil. In this second version, all the wild animals and all the birds of Heaven were created at a later stage, to keep man company, while woman was fashioned last, offered to him as his helper (Genesis 2:7–23).

This garden, about which nothing is said in the former version, was clearly cut off from the rest of the earth. As a result of their disobedience, so

---

[16] For biblical references I have used the English translation of the *New Jerusalem Bible*.

we are told, Adam and Eve were expelled from it, having been provided with animal skins with which to cover their nakedness. God expressed his fear that man would 'reach out his hand and pick from the tree of life too, and eat and live for ever'. To prevent them from re-entering the garden he posted at its entrance great winged creatures and a fiery flashing sword. It was only then, that is, after their fall and their expulsion, that they both found themselves 'free' to fill the earth and to subdue it, as they deemed proper (Genesis 3:1–24). Among other things that they could or should be doing outside the garden, they had intercourse (apparently) for the first time (Genesis 4:1).[17]

This double exposition leads the scrupulous reader to choose between two alternatives. The earth upon which men and women are now living is either the original (and only) place meant for them or a prison in which they have been confined because of their transgression.[18] Of these two alternatives, it is the story of the garden that has proved more fascinating and enduring. The simple idea that men have always lived upon earth as we know it, earning their living by the sweat of their labour, and that women have always experienced intense pain in childbirth has never been very appealing. That men and women derive from dust and that they shall return to dust is an even more disquieting thought. Being assured, however, that in the beginning all was perfect and that the present state of affairs was only established because something went seriously wrong is, in a sense, consoling. It cannot be mere accident that so many ancient peoples have similar stories of an originally perfect state that was lost for one reason or another. Hesiod's myth of the five successive races is a well-known parallel to the biblical account. The poet was sad to have been born in the iron rather than in the golden age when men 'lived with happy hearts, untouched by work or sorrow' while 'ungrudgingly, the fertile land gave up her fruits unasked' (Hesiod 1973: 109–18).[19]

Preoccupation with a lost state of bliss has had important consequences. Extreme pessimism often contains the germ of optimism. Losing generates the prospect of gaining; and falling, the hope of being raised up again. The biblical story of the Garden of Eden is as pessimistic as any creation myth can be. Besides depriving Adam and Eve of their dream-like dwelling place, it did not give them any explicit promise of regaining it—not even a conditional one. But such is the nature of the human intellect that it easily transforms despair into hope and desire into expectation. Most believers or just sympathetic readers of the Bible have been led to the reasonable assumption that the Garden has not been lost forever.

[17] The possibility of having intercourse inside the Garden of Eden has been hotly debated. See Anderson (1989).

[18] For a general presentation of Christian reactions to the creation story, see Pagels (1988).

[19] On the eastern influences in Greek cosmogonical myths, see Kirk (1974).

The word 'garden' used in most English versions of the Genesis account translates the Hebrew word *gan*, a quite obvious and accurate choice, for this is what *gan* really means. It is a word as common and as simple in its usage as garden. However, when in the third century BCE the same story was translated into Greek for the benefit of Greek-speaking Jews living in Egypt, the choice made was neither obvious nor literal. Instead of *kēpos*, that would have immediately come to the mind of a Greek native-speaker, the translators opted for the rather awkward word *paradisos*, from which paradise and other closely related words in most western languages derive. This word was already used by some Greek authors in the fifth century BCE, though its use was not widespread. In fact, it was a loanword from Persian with a very restricted meaning.[20]

From the Avestic root *pairidaēza* or its Babylonian derivative *pardizu*, the word spread to other languages at various stages. In all its early versions it designated an enclosure or a very large fenced park with luxuriant vegetation and wild beasts for the chase. Such enclosures were always created for the pleasure of kings or nobles of very high rank. Since the Greeks of the Classical period never had kings or nobles of great wealth and power, they found little use for the word *paradisos*. The very idea of organizing and maintaining extravagant pleasure grounds was foreign to their culture and beyond their means.

In the few instances where the word appears in Classical Greek literature, it always refers to eastern kingdoms. As the fourth-century historian Xenophon explained to his readers, in all the districts that the Great King of Persia resided in and visited, he took care that there were ' "paradises", as they call them, full of all the good and beautiful things that the soil can produce'. In them the king spent most of his time, except when the season precluded it. While visiting such a paradise at Sardis, the Spartan general Lysander was once greatly impressed with the skilful way everything in it had been measured and arranged. He was even more amazed to learn that king Cyrus himself was responsible for the measurement and arrangement, and that some of the planting was his own personal doing (Xenophon 1923: 4.13–14, 21). As all Greeks knew, kings and noblemen never worked with their own hands, unless it was for exercise or pleasure. But Lysander's astonishment was probably caused by a further consideration. Such harmony as he experienced was beyond his imagination.

It is therefore clear that the translators of the Book of Genesis did not choose the word *paradisos* casually. Although they read *gan* in their text, they clearly understood that this was no ordinary garden or backyard of a commoner. It was really what the Hebrew author should have rendered as *pardes*— the Hebrew derivative from *pairidaēza* or *pardizu*. Interestingly, the choice made by these translators added further ambiguity to the already complex biblical account, for the word *paradisos* and all its offshoots has retained a double meaning: a religious and a secular. Paradise is the original abode of

---

[20] On the original sense of the word, see Bremmer (2002).

Adam and Eve, the God-created garden of innocence and supreme bliss as well as any human creation of surpassing luxury and beauty meant for the felicity of a few privileged members.[21]

The teaching of Jesus obviously owes much of its appeal to the explicit assurance that the kingdom of God is (or rather was) imminent. But as the first Christians started to pass away without having seen the signs of the approaching end, they begun wondering what would happen to them during the (brief) period between their death and the universal resurrection. It was thus argued that some, like the penitent criminal on the cross, would enter paradise at the moment of their death (Luke 23:39–43), as were the martyrs who died for their faith. Others would have to wait longer for the 'second coming'—much longer, as we now know. In his attempt to clarify the matter and to deal with the biblical ambiguity, John the prophet was led to even more complicated doctrines and actually envisaged two distinct paradises: an earthly and a heavenly one.

According to the Book of Revelation the earthly kingdom was an intermediate stage. While the rest of the dead would be still waiting for their resurrection, a few privileged witnesses, having come to life, would reign with Christ for a thousand years. This temporal recompense, as he prophesied, would be succeeded, at the end of time, by a new and everlasting creation, to which all the pious should aspire. Earth and sky, he explained, will finally vanish and their place will be taken by a new Heaven and a new earth. All tears will be wiped away and there will be no more death, no more mourning, sadness, or pain. Those who deserve it will have the privilege of seeing God face to face (Revelation 20:1–6).

But either because the human imagination is less inventive than we usually assume, or because our needs are, in the final analysis, all too mundane, even this most exalted depiction of paradise was presented by John in material terms. In their new abode men and women will still be eating and drinking. Retaining some of the basic characteristics of the Genesis paradise, new earth in Revelation is illustrated as possessing a river of life that will rise from the throne of God with trees of life on either bank bearing twelve crops of fruit in a year, one in each month (Revelation 20:11–22:5, cf. 2:7). As an early expert on such matters, well versed in the biblical tradition, explained, this ultimate paradise was expected to be a world of abundance. 'The days will come', he argued, 'in which vines shall grow, each having ten thousand branches, and in each branch ten thousand twigs, and in each true twig ten thousand shoots, and in each one of the shoots ten thousand clusters, and on everyone of the clusters ten thousand grapes, and every grape when pressed will give five and twenty *metretes* of wine'.[22]

---

[21] Definitions from the *Oxford English Dictionary*.

[22] Thus Papias of Hierapolis in Phrygia who died around the year 130. His words are quoted by Irenaeus, *Against Heresies* 5.33, translation by A. Roberts from *The Ante-Nicene Fathers*, Vol. 1, Michigan 1885. For further details see Kyrtatas (1989).

Other Christians were less content with such ideas and even less satisfied with the hypothesis of the 1000-year reign. Although delightful, paradise should not be envisaged, they thought, in temporal or materialistic terms. Unlike everlasting Hell, in which the body is severely tortured and punished, the kingdom of God must not be expected to offer bodily enjoyment. In it there shall be endless (not to say monotonous) singing and also bright light, but the flesh will not experience sensual delights. Endorsed by orthodox theology, these exalted promises never really caught the imagination of laymen and laywomen. John's 'millenarian' teaching, as it has been called, did not became official dogma of the churches, but most believers have always been inclined to envisage paradise in more or less the way presented in his Revelation.

John's legacy is still with us. In even more secularized fashion we tend to call paradise any place of extreme luxury. In paradises, all good things are offered in abundance; the service is perfect and enjoyment knows no tension and no inhibition. In modern times, a third interpretation of the creation story has, in fact, become popular. As the human mind tends to resolve rather than accept contradictions and as details normally attract more attention than generalities, the two distinct versions given in the *Book of Genesis* have been merged. Influenced by the biblical story, many Westerners (and an increasing number of Easterners) are inclined to believe that the world we are living in had once been the original paradise and at the same time is the definite and only place meant for humans. It lost its glamour and appeal because it was and is still being mistreated and destroyed. By eating the forbidden fruit, Adam and Eve inaugurated a process of reckless devastation. It is therefore our moral and practical obligation to try and make the most of what we now possess. Since earth is our lost paradise, instead of continuing to treat it irresponsibly we must find ways to save it. Save the earth and save all living creatures that are threatened with extinction are common and widely accepted aims.

At the same time, since it is not likely that humans shall ever be able to turn the clock back to time zero, a more realistic project has also been undertaken. Just like the Persian kings, our modern elite has created small (or not so small) paradisiac compartments for leisure, recreation, and amusement: kingdoms of God upon earth, so to say. Our modern paradises are often located in exotic places, as far away from civilization as possible. But also, sometimes, in the middle of our gigantic cities, carefully maintained and guarded. Evidently, such projects call for proper planning and sophisticated organization.

The more democratic our societies become, the more such places are being opened for their less privileged members. More and more Westerners as well as Easterners are seeking cheap and comprehensive tickets to paradise through the expanding tourist industry or, sometimes, by use of drugs rather than by means of regular transportation (Krippendorf 1990; Urry 1990). In one further respect our modern mind has felt it necessary to part company with both John and the orthodox churches. Sex is not excluded from our understanding of uninhibited bliss. Any true paradise should certainly include carnal delights as a major component, including virtual delights as we now tend to call them.

In the years of triumphant Christianity, thousands of believers were ready to make almost any sacrifice required in order to secure a position in the eschatological kingdom of God. In the most extreme cases they abandoned city and village life to settle in the deserts or some other kind of wilderness within their reach. The idea was to avoid the temptations of civilization. If the reward was to be a world of unceasing abundance, then it was small sacrifice to renounce all property and wealth for the brief period of an ordinary lifespan. While still upon earth, these hermits and monks saw themselves and were seen by others as angels on their way to paradise.

Leading lives in almost complete isolation and of almost total deprivation, the holy men and women of late antiquity became particularly sensitized to even the slightest stimulation. They thought that they heard voices and had visions. Some of them were convinced that they were granted the privilege of foresight. A few claimed that they had even visited God's paradise for brief periods. They obviously all knew that such a claim had been made by the apostle Paul in his second epistle to the Corinthians—although Paul had cautiously refrained from disclosing any specific details. (2 Corinthians 12:2–4). Well known was the story told about the fourth century ascetic Macarius, who had lived in the Egyptian desert.[23]

Macarius (i.e. the blessed), it was said, had once strongly desired to get a glimpse of paradise while he was still in the flesh. Realizing, as we may assume, that his desire was somewhat preposterous, he modified it to make it more reasonable and, so to speak, practical. Instead of God's paradise he turned his mind upon a duplicate, known to exist in the desert. It was the creation of two magicians called Jannes and Jambres. In the Book of Exodus, the Pharaoh's wise men and sorcerers had imitated Moses' and Aaron's miracles with great success (Exodus 7:11–13). A further development of the legend gave names to two of them and credited them with even more incredible deeds. Although very popular in its time, this apocryphal Jewish account has only survived in virtually unintelligible fragments, but the basic ideas are clear.[24] The magicians had planted and cultivated a paradise identical to the original (Pietersma 1994).

After much fasting and prayer, Macarius started wandering through the desert for three weeks. As he fasted he found himself on the verge of fainting

---

[23] Actually there were two Macarii living in the same period, one known as the Alexandrian and the other as the Egyptian. The story is attributed by some authorities to the one and by some to the other. For similar visions of the period see Kyrtatas (1998).

[24] We first hear about Jannes and his brother in the first century BCE 'Damascus Rule' of the Dead Sea Scrolls. In the *New Testament* they are mentioned in 2 Timothy 3:8.

when an angel directed him to the place of his heart's desire. Just as there were winged creatures, that is, angels, guarding God's paradise, so there were demons guarding the entrance of the replica. Suitably enough, the Garden covered an enormous area. Macarius prayed again and, making a bold effort, succeeded in entering. Inside he found two holy men. They now all prayed together and embraced each other. The holy men washed his feet and offered him fruit of great size and varied colours. Three large springs watered the huge trees that bore every kind of fruit that exists under Heaven. Macarius remained in the Garden for a week. Then, ignoring the warnings of his companions, he set off again to inform the other monks of his discovery. The return journey was even more difficult and hazardous. Exhausted by the effort he fell asleep.

At long last, having found his fellow monks, Macarius showed them a fruit he had brought with him as proof of his strange discovery. But all his efforts to persuade them that this paradise was a perfect dwelling place for all of them came to no avail. The fathers had strong arguments against this tempting prospect. 'For if we were to enjoy [paradise] in this life', they objected, 'we should have received our portion of good things while still on earth. What reward would we have afterwards when we come into the presence of God?' So they all decided to continue to live in the austere fashion they were accustomed to.[25] The only secure path to paradise was life upon this miserable earth—the more miserable, indeed, the better it prepared men and women for a perfect reward.

The story of Macarius seems enlightening to me in many ways. To begin with, it makes perfect sense as it stands. He who lives in the desert imposing upon himself hardship of every kind in order to enter paradise is quite naturally expected to dream of paradise. For this, at least, is what we may reasonably assume: the whole account is but a dream or hallucinatory vision. Having reached the point of fainting, Macarius finds himself inside the legendary area. The bliss he experiences is so intense that some kind of anticlimax becomes necessary. It is experienced as an urgent need to leave again in the hope of being joined by his friends. The ascetic realises that he has exited at the moment he begins to wake from his deep sleep. Regaining consciousness, he found himself surrounded by his brethren who were clearly worried about his health. They knew that he had been fasting too much. Tactfully, they did not contradict his claims, but tried to bring his thoughts down to earth again.

The Jewish tradition, more strongly than the Greek or the Mesopotamian, took it for granted that the common lot of suffering was the result of a fall or original sin. Christianity was now proclaiming that it was through suffering that paradise would be eventually regained. Eager to secure their destiny,

---

[25] I here offer a paraphrase based on Norman Russell's translation in *The Lives of the Desert Fathers*, London and Oxford 1981, pp. 108–9.

the desert fathers were led to a voluntary sacrifice of all the small pleasures life could offer, as if such pleasures were an obstacle, or rather *the* obstacle, to salvation.

Such attitudes, as the story of Macarius clearly illustrates, brought the desert in surprising and unexpected proximity to paradise. For it was in the wilderness that the gate to the place of desire was found. This gate was a state of mind that allowed the direct transition from a hellish to a heavenly environment. More interestingly, the desert could be described in the same terms as paradise, though as its exact negative: it lacked all that paradise possessed. It was waterless and dry, exceedingly hot or exceedingly cold, it produced no food while the few animals that wandered in it were hungry and dangerous. Paradise, on the contrary, had springs and trees of every variety, especially fruit-bearing ones; it had a mild climate and was felicitous in every possible way.

A story is only a story and a vision only a vision. But stories and visions often have higher meanings and reveal deep structures of the mind. It is precisely because the information provided about paradise was disclosed in a dream that we may consider it as accurate. Dreams, as we now know, are the royal way leading to a deeper reality. Our ascetic was given in a vision what many theologians were trying to formulate in abstract and metaphorical terms.

Macarius was a pious man and his orthodoxy was never really questioned. Yet, he found it possible to believe that humanity could also construct its own paradise, identical to the original—or almost. Of course this particular paradise was the work of sorcerers contesting the deeds of God's agents Moses and Aaron. But their product was widely appreciated and admired. As the legend went, they were both finally converted and saved, while their paradise became a lasting monument of human might.

The adventure in the desert was not recorded to stigmatize vanity. It was neither ridiculed nor condemned. As every sensitive person could realise, it was the expression of a strong desire and the product of a genuine belief. In its own way it repeated the ambiguities and contradictions that are already evident in the Genesis account, in the choice of the word 'paradise' and in the prophecy of John. Life upon earth is harsh; it may become even harsher. But whether one believes in a heavenly paradise or not, men and women have never really completely abandoned the idea that at least in some remote corners upon earth paradises do exist—or can be made to exist.

The quest for paradise during the Middle Ages is a fascinating, albeit complicated, issue deserving special treatment (Cohn 1970). In more recent times, humanity has placed its hopes in industrialization and technological progress. Modern Westerners have secured for themselves comforts that could not even be imagined in traditional societies. Food is offered in such abundance that it is considered rather to be an obstacle than a luxury, giving rise to the creation of slimming centres instead of guaranteeing bliss. Flying like birds or diving like fish are no longer fantasies of storytellers and imaginative poets. We can speak to each other and see each other even when far apart.

People have visited the moon and sent probes into deep space. Any one of these achievements would have been considered by Macarius a far greater feat than planting a garden in the desert. In the Arabian desert whole cities have been built with all kinds of luxuries and amenities. Those who gave life to Las Vegas could be seen as more potent magicians than Jannes and Jambres (Hannighan 1998).

However, as we all know only too well, economic growth, industrialization, and technological progress are not perceived by modern men and women as a sure course to paradise (cf. Chapters 10 and 12). While many people believe that our modern cities are the closest we can get to a world of abundance, there are others who reach the opposite conclusion: civilized life in contemporary cities, with all its amenities and conveniences, is often regarded as a nightmare. The price paid for what comforts have been obtained is overpopulation, pollution, traffic congestion, accidents, illness, and all sorts of anxiety-generating social mischief. City life in most modern societies is increasingly seen as the counterpart of life in an ancient desert. Modern men and women have created their own versions of Hell from which they are constantly hoping to escape. Abandoning everyday life and everyday work for brief periods has become an obsession rather than a privilege.

People go to all kinds of places in order to forget their discontents. They often visit the hellish environment of other people simply to escape from their own—or, perhaps, in the hope that others have made better use of their civilization. Sometimes they find comfort in just travelling or being on the move. But the ultimate aspiration of large sections of the population in western societies is to spend some time in places untouched, if possible, by civilization, places that have remained in more or less their 'original' or 'natural' state. Good vacations, it is often thought, require the exact opposite of what civilization can offer. Not surprisingly, such virginal environments are normally called paradises.

In our modern world, to obtain a ticket to salvation the total renunciation of the early Christian ascetics is not necessary. Our practical mind has also found less demanding ways to secure at least the temporary delights promised by travel agents. In advanced and even not so advanced societies people regularly put money aside from their income throughout the year in order to secure a few days at a tropical island, an exotic beach, a hidden forest, or a magic mountain—although our small sacrifices cannot offer experiences as deep or as fulfilling as were offered to some Christian ascetics.

Paradise is a common name for hotels, beaches, and other exotic locations.[26] It would be futile even to attempt a search of the word in the yellow pages of the huge and expanding tourist industry. The variety of attractions offered

---

[26] Since 28 November 2002, the terrorist attack at the 'Paradise Hotel' in Mombasa, Kenya, which left fifteen dead and scores of injured, has added a deep tragic irony to this observation.

under this label is overwhelming. But we may reasonably assume that any proper claim of the word paradise in our modern and secular sense depends upon a common denominator. It requires some kind of contact with nature, temperate weather, good food, a friendly and unpolluted atmosphere, mobility without congestion, absence of unpleasant noise or smells, and so on. To put it briefly and simply, the paradise built by Jannes and Jambres in the Egyptian desert some 3000 years ago, in which Macarius lived for a spell, might still rank high in the priorities of modern holiday-hungry men and women.

In contemporary society, each person is entitled to have his own private dreams that often differ radically from those of his neighbours. A paradise should thus offer a variety of amusements from which individuals may choose à la carte (Bauman 1988, 1992; Ritzer 1999). But according to a rather common understanding, complete isolation is not desirable. Men and women normally want to share their experiences, especially when they are good and gratifying (but also when they are painful; see Chapter 1, this volume). Those who are privileged to live in a paradise are not expected to feel inhibited by the presence of others. But all of them wish to feel well protected from intruders or indiscreet outsiders. Bliss in heaven, it should be remembered, is a collective rather than a private privilege, which allows entry, however, only to those who deserve it—or have the means to afford it. The entrances to paradise have always been carefully guarded, be it by angels, demons, or, in their absence, security guards (Bauman 2001).

In one of the creation accounts, God commanded Adam and Eve to be fruitful, to multiply, and to fill the earth, implying some kind of carnal knowledge. But most orthodox commentators who concentrated upon the second version came to the conclusion that lovemaking was a punishment not a privilege, the result of the fall and of the expulsion from the Garden of Eden. Consequently, back in Heaven men and women are expected to find again the innocence of Adam and Eve before they ever ate the forbidden fruit. On the other hand, if this were really so, then Hell may be envisaged as a place of unceasing intercourse. It is not accidental that Hell is where Offenbach sets the Bacchanal in his Orphée aux Enfers. The contradiction was clear to all who cared to reflect upon the matter. Some early Christians speculated considerably on the necessity of their sexual organs in paradise. 'If they were not meant for use then why did they exist at all', they asked their religious teachers. Others had second thoughts.[27] But the paradox was never really resolved and, indeed, has left some of its marks. In nudist camps, for example, that are clearly meant to bring men and women closer to the original state of Adam and Eve, sexual activity, at least in public spaces, is normally strictly prohibited. Any sign of carnal desire is felt to be embarrassing and undesirable. Augustine, we may recall, regarded (involuntary) erection a result of original

---

[27] This topic is treated persistently in works attributed (falsely) to Justin, such as the *De resurrectione*. Cf. Clement of Alexandria, *Stromateis* 3.13, 15.

sin (Brown 1983). Sex is also excluded in some modern utopias. Just as Macarius saw no women in his replica paradise, some feminists have aspired to an ideal world without men.

Contrary to what is generally believed, sex was not excluded from the desert life of the early Christian ascetics. Stories were often told about women wandering into the dwelling places of men or of men into the dwelling places of women. For the most part this was done very discretely, but publicity was not always avoided. Just as prostitutes sometimes became nuns, so, too, there was an opposite movement from the desert to the brothels. The villagers, it is recorded, were always ready to attribute the pregnancies of unmarried women to monks and other ascetics. All such behaviour was invariably condemned but it helps us understand that erotic preoccupations were rarely absent from the minds of those living in the hope of regaining paradise (Rousselle 1988).[28]

Besides wishing to exclude unqualified entrants, modern men and women often look forward to discovering places upon earth without policemen, courts, or prisons. In a true paradise freedom should be absolute, especially freedom of desire. Restrictions and prohibitions are seen as incompatible with true enjoyment. The problem is that men and women often experience conflicting desires while the freedom of one person may harm or diminish the enjoyment of others. The Garden of Eden, it may be recalled, was not without its laws. Adam and Eve were clearly asked to take care of all other living creatures. More significantly, they were forbidden to eat from a certain tree. It was by transgressing this law that they provoked their own downfall. It is therefore quite obvious that in a modern paradise there should be some kind of order. Negligence and provocation, no matter how desirable they may be for some people, cannot be (wholly) tolerated. The need for order and aversion for law, rules, and decrees are not easily reconciled.

The solution that seems to be accepted by most modern men and women is once again to be found in the biblical tradition. Proper legislation in an ideal situation is not perceived as oppressive because it is not enforced by policemen and guards. Having been internalized it is experienced as part of a person's own wishes. Adam and Eve were prone to transgressing the law because they had no true, that is, internal, knowledge of it. Through long centuries of suffering and moral instruction the basic obligations of all men and women have been or will be inscribed in their hearts. In his paradise Macarius knew how to behave and how to treat his fellow ascetics just as they knew how to treat the newcomer. Law in paradise exists but is enforced discretely, and rarely (if at all) needs to be explicitly proclaimed. To put it in biblical terms, law shall be planted within men and women, being written in their hearts (Jeremiah 31:33).[29]

---

[28] For a collection of texts see Benedicta Ward S. L. G. (ed.), *Harlots of the Desert: A study of repentance in early monastic sources*, Mowbray, London and Oxford 1987.

[29] Cf. Deuteronomy 6: 4–9.

Such considerations bring me finally to a point that deserves some special attention. Technology is not excluded from our paradises. For our comfort we expect all kinds of sophisticated devices to be employed. Even exotic islands, as we all know, depend for their maintenance upon elaborate programmes and constant human intervention. However, the quality of modern paradises depends heavily on what we may describe as organizational discretion. Technology and other kinds of human intervention should make their presence felt as little as possible. The ideal is to help nature function in its most perfect state. The best possible organization in the best possible place of retreat should appear as a non-organization. The idea is clearly given in the story related about Macarius.

From what little we may surmise about the desert replica paradise, its perfection depended upon the absence of any servants or assistants. There was no one around to plant trees.[30] No gardeners were seen watering the fruit-bearing plants and no workers clearing the banks of the rivers or the channels, as was normal in Egypt. Macarius, just like the Spartan general Lysander, knew well that he had entered a man-made paradise. Yet, having been properly built and organized, this paradise had no need for constant and visible human intervention.

Interestingly, but not surprisingly, the ascetics, too, took good care to make organizational patterns in their desert invisible. It is therefore to the desert that we should once again turn if we wish to locate the roots of some very modern conceptions of our own paradises. For beneath the apparent simplicity of ascetic life there actually lay very complex systems of communication. Precisely because the desert provided little or no water and little or no nutrition and, obviously, no market and no goods, the hermits had to rely upon the help of friends and collaborators. Such friends regularly brought in food in exchange for the artefacts produced by them. Furthermore, although the ideal was a state of almost complete isolation, the holy men and women who lived in the wilderness were in constant and routine movement. They visited each other, served those in need, and exchanged experiences. They all regularly received visitors from nearby villages or towns seeking cures and spiritual advice and were kept informed about developments in the 'civilized' world. When need arose, the ascetics knew which dogma to defend during the long anti-heretical wars that raged in the empire.

In most accounts little is said about all these affairs, but this is only because they were taken for granted. Life in the desert depended upon an efficient though exceedingly discrete organizational network. As I see it, the real magicians were the ascetics themselves. They had managed to build a world of their own and to make it appear as thin as air.

In the high days of triumphant Christianity, the deserts were filled with ascetics, monks, and nuns. Such men and women could be counted in tens of

---

[30] Cf. Baudrillard's discussion of simulations and simulacra (Baudrillard 1983).

thousands, forming small or not so small towns. Through hard work and, especially, a very low cost of living they had found an alternative way of sustaining themselves. It is often overlooked that one of the factors that made life in the desert possible was the absence of tax collectors. 'Tax havens', referring to 'offshore' locations offering profitable investment opportunities, are often considered as 'tax heavens'—and are indeed so called in some languages.

A strong desire to re-enter or recreate paradise is always with us. Just how a paradise works is a matter for improvization and speculation. But (so it would appear) we all still believe that in its perfect form it should convey the idea of being 'natural', that is, without visible human intervention. The Garden of Eden as well as other versions of the story serve as powerful models. Paradise is nature in its most natural condition. Organization, just like hard work and suffering, is seen as the means for regaining the original Garden. While these phenomena contribute to the attainment of paradise, however, they have no place in it. As we all know, the place for enduring suffering and clearly visible organization with unfailing daemon-guards is called Hell.

And yet we do not understand paradise as a simple retreat to primitivism. For all its mischief civilization has never really been considered in purely negative terms. City life is often hellish enough but retains its appeal as a proper place for permanent residence. The adventure of Macarius could be misleading. Humanity is not heading towards a Garden untouched by intelligent intervention. While spending their time inside their paradises, the Persian kings were neither sleeping on the ground nor seeking shelter in caves. The replica created by Jannes and Jambres seems to have missed what the prophet John knew only too well. The new heaven and new earth of which he had a clear vision included a new city as well. Its wall is built of diamond and its base was faced with all kinds of precious stone, while the city itself was made of pure gold, like clear glass (Revelation 21:15–21). Such descriptions convey the idea of luxury, but also of perfection and purity. For its maintenance this city also depends upon some kind of organization, only in this case perfect and pure, if such is possible. But then this is the way our mind and our imagination function: creating and at the same time trying to resolve inconsistencies and contradictions.

References

Anderson, G. (1989). 'Celibacy or consummation in the Garden? Reflections on early Jewish and Christian interpretations of the Garden of Eden'. *Harvard Theological Review*, 82(2): 121–48.

Baudrillard, J. (1983). *Simulations*. New York: Semiotext(e).

Bauman, Z. (1988). *Freedom*. Milton Keynes: Open University Press.

——(1992). *Intimations of Postmodernity*. London: Routledge.

——(2001). 'Uses and disuses of urban space', in B. Czarniawska and R. Solli (eds.), *Organizing Metropolitan Space and Discourse*. Malmo: Liber Ekonomi, pp. 15–32.

Bremmer, J. N. (2002). 'The birth of the term "Paradise"', in *The Rise and Fall of the Afterlife*. London and New York: Routledge, pp. 109–27.

Brown, P. (1983). 'Sexuality and society in fifth century AD: Augustine and Julian of Eclanum', in E. Gabba (ed.), *Tria Corda: Scritti in onore di Arnaldo Momigliano*. Como: Biblioteca di Athenaeum Edizioni New Press, pp. 49–70.

Cohn, N. (1970). *The Pursuit of the Millennium*. Oxford: Oxford University Press.

Hesiod (1973). *Works and Days* (Dorothea Wender, trans.). Harmondsworth: Penguin.

Hannighan, J. (1998). *Fantasy City*. London: Routledge.

Kirk, G. S. (1974). *Greek Myths*. Harmondsworth: Penguin.

Krippendorf (1990). *The Holidaymakers*. London: Butterworth Heinemann.

Kyrtatas, D. J. (1989). 'The transformations of the text: The reception of John's Revelation', in A. Cameron (ed.), *History as Text: The Writing of Ancient History*. London: Duckworth, pp. 146–62.

——(1998). 'Early Christian visions of paradise: Considerations on their Jewish and Greek background', in A. Ovadiah (ed.), *Hellenic and Jewish Arts: Interaction, Tradition and Renewal*. Tel Aviv: Ramot Publishing House, pp. 337–50.

Pagels, E. (1988). *Adam, Eve and the Serpent*. Harmondsworth: Penguin.

Pietersma, A. (1994). *The Apocryphon of Jannes and Jambres the Magicians*. P. Chester Beatty XVI (with New Editions of Papyrus Vindobonensis Greek inv. 29456+29828 verso and British Library Cotton Tiberius B.v f 87), edited with introduction, translation, and commentary, with facsimile of the three texts. Leiden, New York, Köln: E. J. Brill.

Ritzer, G. (1999). *Enchanting a Disenchanted World: Revolutionizing the Means of Consumption*. Thousand Oaks, CA: Pine Forge Press.

Rousselle, A. (1988). *Porneia: On Desire and the Body in Antiquity* (F. Pheasant, trans.). Oxford: Basil Blackwell.

Urry, J. (1990). *The Tourist Gaze*. London: Sage.

Xenophon, (1923). *Oeconomicus* (E. C. Marchant, trans.). Cambridge, MA: Loeb Edition.

II

THE HEROIC NARRATIVES: ACHIEVEMENT, LEADERSHIP, AND POWER

Introduction

HEROISM is the dominant theme of the narratives that animate the chapters in this part of the book. Each chapter presents a distinct aspect of the hero with a thousand faces (Campbell 1949/1988). The rediscovery of heroism by studies of organizations has coincided with increased interest in the cultural life of organizations, their stories, and myths. It has also coincided with a general rediscovery by late industrial capitalism of its heroic heritage, summed up in those independent-minded entrepreneurs who struck out alone, building empires and revolutionizing social and economic life, overcoming crises and leaving lasting legacies. If such entrepreneurs currently vie for the status of contemporary superheroes, ordinary managers who travel business-class and populate the lobbies and business suites of international hotels are lionized as everyday cultural heroes. Between the celebrity manager and the maligned 'fat-cat' who draws astronomical salaries and stock-options, while driving a company to its demise, and eventually gets 'rewarded' by a massive severance payment, the line is a thin one. False messiahs draw upon themselves the rage and the hate of deceived followers, who often turn in hope to new hope merchants, new heroes, who promise to set right the wrongs of their predecessors.

The heroic view of management often lapses into what I call the 'hubris of management'—the view that everything, ranging from information to feelings and emotions, from natural resources to cultural heritage, from business enterprises to amorphous social systems, can be controlled, planned for, and taken advantage of by management (Gabriel 1998). Managers, then, far from being dismissed as vulgarians or philistines, are widely hailed as cultural heroes responsible for some of our civilization's greatest achievements and embodying its core values. Not for nothing then Alasdair MacIntyre cast the manager as one of our three contemporary cultural archetypes, the character for an era which elevates efficiency and effectiveness as supreme values:

The manager represents in his *character* the obliteration of the distinction between manipulative and non-manipulative social relations; . . . The manager treats ends as given, as outside his scope; his concern is with effectiveness in transforming raw materials into final products, unskilled labor into skilled labor, investment into profits. (MacIntyre 1981: 30)

Each of the three chapters in this section uses a well-known hero from Greek, Scriptural, and Celtic mythologies, to highlight certain core features of organizational and political leadership today.

Keith Grint (Chapter 5) draws his inspiration from the second of Hercules' twelve labours, in which the hero defeats the many-headed hydra, whose heads have regenerative qualities, so that when one is cut, two appear in its place. Hercules only manages to kill the hydra when he adopts a flexible multi-pronged approach, cutting, cauterizing, and burying. The hydra readily becomes a metaphor for network-based organizations, that have regenerative qualities and are difficult foes to defeat. Drug cartels, the mafia, and terrorist organizations, like al-Qaida, easily slip into a hydra metaphor, and, as Grint shows, reliance on the single strategy of brute force is unlikely to succeed. More disconcertingly, Grint demonstrates that the roles of Hercules and the Hydra readily cross-migrate, so that one person's Hydra becomes another person's Hercules, just as one person's terrorist becomes another person's terror-fighter. Using numerous historical examples, Grint illustrates how neither triumphalism nor defeatism, but flexibility and inventiveness are required whenever the political leaders confront hydra-like enemies. He offers strong evidence that while individual hydras can be conclusively defeated, it is in the predicament of a hero never to be free of confrontation with hydra-like situations.

If Grint examines the hero when undertaking a difficult exploit, Robert French and Patrick Moore (Chapter 6) illuminate a different aspect—the hero as a friend. Heroic friendship is a theme featuring widely in relations that bind Achilles and Patroclus, or Orestes and Pylades. French and Moore, however, look at friendship not only as a private bond between individuals, but as a very public bond upon which the legitimacy of the leader rests. Such is the friendship of David and Jonathan, a friendship which drives Jonathan to relinquish the rights to royal succession of his father, Saul, in favour of David; this gesture, through which Jonathan recognizes David's greatness, becomes the foundation of David's own greatness as a leader. David feels a spiritual obligation to rise to the level to which his friend has elevated him, and this enables him to deal with the crises and ordeals that fate puts in his path.

It is interesting that while hydra-like situations seem to confront many of today's leaders (even if few of them dispatch them with the aplomb or finality of Hercules), few of today's leaders seem to have the spiritual support of a dedicated friend who is a public figure and one on whose support they can rely. Even when specific political or business partnerships steal the limelight, the suspicion is invariably that theirs is a marriage of convenience rather than a profound spiritual bond. As MacIntyre suggests in the above quotation, such partnerships are driven by expedience, in a moral order which has lost its sense of absolutes and is driven by mere emotivism. French and Moore seek to redeem friendship as a political relationship that does not degenerate into mutual back-scratching and the building of exclusive types of old-boy networks (hydras in their own right), but is instead one that supports the leader through periods of uncertainty and self-doubt, bolstering his/her integrity and dedication to the common good.

In the third chapter of this section (Chapter 7), Donncha Kavanagh and Majella O'Leary use a great Irish hero, Cú Chulainn, as the starting point for an examination of heroism and its relevance to our relatively unheroic age. The study of a Celtic hero enables the authors to tease out certain qualities that may not be so evident in other heroes—courage, versatility, total self-confidence, but also, for the most part, indifference to the common good and a remarkable degree of impetuosity or even stupidity that makes him/her susceptible to being outsmarted by lesser opponents. The great rebirth of interest in Celtic mythology and folklore in the nineteenth century coincided with the emergence of the romantic hero as the great human being who, in politics (like Napoleon), art (like Beethoven), or any sphere of social life, leaves his or her stamp on his or her time, dramatically and indelibly altering boundaries, internal as well as external. What the romantic hero loses in versatility, fierceness, and sheer valour compared to the Celtic prototype, he or she gains in a sensibility, which casts him or her not just as the champion of justice and truth, but more importantly as the champion of emotion over rationality, of the human spirit over mechanical and bureaucratic forces. This is not to say that the Celtic hero is unemotional or lacks friendship or love interests. What sets apart the Romantic hero is that he and very often she broods, dreams, and suffers for love. One can find many impersonations of the romantic hero and heroine, though few can match Goethe's Werther, a truly heroic figure who rebels against Enlightenment Rationalism through a doomed and tragic emotional attachment. As Kavanagh and O'Leary show, where pride was the Achilles heel of the Celtic hero, the romantic hero is susceptible to a gloomy melancholy (a 'mal du temps'), which can easily turn into self-destruction or even into a total corruption of the romantic ideal ending up as megalomaniac tyranny.

If the romantics redefined the idea of heroism and invented a new kind of hero, so too, argue Kavanagh and O'Leary, did the twentieth century, which invented two distinct models of heroism—the neo-romantic hero is a version of the romantic who has tempered his or her aversion for money with a healthy ambition for monetary success, and the postmodern anti-hero, who may be a cynic or a narcissist. Twentieth century anti-heroes sometimes eschew heroic achievement altogether, being merely style leaders or celebrities, imitated for their looks or opinions rather than any directly heroic exploits. Kavanagh and O'Leary rightly point out an additional line in twentieth century heroism—the heroism of the ordinary man or woman, who struggles, endures, and usually survives, often side-stepping the hydras instead of taking them on in direct confrontation. As Kavanagh and O'Leary remind us, this is the basis of a model of heroism, which was extolled primarily by Russian authors, like Gorky and Solzhenitsyn. The variant of the socialist hero is not so very distant from this.

The chapters in this section undoubtedly sound a note of caution towards the unconditional veneration of the hero as a benevolent influence in business, politics, or culture. They also highlight how different eras do not merely discover their own heroes, but redefine the idea of heroism and invent new kinds of heroes whom they alternately venerate or dread.

References

Campbell, J. (1949/1988). *The Hero with a Thousand Faces*. London: Palladin Books.
Gabriel, Y. (1998). 'The hubris of management'. *Administrative Theory and Praxis*, 20(3): 257–73.
MacIntyre, A. (1981). *After Virtue*. London: Duckworth.

FIVE

Overcoming the Hydra: Leaderless Groups and Terrorism

Keith Grint

Introduction

T HE Hydra in Greek mythology represented that most difficult of creatures to overcome: not just a creature with multiple heads, and therefore no apparent leader and no one to hold responsible or to focus upon, but also a creature whose structure appeared to make it immortal because each severed head grew two more. This paradox was eventually transcended when Hercules changed his strategy both for dealing with the mortal heads and for despatching the immortal head.

A similar problem now faces those targeted by terrorists that resemble just such a creature. Since 11 September much blood and many resources have been expended in trying to find, understand, and eliminate the perpetrators. Much has also been written on the development of the network both as a form of organization and as a metaphor for future global business: the traditional organizational hierarchy is dead; long live the non-hierarchical network! My purpose here is neither to debate the dubious nature of the latter nor the premature burial of the former, but instead to consider how the historical myth of the Hydra might provide us with a metaphor to facilitate organizational analysis. In particular, I am concerned with the strengths and weaknesses of what has come to be regarded as a contemporary Hydra and an archetypal network organization: the al-Qaida group.[31]

This chapter takes the myth of the Hydra as a starting point from which to explore the issues and traces the double strategy that Hercules is forced to adopt in his original fight with the beast. While Hercules is able to decapitate

---

[31] See: http://web.nps.navy.mil/~library/tgp/qaida.htm; http://cns.miis.edu/research/wtc01/alqaida.htm; www.au.af.mil/au/aul/bibs/tergps/tgaqai.htm.

the multiple heads, their regenerative powers force him to cauterize the stumps to prevent their regrowth. However, the central—and immortal—head requires a different strategy because severing and cauterizing it is not enough to prevent regrowth; instead it has to be properly buried. This double strategy I call 'the Hydra paradox' because deploying either one simply encourages regeneration—a lesson we are in danger of overlooking with regard to the contemporary threat of terrorism. But first let us explore what kind of things the Hydra represents.

The Five Hydras

The 'Hydra' has (at least) five embodiments: star formation, myth, metaphor, polyp, and organizational design. First, the largest (and for my purposes the least significant) version of the hydra is the extremely long star formation in a very distant constellation, primarily in the southern hemisphere.[32] Second, it is a mythical monster: a multi-headed regenerative creature that formed the second of Hercules' 'labours'. Third, it is biological creature, a polyp: a freshwater hydroid with tentacles around its mouth and the beloved aquatic animal of biology students, which can regenerate the parts of its body that have been cut off. Fourth, the Hydra has been adopted as a metaphor for the underworld, the mob, or the devil incarnate. Lastly, the Hydra represents the design blueprint for a new form of organization—a network of loosely aligned groups with little formal structure or central leadership. With the exception of the star formation, all the other embodiments have some resonance with the analysis of the al-Qaida Group that follows below: it is steeped in myth, it is a monster, it is regenerative, and it represents a novel form of organization.

The Mythical Hydra

In Greek mythology, Hercules was the son of Zeus and the mortal woman Alcmene. Zeus's immortal wife, Hera, tried to kill her husband's earthly off-spring by putting two snakes into Hercules' crib—but he strangled one with each hand. Not to be outdone, she appointed Eurystheus not Hercules as King of Mycenae and then drove Hercules mad, inciting him to kill his own children. To atone for the crime Eurystheus promptly ordered Hercules to perform a series of twelve 'impossible' labours, the second of which was killing the Lernaean Hydra. If he completed the labours successfully Hercules would atone for his guilt and achieve immortality.

[32] Hydra: Abbreviation: Hya; Genitive: Hydrae. Right Ascension: 10.12 h; Declination: − 19.36°. See www.astronomical.org/constellations/hya.html.

The Hydra was a multi-headed water serpent born from a union between Echidne and Typhon. While Echidne, related to the mermaids, was half-woman and half-serpent, Typhon was a terrible giant. The Hydra inhabited a cave, or alternatively the roots of a giant plane tree, in Lake Lerna in Argolis, near the city of Argos. Lerna's waters were bottomless and provided access to the underworld for all who could get past the gatekeeper—the Hydra, whose elder brother was Kerberos, a three- or sometimes five-headed creature. The precise number of heads on the Hydra is also debated: most versions suggest nine, some five, and some increase the number to several hundred.[33] Whatever the number, one of the heads was immortal and the Hydra spent most of its time destroying the livestock and crops of the surrounding farmers—often killing people simply by breathing on them, so poisonous was its breath, as indeed was its blood.

Guided by Athene, Iolaus, the son of Iphicles (the twin brother of Hercules), drove Hercules to the creature's lair in a chariot. There the Hydra was forced out of its cave by flaming arrows. But Hercules soon found that cutting off any of its existing heads simply compounded his problems because each stump grew two more heads. In effect, the more he attacked the creature the stronger it became. Eventually, Hercules called upon his nephew to help and Iolaus started a fire (having cut down an entire forest) and duly cauterized each of the Hydra's headless stumps as they fell to Hercules's sword. However, the last head was immortal so when Hercules cut it off he buried it under a large rock on the road between Lerna and Elaius (Kerényi 1974: 143–5).

The Biological Hydra

The regenerative heads of the mythical hydra were precisely where the biological hydra derived its name, and it has been known for some considerable time that certain species have the ability to regrow parts of their bodies. Indeed, flatworms seem to have perfected the art to the point where a theoretical immortality appears to exist. But, it is not coincidental that the metaphorical hydras of anarchy only entered the language in the eighteenth century, for the polyp (a hollow cylindrical body with a ring of tentacles around the mouth, which occurs in freshwater ponds and lakes) was only discovered by the Dutch inventor of the microscope, Anton von Leeuwenhoek, in 1702. In 1740, Abraham Trembley, a Swiss naturalist, discovered the green species but he was uncertain whether it was a plant—because it was green—or an animal—because it moved. Although the regenerative powers of lizards (tails) and crayfish (claws) were also well known at this time, Trembley thought that only a plant could regenerate more than half its body, but cutting a polyp in half horizontally led the old head to grow a new bottom and the old bottom to grow a new head. Indeed, whichever way he cut it the

[33] See http://astro.sci.uop.edu/~sas/Newsletter/CON_Hydra.html.

polyp regrew itself until one polyp had seven heads. In 1758, Linneaus named the polyp a Hydra.

Hydras live in most streams, lakes, and ponds, they are from 3 to 50mm in length, and they use their four to eight tentacles to feed on crustaceans, insect larvae, worms, and similar small animals (www.aaskolnick.com/hydra.htm). And there's more to Hercules' strategy than just brute force. According to Shimizu's (2001) experiments, the regeneration of a Hydra's head after decapitation depends upon the state of the injured tissue. In effect, the greater the injury the less chance of regeneration—Hercules was right: chopping the head off is insufficient but cauterizing the stump (inflicting greater tissue damage) may well prevent regeneration. It may have worked for Hercules, and it may work in the laboratory, but does this help us understand, or deal with, either the historical or contemporary political threats to the establishment, the state, or society?

The Metaphorical Hydra

Labelling groups that threaten the establishment as Hydras is hardly new; indeed, the juxtaposition of Hercules and the Hydra has provided a richly woven mythical tapestry for many writers, monarchs, and militants. Hercules was frequently represented as the hero in whose image laboured the builders of the Old and New Worlds. The British king, George I (1660–1727), George III's (1738–1820) brother, and King William III (1765–1837) all modelled themselves on Hercules. While in America, in 1776, John Adams called for 'The Judgement of Hercules' to be the seal of the future United States of America. Francis Bacon even suggested that Hercules was the inspiration of modern science and capitalism.

In contrast, the many-headed Hydra was deemed to embody the opposite: the Lord of Misrule. As J. J. Mauricius, the ex-governor of Suriname, lamented on his return to Holland in 1751—having failed to destroy a group of rebellious runaway slaves encamped in the swamp:

> Even if an army of ten thousand men were gathered, with
> The courage and strategy of Caesar and Eugene,
> They'd find their work cut out for them, destroying a Hydra's growth
> Which even Alcides [Hercules] would try to avoid
>
> (quoted in Linebaugh and Rediker 2000: 2–4)

Similarly, Andrew Ure contended that he (and for that matter every other manufacturer of the early nineteenth century) was the contemporary Hercules—not just in constructing machines with powers that matched Hercules, but also in using such inventions to tame or 'strangle' the 'Hydra of misrule', that is, the contagion of rebellious workers. But, one might argue, 'is not one person's hydra just another person's Hercules?'.

The definitional quagmire that surrounds 'terrorism'—aka 'freedom-fighter', 'separatist', 'rebel', 'guerrilla', and, increasingly with regard to media descriptions of armed supporters of al-Qaida, 'fighter'—was raised by Sir Jeremy Greenstock, Chair of the UN Security Council's Committee on Terrorism on 28 October 2001. He suggested that terrorism should include: 'The indiscriminate use of violence, particularly against civilians, to further a political aim'. In fact, the original use seems to have been recorded by the Académie française in 1789, as 'a system or rule of terror'—an interesting definition since it includes the use of terror by a state against its own citizens. Indeed, for much of the post-1945 era the United Nations has failed to agree a definition of terrorism precisely because such a definition may implicate some member states, and because some definitions imply a justification of terror. Since 1963 twelve international conventions on terrorism have been drawn up against specific acts of terrorism, hijacking and hostage taking and so on, but no definition has ever been agreed upon (Roberts 2002: 18–19), though resolution 1373 (2001) on terrorism was adopted by the Security Council at its 4385th meeting, on 28 September 2001.[34] The nearest thing to a consensus on the definition of terrorism talks of: '…criminal acts intended or calculated to provoke a state of terror in the general public, a group of persons or particular persons for political purposes…[these are] in any circumstances unjustifiable whatever the considerations of a political, philosophical, ideological, racial, ethnic, religious or other nature that may be used to justify them' (quoted in Roberts 2002: 19).[35]

Fisk (2001) insists that linguistic gyrations around the word 'terrorism' are common and contemptible on the part of all involved in such conflicts. In other words, the problem is not using the word 'terrorist' to say what we mean, but that competing groups try to delineate their 'legitimate' acts in contrast to the 'terrorism' imposed by the other side. In most cases both sides seem to be involved in acts of terrorism. For example,

> …when Israeli soldiers were captured by Lebanese guerrillas they were reported to have been "kidnapped", as if the Israeli presence in Lebanon was in some way legitimate. Suspected resistance men in southern Lebanon, however, were "captured" by Israeli troops… By the mid-1980s, the AP [Associated Press] used "terrorists" about Arabs but rarely about the IRA in Northern Ireland, where the agreed word was "guerrillas", presumably because AP serves a number of news outlets in the United States with a large Irish-American audience. The BBC, which increasingly referred to Arab "terrorists", *always* referred to the IRA as "terrorists" but scarcely ever called ANC bombers in South Africa "terrorists"… *Tass* and *Pravda*, of course, referred to Afghan rebels as "terrorists"… In September 1985 a British newspaper reported that a [Soviet] airliner carrying civilian passengers [over Afghanistan] had been "downed by rebels". "Terrorists" are those who use

---

[34] Resolution 1373 (2001) on terrorism was adopted by the Security Council at its 4385th meeting, on 28 September 2001. It can be viewed at: www.un.org/Docs/sc/committees/1373.

[35] 'Terrorism'—as currently defined by the US government—can be viewed at http://civilliberty.about.com/library/weekly/aa082902a.htm (thanks to Kris Grint for pointing this out).

violence against the side that is using the word. The only terrorists whom Israel acknowledges are those opposed to Israel. The only terrorists the United States acknowledges are those who oppose the United States or their allies. The only terrorists Palestinians acknowledge—for they too use the word—are those opposed to the Palestinians. (Fisk 2001: 438–41).[36]

Under any of these definitions the 11 September attacks were acts of terrorism, acts of violence perpetrated against non-combatants for political and religious ends. But clearly the members of al-Qaida do not regard themselves as terrorists, so irrespective of the lexicon of terror, can conventional organizations defeat unconventional organizations that have some degree of popular support?

The Organizational Hydra: Hierarchies and Networks

The difficulties of conventional—and thus hierarchical—organizations in dealing with more flexible and fluid opponents operating in territory unfamiliar to the former have long been mooted. For instance, one of the reasons why management sometimes prefers to deal with organized trade unions, rather than a disorganized mass, is because a 'leaderless' group is far more difficult to control or negotiate with than an organization with a recognizable hierarchy and some degree of control over its members. In the British fuel crisis of September 2000, for example, a small number of self-appointed militants, intent on disrupting the transportation of petrol to force down the tax, virtually held the country to ransom for several days. And while the government struggled to respond, their main problem was that the protesters appeared to have no recognizable leadership that could at best either negotiate a settlement or at worst provide a recognizable target for some form of legal constraint (Burke *et al.* 2000).

Military overlords have long struggled with such unconventional opponents grounded in what is now called 'Asymmetric Warfare'. In fact the contemporary threat from al-Qaida has rather more resonance with the Order of Assassins, the *batiniyya*, from the twelfth-century Middle East, notably Persia and Syria. 'Assassin' was a derogatory label applied by the Crusaders from the Arabic word *hashshashin*, meaning 'taker of hashish' (cannabis), but it seems doubtful that the perpetrators of terror were drug-induced. Instead they were comprised of fanatical Shi'ites led by a Persian, Hasan-i-Sabbah, whose primary targets were the Turkish Seljuq sultans, Sunni Muslims, though Crusaders were also their victims. And like the contemporary suicide bombers,

---

[36] 625 Israelis have been killed and 4500 injured in 14,280 Palestinian attacks between 1999 and 2002. Over 1372 Palestinians have been killed and 19,684 injured in Israeli attacks (Grossman 2002).

the Assassins accepted their own deaths as a duty and in the expectation of entry into paradise (Blow 2001).

One thousand years later the difficulties posed to conventional authority by unconventional organizations increased—but it was by no means clear that conventional force would succumb to the unconventional. For instance, the US government fought a long campaign against terror allegedly linked to an anarchist network in the first three decades of the twentieth century. This ultimately fizzled out, marked—though not caused—by the (in)famous execution of Nicola Sacco and Bartolomeo Vanzetti in 1927 for a murder that occurred in 1920 in Boston.[37] Forty years later, a rather more organized attempt to overthrow the political establishment was successfully defeated by the British after a twelve-year communist insurgency in Malaya—but only by putting 105,000 full-time and 250,000 part-time soldiers and police into action to kill over 10,000 insurgents (losing 1865 men themselves in the process). Yet alongside the overt strategy of force was a more subtle one: the British promised independence to Malaya and their strategy worked because the Chinese-led insurgents failed to ensure significant Malay support (Grey 2002). Where the response was more military than anything else, the British were less successful: in 1967, for example, British forces withdrew from Aden after three years of insurgency had stimulated the then Conservative government to declare that, although Southern Arabia would be granted independence by 1968, Britain would maintain a military base there, though it did not.

Indeed, one reason that most of Europe has remained so peaceful since the Second World War may well be that what came to be known as the Marshall Plan provided such a different inheritance to that laid down by the Treaty of Versailles in 1919. As Marshall said in 1947, 'our policy is directed not against any country or doctrine, but against hunger, poverty, desperation and chaos. Its purpose should be the revival of a working economy in the world so as to permit the emergence of political and social conditions in which free institutions can exist' (quoted in Carruth and Eugene 1988). In effect, the assault upon fascism in general and Nazi Germany in particular comprised two elements: destroying the enemy's capacity for war and undermining the context that had helped it to grow in the first place. This double strategy both reflects Hercules' differentiated approach to the Hydra and is echoed in Amartya Sen's (2002: 25) recent call for a global alliance to combat not just terrorism but also 'for more positive goals, such as combating illiteracy and reducing preventable illnesses that so disrupt economic and social lives in poorer countries'. In other words, the immortal head—the cause—has to be buried along with the mortal heads—the means. So if neither networks nor hierarchies are invincible, what kind of organization is the al-Qaida group?

[37] For a brief review of events see www.english.upenn.edu/~afilreis/88/sacvan.html.

Hierarchies and Networks: The al-Qaida Group

Few people predicted the rise of a qualitatively different kind of terrorist group, one that was religiously inspired, globally located, and intent on maximizing rather than avoiding the mass death of innocent civilians. Certainly Paul Wilkinson (2000: 59–60), a noted British expert, seemed to dismiss the probability of Islamic terrorists primarily targeting anywhere other than the existing Middle East states because the existing groups at the time of writing had a fundamentally political agenda. So why did al-Qaida take a different turn?

The source of al-Qaida seems to lie in two critical events of 1979: the fall of the Shah of Iran to an Islamic Revolution and the Soviet invasion of Afghanistan. Both events encouraged the flowering of many radical groups intent on creating other fundamentalist Islamic societies, amongst whom was Al Qaida al-Sulbah (The Solid Base) formed by Abdullah Azzam, a mentor to Osama bin Laden. The group, comprising a self-styled 'pious vanguard' (in some ways similar both to the early Bolshevik party and the New Model Army of the English civil war) operating under the name of MAK (Afghan Service Bureau) recruited, financed, trained, and placed perhaps as many as 100,000 for the *jihad* (holy war) against the Soviet Union and then into several flash points, including: Kashmir, Chechnya, the Philippines, Indonesia, Georgia, Somalia, Uzbekistan, Yemen, Algeria, and Egypt. Around 3000 were then selected for further operations and al-Qaida fighters were involved in the bombing of US embassies in Tanzania and Kenya and against the USS Cole. This diaspora is critical in determining what the aims of al-Qaida are: they are not focused on particular territorial ambitions as manifest in a specific state but rather on the regional construction of a fundamentalist pan-Islamic state, a regenerated Caliphate, to replace what they regard as corrupt Islamic states and displace all those that inhibit this, most notably the United States (Gunaratna 2002: 1–15). In fact, as Bergen (2001: 242–3) suggests, bin Laden's propaganda does not attack the West for what he might see as its cultural depravity, but for its support of what he regards as corrupt Muslim states. Indeed, the idea of a Caliphate—a political–religious structure for all Islamic people that was originally constructed after the death of the Prophet Muhammad—is theoretically boundaryless and certainly unrelated to the idea of territorial nation states (see Hill 2001: 98–100).

More problematically, the horror of 11 September has been considerably compounded by the difficulty of discerning those responsible for planning it and the likelihood of such attacks stopping if bin Laden was apprehended. It has often been suggested that al-Qaida is a leaderless group and thus removing Osama bin Laden from the scene will do little to undermine its effectiveness. There are, indeed, leaderless groups in existence, especially bands of hunter-gatherers like the Hadza of Tanzania, but al-Qaida does not seem to be one of these 'conventional' leaderless groups. The structure of al-Qaida is not an egalitarian network, then, but nor is it an authoritarian hierarchy; instead it seems to be a hybrid of the two: Osama bin Laden provides the central command structure, the strategic direction, and the financial and ideological resources for the entire network but he sits within a horizontally derived network of semi-independent terrorist cells of between two and fifteen people who are called upon as and when necessary for tactical deployments and action. The relatively loose coalition remains coherent in and through its ideological glue, not through formal hierarchies or structures, and this philosophical similarity, a religious identity, transcends whatever diversity exists; as long as al-Qaida remains internally coherent, individuals will remain committed to it. As Gunaratna (2003*b*: 21) suggests, 'it is not poverty or lack of literacy that drives people to join terrorist groups, but ideology; the poor and ill-educated simply being more susceptible'. At most, then, perhaps bin Laden or even al-Qaida plays a gatekeeper role for those seeking martyrdom, much as the Hydra did in the original myth.[38]

Thus, rather like the *Waffen* SS units in the Second World War, the disciplinary system is internally accepted rather than externally enforced: individual units do not need to be told what to do because their common philosophy acts as an ideological compass. However, unlike the *Waffen* SS, the global cells of al-Qaida have a very limited hierarchy amongst or between themselves and tend to be organized along ethnic lines, with each ethnic 'family' responsible for a different function: training, weapons procurement, finance, and so on (Gunaratna 2002: 95–166). In this sense al-Qaida is closer to a heterarchy than a hierarchy, that is, a flexible hierarchy where control is temporarily taken by ostensibly subordinate elements, but the structure of the group remains coherent if flexible. Moreover, the absence of a conventional hierarchy makes detection and pursuit very difficult, for the cells are unlikely to know of other cells and, like the Hydra's mortal heads, are neither subordinate nor superordinate to them. In short, you cannot destroy a heterarchy or a network with a Cruise Missile.

However, you may be able to destabilize it by removing pivotal nodes and that pivotal node in the al-Qaida heterarchy remains the core group around Osama bin Laden, the *shura majlis* or consultative council comprising around 12–14 individuals (all men of course), which oversee four subgroups: military, finance, religion, and publicity. The military committee appoints agent-handlers to oversee and coordinate groups outside the centre. Consequently, while the centre does not necessarily determine what the cells do, it can impose its will. For example, in April 1996, a cell intended to attack western targets in Singapore but on 18 April, after members of the Israeli Defence Force killed 109 Lebanese civilians, bin Laden apparently cancelled the operation to prevent it undermining the global condemnation of Israel (Gunaratna 2002: 100).

---

[38] Thanks to the collective authors for pointing this out.

When the trail from Ground Zero in New York purportedly led to Osama bin Laden's al-Qaida network in the middle of Afghanistan, many argued that a conventional assault would be both costly and ultimately fruitless: you could not destroy a Hydra-like organization such as al-Qaida, by lopping off its head, first, because it would be inordinately difficult to find, and second, because eliminating any element of it would not destroy it, but, on the contrary, only serve to stimulate further growth and resistance. In effect, force was counterproductive—surely the most frightening of all possibilities for those intent on a military solution—thus only reconciliation would work. Either way, it seemed the Americans were doomed: if the Taliban fought to the end there would be unsupportable casualties going home to Washington, and if the Taliban disappeared then the assault would be irrelevant and just the beginning of another protracted guerrilla war. The result could only be that Afghanistan would be America's second Vietnam; and as Vladimir Putin found to his cost in the Moscow theatre siege in October 2002, 'winning' the war against Chechen terrorists in Chechnya was only the first move not the last. Thus at the extreme end of the reconciliation approach could Alice Walker, in *The Village Voice*, 9 October 2001, wonder 'what would happen to him [bin Laden] if he could be brought to understand the preciousness of the lives he has destroyed? I believe the only punishment that works is love'.

Two weeks into November 2001 the bombing campaign had little to show, other than film footage of bombs exploding in the distant hills, and the opponents of the military campaign took comfort from the beginnings of 'Vietnam II'. Yet four months after the attacks on the US mainland, and barely four weeks after the campaign began, the American-led assault had effectively displaced the al-Qaida–Taliban network (AQT), even if the search for its leaders continues. The temptation of the hawks to remind the doves of their misunderstanding of the military situation could only be matched by the doves' subsequent concern that nothing has been achieved as the United States and Royal Marines endlessly scoured the Afghan countryside for their invisible enemy. Even overt hawks were not always convinced that the war had been won, as Colonel David H. Hackworth (a veteran critic of the current US armed forces) suggested, 'We are in round one—which is not even over—of a 30-round fight. I think my grandkids, who are five and eight, will be in college before we're in round 30... It's a mistake to believe you can stop a terrorist movement by taking out its leader. You can cut off the head but the body will still live on' (quoted in Scriven 2002: 7). So can the Hydra myth help us analyse the issues involved here?

Reassessing the Myth

The rapid collapse of the AQT might imply that their hold over the population and the territory was never deep rooted, and, indeed, was itself a myth.

Since the power of myths remains only as long as people believe in them, the military collapse of the group demonstrated that its much-vaunted 'monopoly of support' was nothing of the sort. Just as the Berlin Wall fell when the East German population stopped being cowed by it, so the role of the Hydra myth in this situation was to demonstrate that myths are powerful, but not as powerful as bombs. But the Hydra myth provides us with several other ways of understanding the problem of terrorism.

A first and literal application of the myth might perceive an American Hercules coming to wreak revenge on the AQT, guided there by the Northern Alliance as Iolaus. At first the task appears impossible; the Hydra cannot even be located and its lair is so deep that it cannot be reached. But when the flaming arrows of the US air force enter the complex the creature is driven into the open. Although difficult, the overwhelming power of the American Hercules eventually grapples the Hydra to the ground, and begins to sever the heads of the monster, only to find that for each problem solved (e.g. getting the agreement of the Pakistani government to use their air space), two more emerge (e.g. the target has moved and Taliban supporters in Pakistan are threatening to destabilize Pakistan itself.) Eventually the American Hercules realises that it alone cannot defeat the Hydra and after each head is removed the Northern Alliance (Iolaus) cauterize each headless stump in turn until victory is achieved; force worked.

A second, and contrary, interpretation is that the problem remains because the immortal head—Osama bin Laden or the hatred of the United States that motivates such groups—cannot be so easily disposed off, and Hercules has simply buried the problem under the rubble of the Tora Bora cave complex. If the immortal head is Osama bin Laden, then his elimination will remove the problem—or at least undermine the focus of the group in the same way that Hitler's death contributed to the elimination of the myth of Nazi invincibility. But if the immortal head is the hatred of the United States and the existing Islamic regimes, then the tactical focus of the military assault by the West can only ever be a prelude to a strategic resolution of what many Muslims appear to consider an intolerable situation. And that situation undoubtedly involves not just the problems of the Palestinians—and Yasser Arafat publicly denounced bin Laden in December 2002—but the form of governments that currently control some Muslim societies. As Meek (2001: 3) suggested, a year after 11 September there were 'signs that the Bush administration [was] beginning to accept the absurdity of characterising bin Laden as "the CEO of Terrorism Incorporated". Yet when Khalid Sheik Mohammed ('al-Qaida's number three') was arrested in Rawalpindi on 2 March 2003, precisely the same assumptions pervaded Gunaratna's (2003c: 3) response: 'His arrest will gravely diminish al-Qaida's ability to plan, prepare and execute large-scale operations of the scope of September 11'. However, the Herculean task facing the United States lies in Gunaratna's final paragraph: 'with the erosion of core leadership of al-Qaida in Afghanistan and Pakistan, al-Qaida cells in at least 98 countries are likely to learn to function wholly or partly on their own'. Using yet another Hydra metaphor, Paul Rogers has suggested, 'if the coalition succeeds in its aims, and manages to get rid of the whole bin Laden operation, it will be perhaps three years before the next similar group rears its head' (quoted in Meek 2001: 3). In effect, only by ceasing support for auto-cratic oil-rich gulf regimes and by guaranteeing a Palestinian state will the United States ever undermine support for al-Qaida-like groups. In this approach, the double strategy of Hercules is necessary because the target groups and their motivations are different.

A third, more worrying analysis might be that the Hydra has no head, no central cause, and therefore no method for permanent destruction, least of all a conventional military 'defeat', for each assault upon it stimulates its regenerative capacity to the point where, as in some stages and forms of cancer, attacking it ensures its proliferation.[39] Here the Hydra myth is more appropriate in terms of its biological manifestation. That is to say that the multiple heads of the Hydra actually represent the malleable nature of the threat in which al-Qaida is just one of the heads. This threat is not rooted in one place, nor does it restrict its forms of attack to a particular format, and its support systems encompass significant financial assets, a considerable num-ber of fighters, and supporters right across the world. The bomb attacks in Bali in 2002, the arrests of a number of Algerians for allegedly developing Ricin in Wood Green, London, and of ten suspected terrorists in Spain, all in January 2003, together with the almost simultaneous murder of a police officer in Manchester whilst arresting suspected North African terrorists, all suggest that the 'hierarchy of terror' is rather more like a 'heterarchy of terror', for there exists a proliferating number of individuals and groups whose only allegiance to al-Qaida is fraternal support, not organizational subordination. Thus although 3000 people in 98 countries had been arrested for alleged member-ship of al-Qaida by January 2003 (Gunaratna 2003a: 9), this does not neces-sarily imply the end of terrorism any more than the arrest of 3000 burglars necessarily implies the end of burglary. Indeed, one could suggest that even if al-Qaida was destroyed it has already provided the leadership for others by demonstrating the direction to be taken. Similarly, the Anglo-American attack on Iraq may result in an increase in recruits to terrorist organizations, which will more than compensate for the elimination of any alleged direct threat posed by Saddam Hussein.

We might take comfort from Northern Ireland and from Sri Lanka here—both ostensibly intractable problems involving religion and terrorism that appear to have burnt themselves to a recognition that the strategy cannot succeed (Woollacott 2002: 18). However, up until now, at least, al-Qaida's reli-gious fanaticism means that it remains uninterested in compromise, unde-terred by death, unconcerned by the unlikelihood of success in the short

---

[39] Thanks to Yiannis Gabriel for this insight.

term, yet willing to change the focus of its target to the point where it is polit-ically impossible to satisfy. Within this analysis the parallel with Hercules is the apparent willingness of the Hydra to sacrifice its mortal heads in the cer-tain knowledge that two more will grow in its place. The only response, there-fore, is permanent vigilance and preparedness because the 'beast' appears to be literally immortal.[40] This might actually be worth contextualizing rather more deeply, for there are precious few years in which war has not been a fea-ture of the world, and more people have died as a result of war in the last 100 years than in any other period that we know of. In short, as Machiavelli implied, the threat of violence is an endemic feature of human society and not something linked to the recent rise of religious fundamentalism.

Finally, it is worth considering a reverse perspective of the myth such that bin Laden would presumably perceive himself to be Hercules fighting the American Hydra, the only global superpower remaining. And in this form it is the multiple military, economic, political, and cultural arms of the US 'empire' that strike terror into the hearts of its neighbours. 'The fact is', sug-gested Krauthammer in the *New York Times*, 'no country has been as domi-nant culturally, economically, technologically and militarily in the history of the world the Roman Empire' (quoted in Freedland 2002: 2). And although the United States does not have the colonies normally associated with empires, it does have a military unit of some kind in 132 of 190 member states of the United Nations, and it is the predominant technological and eco-nomic power, to say nothing of the cultural domination of icons like Coke and McDonalds. We also face a global threat to the environment that can only really be resolved at a global level, preferably through something like the Kyoto agreement. Yet the United States has chosen to ignore most of the rest of the world community on this and on the International Court of Justice, on steel imports and on what to do about Saddam Hussein.

For Castells (1997), such exclusionary practices in turn generate attempts by the excluded to 'exclude the excluders', or rather to eliminate the excluders, and, moreover, to route that elimination along the network channels that the excluders have long sought to use for their own purposes. Here we would expect increasing links between the various mafias and organized crime syn-dicates and al-Qaida. But it may be that no such links are necessary for the glue that holds al-Qaida together is rooted in ideology, not self-interested networks. Baudrillard (2002: 6–7), for example, has suggested that all such 'definitive orders' like the United States induce the will to destroy them; in some bizarre way although 'they did it...we wished for it', as he calls it.[41] In short, and in very Hegelian terms, 'every machinery of domination [has] secreted its own counter-apparatus, the agent of its own disappearance' (Baudrillard 2002: 10).

---

[40] Thanks to Yiannis Gabriel for pointing this parallel out.
[41] A point that Gore Vidal (2002) makes the centrepiece of his conspiratorial case against the US government—the 'Bush Junta'.

In fact, Baudrillard claims we are now entering the Fourth World War (the third being the Cold War that eliminated Communism), and as with each preceding world war the end result is the greater integration of the world order (cf. Bobbitt 2002). Yet, in distinctly un-Hegelian terms, there is no victory of Good at the end of this story because Good and Evil are permanent members of the world community and whichever side of the fence we may find ourselves, we are fated to the permanent recurrence of the myth of Hercules and the Hydra.

Conclusion

The Myth of the Hydra provides us with (at least) three different ways of understanding the United States' and the West's perspective on terrorism and al-Qaida. First, as Hercules initially believed, military force is adequate for the job because force is the only thing that terrorists understand. There is, after all, little point in trying to negotiate with hijackers who intend to kill themselves as well as their victims. The problem here is not ensuring the means to despatch the terrorists but generating the political will to go through with the task. Indeed, the longer the West procrastinates over the moral case for intervention the more likely terrorists are to get hold of and then use weapons of mass destruction. And, following Hercules, the issue is not *if* he will attack the Hydra but *when*.

Second, and alternatively, the violent response is to misunderstand the nature of the problem: al-Qaida can only continue because some people regard its cause as just, therefore that cause needs to be addressed through some form of reconciliation. And even if al-Qaida is destroyed the motivations that drove its members will remain and a new group or network will emerge like a Phoenix from the ashes. Here the problem relates to the difficulties Hercules faces when dealing with the Hydra—it is literally 'headless' in the sense of seeking out leaders to decapitate because for every 'terrorist' killed, another two 'freedom fighters' will emerge as replacements; this is not a clash of civilizations but a consequence of perceiving 'the other' as the enemy.

Third, neither of these responses is adequate because, like Hercules, you have to employ a dual strategy against different kinds of opposition: force worked for the mortal heads—providing they were cut off and the necks cauterized—but force alone was inadequate for the immortal head; that required a different resolution. Thus force is inadequate to prevent terrorism that has some popular support because its heterarchical and network manifestations are less susceptible to conventional force, but addressing the problems that generate support for terrorism will not remove the problem; there are simply some problems for which violence may be an unfortunate but necessary response. This is the Hydra paradox that Hercules can only resolve by engaging in different strategies for what appears at one level to be the same enemy. Indeed, in deference to the myth, even if this set of political problems is resolved the American Hercules cannot rest in peace forever, for there are another ten labours yet to complete. This permanent engagement is a consequence of the United States taking upon itself the role of global police force and, as all police officers know, activity deemed to be criminal by the law can never be permanently eliminated, though it can be constrained.

References

Baudrillard, J. (2002). *The Spirit of Terrorism*. London: Verso.

Bergen, P. L. (2001). *Holy War Inc.: Inside the Secret World of Osama bin Laden*. London: Weidenfeld and Nicolson.

Blow, D. (2001). 'A dagger in the dark'. *History*, 2(11): 40–1.

Bobbitt, P. (2002). 'The Shield of Achilles: The Long War and the Market State', London: Anchor.

Burke, J., Ahmed, K., Barnett, A., Sweeney, J., Paton, N., Harris, P., and Millar, S. (2000). 'A few angry men'. *Observer*, 17 September.

Carruth, G. and Eugene, E. (eds.) (1988). *The Harper Book of American Quotations*. New York: Harper and Row.

Castells, M. (1997). *The Power of Identity: The Information Age: Economy, Society and Culture*. Oxford: Blackwell.

Fisk, R. (2001). *Pity the Nation*. Oxford: Oxford Paperbacks.

Freedland, J. (2002). 'Rome AD ... Rome DC?'. *Guardian*, 18 September.

Grey, J. (2002). 'Malaya, 1948–60: Defeating the Communist Insurgency', in Thompson, J. (ed.), *The Imperial War Museum Book of Modern Warfare*. London: Sidgwick and Jackson.

Grossman, D. (2002). 'Israel has won for now but what is victory when it brings no hope?'. *Guardian Unlimited*, 30 September.

Gunaratna, R. (2002). *Inside Al Qaeda: Global Network of Terror*. London: Hurst & Co.

——(2003a). 'And now, a little local jihad'. *Sunday Times*, 26 January.

——(2003b). 'Cooking for terrorists'. *The Times Higher*, 14 February.

——(2003c). 'Womaniser, joker, scuba diver: The other face of al-Qaida's No 3'. *Guardian*, 3 March.

Hill, C. (2001). 'A Herculean task', in Talbott, S. and Chanda, N. (eds.), *The Age of Terror: America and the World after September 11*. New York: Basic Books

Kerényi, C. (1974). *The Heroes of the Greeks*. London: Thames and Hudson.

Linebaugh, P. and Rediker, M. (2000). 'The Many Headed Hydra: Sailors, Slaves, Commoners, and the Hidden History of the Revolutionary Atlantic'. London: Beacon Press.

Meek, J. (2001). 'Why the management style of a Danish hearing-aid maker may hold the key to stopping Bin Laden'. *Guardian*, 18 October.

Roberts, A. (2002). 'Can we define terrorism?'. *Oxford Today*, 14(2)(Hilary Issue): 18–19.

Scriven, M. (2001). 'These men are feted as America's elite troops'. *Guardian*, 29 October.

Sen, A. (2002). 'Why half the planet is hungry'. *Observer*, 16 June.

Shimizu, H. (2001). 'The effect of injury on hydra head regeneration'. *Forma*, 4(1): 21–5

Vidal, G. (2002). 'The enemy within'. *Observer*, 27 October.

Wilkinson, P. (2000). *Terrorism Versus Democracy: The Liberal State Response*. London: Frank Cass.

Woollacott, M. (2002). 'Al-Qaida's hatred will burn out—unless we stoke the fire'. *Guardian*, 26 September.

http://nikki.sitenation.com/creatures/hydra.html

SIX

Divided Neither in Life, Nor in Death: Friendship and Leadership in the Story of David and Jonathan

Robert French and Patrick Moore[42]

Introduction

IN this chapter, we offer the story of David and Jonathan's friendship as a lens through which to view some issues that seem to us to be central to organizational life today. The story challenges some of our assumptions about the separation of public and private, person and role, individual and 'system' or organization, and offers a framework for thinking about commitment and authority in role, especially the role of a leader.

Friendship at work is one of the great and ignored themes of our day— ignored, that is, in the mainstream literature on organizations, management, and leadership, and in the curricula of degree and training courses. In our own experience, by contrast, it has been a central pillar around which our learning and working lives have revolved. And we are not alone. When we raise the topic with others, it invariably evokes an animated response: enthusiasm, eagerness, or incredulity—and a flood of associations and stories.

Our eagerness to contribute to this book came from the opportunity it offered to open up the theme by exploring the remarkable story of David and Jonathan's friendship, as told in the Hebrew Scriptures.[43] For centuries these men have been symbols of deep and faithful friendship. However, the organizational implications of the friendship have been obscured by modern assumptions.

[42] We would like to express our gratitude to Dr. Peter Simpson for his invaluable help in the preparation of this chapter.
[43] Their story is told in the two Books of Samuel.

The key shift in our minds has been to shed the modern image of friendship simply as an 'interpersonal relationship', and to think of it instead—or rather, as well—as an *organizing principle*. What is exciting about the story of David and Jonathan is that their friendship is presented as just this. It is the organizing principle that enabled a remarkable political transformation, whereby Saul, the first King of Israel, was succeeded not by his son, Jonathan, but by Jonathan's friend, David. Yet not only did David have no claim to the throne, he did not even have the status that would have made him a leader within his own family or tribe.

This friendship takes us back to the true meaning of *Eros*, locating it in the realm of beauty, energy, and generativity, rather than limiting it exclusively to the area of sexuality. In this sense, Eros is at the creative and life-giving edge between, on the one hand, richness, completeness, and resourcefulness, and, on the other, poverty, want, and desire (McGinn 1991: 26). The outcome is a vitality so all-pervasive that the Greeks recognized Eros not merely as a god but as the informing god of all things: 'for no one achieves excellence in his life task without love for it ... Love brings everything to flower, each in terms of its own potential, and so is the true pedagogue of the open, free society' (Campbell 1976: 227).

In our day, by contrast, obsessed as it is with sexual scandal among 'celebrities', readers are likely to look for a sexual subtext to this 'friendship'. However, this misses entirely the fact of a great tradition, which includes David and Jonathan, but also stretches from ancient Greece through to the Middle Ages and the Italian Renaissance. It is exemplified, for example, in Plato's work, and in the love of Dante and Beatrice, or Petrarch and Laura.

What we wish to explore in this chapter, therefore, is the place and significance of the friendship between David and Jonathan in the leadership succession that led to David becoming King of Israel—and also to analyse its impact on him as king, because David became *the* outstanding leader in Hebrew history and also the direct leadership model, historical and symbolic, for Christianity.

In short, the story suggests that it was the friendship with Jonathan that made the difference between Saul and David. The whole focus of the story is on the depth of the relationship and its systemic impact. The friendship crossed boundaries: across age and social standing, across self-interest and the interests of state and family, and even across life and death. This makes little sense, unless one is prepared to conceive of human relationships occurring at a very different level from that suggested by the modern languages of organizations and of friendship.

Before looking further into the significance of the friendship, however, we must first retell the story. It was recorded in the form in which we now know it around 600 BCE. However, the events themselves occurred some 400 years earlier. Clearly any work of such antiquity presents multiple issues of interpretation, particularly when we recognize that it emerged from an oral not a literary tradition. Many apparent anomalies or contradictions in the text can be traced to its origins in that tradition.

The Story

Jonathan was the son of Saul, the first, and therefore ground-breaking, King of Israel. When he and David first met, Jonathan had already proved himself as a fighter and an outstanding military leader and strategist, quite ready to follow in his father's footsteps.

David, by contrast, simply had no place in the political scheme of things. He was the last of eight sons and still too young even to be considered as a soldier. When important visitors were introduced to his family, his father did not even bring David in from his work to meet them. In addition, Bethlehem, his home village, was only affiliated to Saul's kingdom—useful for supplying soldiers and taxes, but with no say in political affairs. This is why, when the prophet Samuel arrived in the village, he was immediately recognized as associated with King Saul, so that the elders came 'trembling to meet him, and asked, "Seer, is your coming favourable for us?"' (16:4).[44]

It was, therefore, not surprising that this unknown boy, David, made an impression on everyone, including Jonathan, when he killed the Philistine champion, Goliath—who was well over two metres tall, well-armed, and had been 'a warrior since his youth' (17:33). In military terms, Goliath's death released the Israelite army from the terror that had disabled them, and they inflicted a heavy defeat on the Philistines. Understandably, Saul 'would not let him [David] go home to his father' (18:2), but kept him on as a military commander.

When, with Goliath's severed head still in his hand, David was introduced to Saul and Jonathan, something sudden and unexpected happened: 'Jonathan felt an instant affection for David; Jonathan loved him like his very self' (18:1). Generations of people have had an intimation of Jonathan's experience when they see Michelangelo's *David* for the first time, a classic representation of the tradition associating friendship with beauty. From his own intuition—what Keats called 'the holiness of the Heart's affections'[45]—Jonathan knew that David was functioning on a different level; in Biblical language, he could see that God was with David as he had once been with Saul.

---

[44] Except where otherwise indicated, chapter and verse references are to the first Book of Samuel; translation, *The New Jerusalem Bible* (London: Darton, Longman & Todd, 1985).

[45] Letter to Benjamin Bailey, 22 November 1817.

Acting on this intuition—the earlier phrase is repeated: 'since he loved him like his very self'—Jonathan then 'made a pact' of friendship with David. In a symbolic gesture of great significance, 'Jonathan took off the cloak which he was wearing and gave it to David, and his armour too, even including his sword, his bow and his belt'. (18:4.) In this agreement beyond words, the assumed heir to the throne[46] handed over the symbols of his status to an unknown stranger he had only just met.

Before the fight with Goliath, Saul too had given David his armour. David had put it on, but found it did not fit: 'David tried to walk but, not being used to them [armour, helmet, breastplate, sword], said to Saul, "I cannot walk in these; I am not used to them." So they took them off again'. (17:38–9.) David 'knew his place', as it were. Rejecting the king's clothing would have been understood by those listening to the story as symbolically refusing to set himself up as a rival. The narrator is clearly signalling to the audience that David will not displace Saul as king, but follow him.

While the scale of Jonathan's response to David is, perhaps, hard for us to imagine, Saul's is not. Initially enthusiastic, he quickly began to change when David's popularity outgrew his own. David inspired huge passion, captured in the well-known, repeated couplet, which fired Saul's jealousy (18:7; 21:12; 29:5):

> Saul has killed his thousands,
> and David his tens of thousands.

Saul had already been showing the effects of what we might call 'stress-related' illness or 'burn-out'. Now he projected onto David all the self-hatred generated by his own failures—and his frustrated desire. He came to hate and fear David so intensely and obsessionally that his one thought was to get rid of him: he tried to kill him himself, to set him up to be killed by the Philistines, and to have him assassinated by his own agents. On more than one occasion, it was Jonathan who rescued David from Saul's murderous rage—even endangering his own life by doing so. Not only had he handed over to David his right to lead the nation, he also used his position to ensure that David stayed alive to be able to become a leader.

Apart from the record of Jonathan's protective actions, we simply are not told what these two men actually *did* together. In terms of modern expectations of friendship, and of the more or less intimate stages of its development, we learn nothing—except for two moments. The first is their grief on parting for the last time: 'They then embraced each other, both weeping copiously' (20:41). The second is David's famous lament for Jonathan and Saul after both had died in battle (2 Samuel 1:19–27):

---

[46] At this stage, only the prophet Samuel had the authority to appoint a king. However, there is a clear expectation in the text (e.g. 20:31, 28:17) that Jonathan would follow his father.

> Does the splendour of Israel
> lie dead on your heights?
> How did the heroes fall?
> Do not speak of it in Gath,
> nor broadcast it in the streets of Ashkelon,
> for fear the daughters of the Philistines rejoice,
> for fear the daughters of the uncircumcised gloat.
>
> . . .
>
> Saul and Jonathan, beloved and handsome,
> were divided neither in life, nor in death.
> Swifter than eagles were they,
> stronger than lions.
>
> O daughters of Israel, weep for Saul . . .
>
> Jonathan, by your dying I too am stricken,
> I am desolate for you, Jonathan my brother.
> Very dear you were to me,
> your love more wonderful to me
> than the love of a woman.

After this, the friendship continued to influence David. For example, many years into his reign as king, he sought out any remaining members of Saul's family 'to whom I might show faithful love for Jonathan's sake'. When he was told of Jonathan's one remaining son, Meribbaal, who was disabled, he brought him to court, reinstated him with all his family's property, arranged for a former family servant (with his fifteen sons and twenty slaves) to work the land for him, and, as a final symbolic gesture of reconciliation, invited Meribbaal himself to take his meals at the king's table (2 Samuel 9:1–13). The phrase, 'divided neither in life, nor in death', applies as well to David's own friendship with Jonathan, as it does to the relationship between Jonathan and Saul.

The Place and Significance of the Friendship

There is no doubt that in the mind of the narrator the friendship between David and Jonathan is the fulcrum around which the whole story of leadership and leadership succession revolves.

The overarching context for the friendship is the history of David's success as a leader. No other leader in Hebrew history managed to combine so successfully the competing secular and spiritual demands of the role of a king. As a result, his impact has been immense within Judaism and Christianity, both through the model of his kingship and through the influence of the Psalms, many of which are attributed to him. However, he is certainly not portrayed as perfect. There is no simple equation: Saul bad, David good. In the second half of the

Second Book of Samuel, the narrator is at pains to describe just how badly wrong things went for David, his family, and the nation after he seduced Bathsheba, a married woman, made her pregnant, and had her husband killed.

Nonetheless, the two men are contrasted. Whatever moral judgements we might apply to the relative strengths and weaknesses of the two, Saul's reign is portrayed as essentially unhealthy because of his mistakes, whereas David's is essentially healthy despite his. Saul's failure is reflected in his rejection of reliable advice, his resort instead to witchcraft and necromancy, and his descent into madness. In biblical language, this is attributed to a failed relationship to the Divine: 'the spirit of Yahweh had withdrawn from Saul, and an evil spirit from Yahweh afflicted him with terrors' (16:14). His sons and the family succession die with him. By contrast, David's son, Solomon, is probably second only to his father in status in the history of Jewish leadership. Again in biblical terms: 'Yahweh was with David' (18:12).

At the level of belief, David's legitimacy came from Yahweh. However, in terms of organizational politics, his legitimacy came from Jonathan, stimulated by his recognition of something in David that he knew made the difference. It was not only the bravery David had just demonstrated, although this was the immediate cause of their meeting; it was also Jonathan's intuition at the moment of meeting. Parting with his clothing was the gesture he chose both to hand over his role as 'natural' heir and to make a pact of friendship. In this narrative tradition, clothes represent both the role and the inner person. Thus, Saul's armour did not fit, but Jonathan's clothes did, because now, following the fight with Goliath, the fit of person and role was a good one.

By placing Saul, Jonathan, and David together at this first meeting, the friendship is located at the centre of the whole political and personal matrix that is about to unravel. David only got where he did because of Jonathan. And yet this intense moment of meeting also contains an intense ambiguity: to what extent was Jonathan's friendship inspired by already formed capacities that he saw in David? Or: did Jonathan's love stimulate the development in David of capacities that were only there in potential? As the writer Hugh of St Victor said in the twelfth century: 'I was a foreigner and met you in a strange land. But the land was not really strange for I found friends there. I don't know whether I first made friends or was made one' (quoted in Illich 1993: 27, n.53).

We shall return below to the figure of Jonathan. However, it is worth noting here that he not only gave up the throne to David, and helped him survive to become king, he also never stopped supporting his father, the nation's anointed king, even dying alongside him in battle.

In the following sections, we shall highlight those aspects of this story which bring out the significance of friendship for our postmodern world. The issues to be discussed involve the following:

• the issue of 'depth' in human relationships and the psyche;
• the 'levels' of friendship, personal/impersonal, private/public;

- the relationship to context: friendship and the capacity to tolerate contradiction;
- the contrasting leadership models of Saul and David;
- the possibility that leaders can experience leadership as a threat to their power.

Depth in Human Relationships and the Psyche

A major obstacle to understanding the narrator's intentions is that today we no longer have a language to explain the 'depths' of human relatedness. As a result, a contemporary reader may misunderstand the true impact and meaning of this friendship. For example, a text (almost certainly a pre-modern one) that includes a phrase such as 'thoughts of the heart' may be understood as referring to the affective life, rather than the profound insight of Pascal that, 'Le cœur a ses raisons que la raison ne connaît point': 'The heart has reasons of which reason knows nothing'. In the story of David and Jonathan, however, the whole focus is on the depth of the relationship and on the systemic impact of deep human friendship: its capacity to cross the boundaries of age and status, and the competing interests of self and other, family and state.

The modern phrase 'intimate relations' emphasizes inwardness to the exclusion of others—the Latin 'intimus' being the superlative of 'interior'. This friendship, by contrast, demonstrates a psychic and emotional depth, which is actually *inclusive* of others. At this level, the potency and generative vitality of Eros are released and made available to all; that is, the power of the erotic in its original sense, not with its secondary, merely sexual connotations.

A clear expression of this idea of depth in relation to friendship can be found in the title of a letter written by Marsilio Ficino, one of the most lyrical voices of the fifteenth century Florentine Renaissance: 'Friendship between men cannot be kindled unless God breathes upon it' (Ficino 1981: letter 31). To convey his belief in the depth and central significance of friendship in all human affairs, Ficino suggested that it is an experience that somehow participates in the Divinity. In his view, true friendship is located at such a deep level of the personality that it must be thought of as involving not two but three: that is, the two friends in the presence of the Divine. It is at this level that David and Jonathan were linked, and it is as a result of this depth of relationship and relatedness that their friendship acted as an organizing principle, both personally and politically.

It was Ficino who first identified a depth of friendship or love that he called 'Socratic', and that we have renamed 'Platonic love'. However, we define a Platonic relationship as one from which something—sex—is *excluded*, whereas Ficino's definition is clearly the opposite. The creative and generative impact of the friendships that developed under Ficino's influence is obvious in every field: the arts, including architecture, music, politics, philosophy, religion, medicine, and even commerce.

'Depth psychology'—that is, psychoanalysis and its near cousins—is one of the few places, other than in the arts, perhaps, where the notion of depth in the human psyche and in relationships has been developed. While their primary focus is interpersonal, rather than political or organizational, the whole mechanism of learning and healing is based on the depth of the therapeutic relationship. This depth is named in such concepts as the unconscious, projection, transference, and counter-transference.

Levels of Friendship: Personal/Impersonal, Private/Public

At the core of the story of David and Jonathan is the view that their friendship is not just a private affair. The predominant modern conception of friendship, by contrast, locates it firmly in the private sphere—although there is a growing recognition of its systemic potential to act as 'the necessary cement to hold the bricks of an increasingly fragmented social structure together' (Pahl, 2000: 11).[47]

The relationship between these 'levels' of friendship is clearly demonstrated within the story itself, but also at the level of language. Ancient Hebrew had a more limited vocabulary than modern English, so that words had to 'work' harder and were open to multiple interpretations. One consequence is that the English words 'friendship' and 'love' do not convey the levels of significance attached to the equivalent Hebrew term, *hesed*.

The noun *hesed*, which appears frequently (approximately 250 times in the Hebrew Scriptures overall), has no verbal counterpart. It is often used with the verb 'to do': 'to do friendship' or 'to do love' for someone, as with David's question, 'Is there anyone belonging to Saul's family left, to whom I might show faithful love for Jonathan's sake?' (9:1). As no English term corresponds precisely to *hesed*, translators over the centuries have tried many ways to capture the nuances of the word, such as 'mercy', 'kindness' or 'loving kindness', 'love', 'steadfast love' or 'faithful love', 'devotion', and 'faithfulness' or 'loyalty'. As a result, the lengthy entry in the *Anchor Bible Dictionary* opts to use the word *hesed* rather than any one of the English words, 'each of which is misleading in a different direction'.[48] (No doubt an analysis of translations into other languages would bring out other distinctions.)

---

[47] The power of friendship as a cohesive factor in military contexts has been acknowledged from the ancient world, whose traditional icons were often pairs of heroes, to the modern day (Little 1970; Keegan 1976).

[48] The *Anchor Bible Dictionary* (1992), Editor-in-Chief, David Noel Freedman, New York: Doubleday. See pages 377–80 for the full entry on *hesed*.

The key point is that the concept of *hesed* stood at an edge between several experiential fields: between person and person in private relationships, between person and system in secular, public relationships, and between human and divine in the spiritual realm. Thus, there could be *hesed* between individuals, there was human *hesed* towards both Yahweh and neighbour, and there was Yahweh's *hesed* towards humanity and creation generally. *Hesed* could describe intimate loving relationships between individuals, whether in friendship, in family, or in marriage, but could also refer to political bonds or contractual relationships, such as that made by Jonathan when he first met David: 'Jonathan made a pact with David'.

This 'pact' is restated at several points in the story (20:8, 17, 23, 42; 2 Samuel 9:1). It reflects the depth of love and friendship between the two men, but also implies their joint commitment to the will of Yahweh, and finds expression in Jonathan's actions towards David, and in David's towards Meribbaal. Their 'faithful love' would have been a powerful reminder to listeners of Yahweh's 'faithful love' for the Hebrew people.

In this way, the term *hesed* stood for integrity and commitment both at the deeply personal level—towards Yahweh, for instance, or in friendship or marriage—and, at the more impersonal level, in a range of contractual arrangements of a social or political/organizational nature—at the level of the nation, for example, or, again, in marriage. The word, therefore, crosses individual and systemic boundaries that the rational project of modernity increasingly kept separate. Its flexibility, and especially its 'impersonal' aspect, may help to make more sense of the idea of friendship as an organizing principle.

A 'disposition' of friendship can exist, even where the feelings we normally associate with friendship may be missing. For example, one woman reported to us that, when she recently left an organization, she was taken aback by the strength of her emotional response to parting from one of her colleagues. This was a woman she did not like and never had, and yet there had been a kind of unspoken agreement between them to work as well as they could together despite the antipathy at a personal level. And the working relationship had indeed been good. In discussing friendship as an organizing principle, not just an interpersonal relationship or a feeling state, she found herself redefining her 'pact' with her former colleague as characterized—and organized—by friendship-in-role.

The Relationship to Context: Friendship and the Capacity to Tolerate Contradiction

Contradiction may be a defining experience of our postmodern world, whether in relation to family or work, and to local, national, or global issues. For example, merely in buying a loaf of bread, we may find ourselves faced by more than just questions of price and taste. There are also issues such as health (genetically modified (GM) or organic ingredients; fat, sugar, or salt content), equity (fair trade, locally grown or prepared), politics (supermarket chain versus local trader), and pollution (do we walk or go by car, public transport, or bicycle).

In view of the complexity of modern society, the same pattern of competing demands, often contradictory, permeates our organizations. Although it may seldom have existed in a pure form, the rationalist project of modernity did aim for uniformity and clarity in organizations, with carefully tiered hierarchical structures, strong bureaucratic control systems, and standardized role differentiation. To the extent that such organizational arrangements still had a foundation in traditional societal roles and expectations, especially in relation to gender, age, class, education, and religion, the range of demands on the individual remained relatively restricted.

Postmodern organizations, by contrast, are fragmented, political arenas, constantly on the move and lacking clarity of structure or relations with others. As remnants of the traditional organization have also continued to fade, we are left in a situation characterized by Bauman as 'liquid': 'patterns and configurations are no longer "given", let alone "self-evident"; there are just too many of them, clashing with one another and contradicting one another's commandments' (Bauman 2000: 7).

In the drama of this story, David and Saul are the major historical figures. However, the more one looks at the events, the more Jonathan stands out as a truly remarkable figure, demonstrating not only an extraordinary level of loyalty and commitment, but also the capacity to take up contradictory roles with authority. He experienced great tensions: between personal and family loyalties, between father as person and father as king, and between his own personal ambition and his ambitions for his nation and his friend. In addition, the social and political world of the day was in constant danger of attack from outside, and of disintegration and fragmentation from within. In this respect, his experience seems more in tune with life today than one might expect.

Against the wishes of his father, Jonathan remained loyal to the friend he had committed himself to, and for whom he had been ready to give up any claim to the throne. He recognized that his father was abusing his authority as king by engaging in a personal vendetta against David—who, for his part, always remained loyal: 'The king should not harm his servant David; far from harming you, what he [David] has done has been greatly to your advantage' (19:4). At the same time, however, Jonathan also supported his father right up to his death, as the king anointed by Yahweh, to lead the nation.

The rather unfamiliar language of kingship should not distract us from the very unusual nature of Jonathan's action and from its powerful organizational effects. He demonstrated the readiness to give himself to the organization at the expense of personal benefit. He lived with contradictory commitments for the sake of the friendship and his own understanding of the good of the nation, and, in a remarkable way, was able to hold together the tensions of his position. One is reminded of E. M. Forster's famous statement that if he had to choose between friend and country, he hoped he would always choose the friend. This was precisely the choice faced by Jonathan, and the story illustrates a way of understanding friendship that allowed him to hold the tension in a creative frame that Forster clearly could not know.

The Contrasting Leadership Models of Saul and David

The significance of this story for postmodern organizations is brought sharply into focus by the way the narrator presents two contrasting models of leadership in Saul and David, one centred on politics, the other on friendship.

The nature and implications of the contrast are stark and challenging for a world in which Saul's political behaviour is so familiar as to seem 'normal'. The monarchy had, after all, been established for reasons that sound remarkably familiar today: 'so that we can be like the other nations, with our own king to rule us and lead us and fight our battles' (8:20).

Clearly there is no organization—no 'polis'—without politics. However, the loosely coupled, contingent character of the postmodern world means that the dominant leadership model today is indeed a political one. However, our excitement in working with this story has stemmed from the way it challenges the familiar and has allowed us to see the 'golden thread' of friendship that stands out brightly in the fabric of our own best work experiences.

In Saul, we are presented with a model of leadership as political activity. The measure of the model's familiarity today is the fact that many modern readers find it hard to see what it was that made Yahweh 'reject' him. We can easily understand Saul's motives—and even approve of them, as did his army, when they did not kill every living thing belonging to the Amalekites, but kept the best animals to sacrifice to Yahweh (15:9). At an immediate, political level, Saul's mistakes, retold in 1 Samuel 13 and 15, are quite understandable.

David, by contrast, represents a friendship model of leadership. The measure, in turn, of its unfamiliarity is the fact that most commentators on the story ignore any connection between David's friendship with Jonathan and his success as a leader.

This friendship model gives primary importance to the relational rather than the political. It is not that David does not act politically. Clearly he does. However, his leadership is presented as essentially healthy because it was legitimized, enabled, and sustained by his friendship with Jonathan. In place of the pursuit of self-interest, this model keeps together the interests of self and other. The balance we have discussed above between the personal and impersonal dimensions of friendship echoes throughout: relationship and relatedness coexist in a symbiotic balance.

With Ficino's statement in mind, that friendship 'cannot be kindled unless God breathes upon it', we can begin to present schematically the characteristics of the friendship model.

First of all, it is friendship with God that enabled Jonathan and David to put self aside for a greater good. The pursuit of truth or the real precedes the pursuit of political goals, self-interest, or popularity. Thus defined, the friendship between David and Jonathan enabled Jonathan to see David as having authority, and therefore to hand over the leadership succession to him. It also meant that each saw the other, in Aristotle's terms, as 'another self'—or an 'other-self'.

At the same time, the capacity of their friendship to contain contradiction enabled the two men also to recognize Saul as having authority as 'God's anointed'. As a result, they did not, for example, attempt to seize power through organized resistance. What is more, their friendship continued to have an impact on David, even after the deaths of Jonathan and Saul, so that David continued to honour Saul's family and to 'show faithful love for Jonathan's sake'. One could say that David's friendship for God and for Jonathan enabled him also to be a friend to Meribbaal and, despite everything, to Saul himself.

In terms of the organizational framework of this discussion, we might, then, also say that whereas in the political model leaders mobilize power for the sake of control, in the friendship model they are prepared to give up control for the sake of learning. The principle and importance of learning are now widely recognized in postmodern leadership and management—but the role of friendship in learning is not (French and Thomas 1999).

The importance of this would be crucial, since friendship replaces the organizing personality with an organizing principle. Most importantly, friends who lived in a pre-modern society—for example, Aristotle, Cicero, Aelred of Rievaulx, and Marsilio Ficino—lived within a context which supplied them with agreed ethical norms. Since this is not the case in contemporary society, those whose friendship exists in the public, political sphere may have to discover or create such ethical boundaries for themselves, rather than receive them from the 'community'. One outcome of this quest can be the re-emergence of a fresh level of ethical awareness in the system as a whole.

This, in effect, would be a quintessential new point, since friendship not only offers an alternative to the political model of leadership, but also constitutes a political act by itself. Jonathan's commitment to David was essential for his friend's very survival, as well as keeping open the space for him in the leadership succession. However, the story illustrates the radical nature of the model: the friendship must be primary; if it is, then benefits and solutions also arise at the political level.

The fragmented nature of postmodern organizations creates anxiety that feeds political activity as a way of coping. However, such activity inevitably also produces further fragmentation. Friendship as an organizing principle, on the other hand, not only mobilizes or constructs necessary political connections, but also has the capacity to enable some repair to the fragmentation. This healing effect is graphically illustrated when David had the opportunity to kill Saul, but did not do so:

Saul began to weep aloud, "You are upright and I am not," he said to David, "since you have behaved well to me, whereas I have behaved badly to you... May Yahweh reward you for the good you have done me today! Now I know that you will indeed reign and that the sovereignty in Israel will pass into your hands. Now swear to me by Yahweh that you will not suppress my descendants once I am gone, or blot my name out of my family." This David swore to Saul. (24:18–25)

The Possibility that Leaders can Experience Leadership as a Threat to their Power

Finally, we turn to the relationship between *leadership* and *the role of a leader*. In stark terms, the story is this: Saul was leader, and Jonathan his designated and unquestioned successor. David, however, offered leadership—*appropriate* leadership, as symbolized in his refusal to wear Saul's armour. Recognizing David's capacity as more suited to the situation than his own, Jonathan was prepared to forego his own claim. In doing so, he allowed leadership from a very junior position in the system to replace his own.

Saul's reaction was quite different. Although he responded positively at first to David's bravery, and was ready to give him a military leadership role, he quickly perceived David's success as a threat to his own position and status as the leader: 'As long as the son of Jesse lives on earth, neither you [Jonathan] nor your royal rights are secure' (20:31).

Jonathan and Saul both recognized the impact of the leadership David gave. What made the difference in their responses, however, was the fact of the friendship. Jonathan's investment in this friendship enabled him to keep in mind the need for leadership at the national level, but, at the same time, to separate this from his personal ambition and from his own and his family's association with the role of a leader. Saul was unable to make this separation, and therefore could not let go of his personal investment in the role. With this mindset, the only possibility open to him was to act politically, and to do anything he could to remove the threat.

Many leaders express the desire to tap into leadership potential at all levels of the organization—often captured in the idea of 'empowerment'. In this context, Saul's response to Jonathan's legitimization of David has a familiar ring. Without an alternative model by which to assess the situation, leaders often experience leadership from others, whether senior colleagues or junior organizational members, as a threat to their position and power.

Conclusion

The more we have worked on this story, the richer the friendship has seemed in its relevance to the postmodern world. At one level, it seems all too familiar: an organization under constant threat from a turbulent environment is paralysed by a leadership void and lacks creativity. In response to the threat from outside and from internal disarray, a new structure and style of leadership is introduced—in this case, the appointment of Saul as the king, 'so that we can be like the other nations, with our own king to rule us and lead us and fight our battles'. After an initial period of success, however, this once transformational leader loses touch with the organization's purpose and is driven by paranoid self-interest into the micropolitical world of power politics.

The question, now as then, is whether more of the same is required, or something different. An extraordinary aspect of the story of David and Jonathan, and, ironically, one which can be problematic to modern readers, is that although an ideal is presented—a model of leadership, which puts friendship first, as the epitome of the relational—David's leadership is not idealized, in the sense of being portrayed as perfect. David made serious mistakes, which could easily have destroyed all that had been achieved. Despite his failings, however, his leadership was rooted in friendship, experienced as deep personal love and expressed in a lasting pact. This made the difference that was required.

The term friendship does occur in political contexts today, such as the 'friendship' between two nations at a particular moment in their histories. It is also recognized that political and business leaders can form friendships across the boundaries of the systems they represent. However, the first is a rather watery notion, and the second is tolerated or becomes the object of gossip rather than genuine interest. They are at an entirely different depth or level of significance than that indicated by this story. They do not present the (to us postmoderns) problematic richness of the personal, the political, and the spiritual contained in the friendship of David and Jonathan.

This friendship was rooted in true Eros. Its energy and generativity precluded an exclusive narrowness or self-interest. However, friendships in contemporary organizations can be a problematic and difficult affair. They can be—and can certainly appear to be—exclusive of others. When they occur between those in power, the effect can deaden the critical questioning that all organizations require if they are to remain in good health. On the other hand, they can also release the power of envy, which does not seek to emulate but to destroy.

What we have tried to show here is the way in which the friendship between David and Jonathan worked at many levels—practical, emotional, and spiritual. It allowed for the integration of conscious and unconscious dynamics, and therefore released energies that go beyond the rational. The connections made in friendship are not irrational but a-rational. It is because they do have their own order, however, that friendship can prove so effective as an ordering principle.

References

Bauman, Zygmunt (2000). *Liquid Modernity*. Cambridge: Polity Press.

Campbell, Joseph (1976). *The Masks of God: Occidental Mythology*. Harmondsworth: Penguin.

Ficino, Marsilio (1981). *The Letters of Marsilio Ficino* (Vol. 3). London: Shepheard-Walwyn.

French, Robert and Thomas, Jem (1999). 'Maturity, education and enlightenment—An introduction to Theodor Adorno and Hellmut Becker: Education for Maturity and Responsibility'. *History of the Human Sciences*, 12(3): 1–19.

Illich, Ivan (1993). *In the Vineyard of the Text: A Commentary to Hugh's 'Didascalicon'*. Chicago: University of Chicago Press.

Keegan, J. (1976). *The Face of Battle*. Harmondsworth: Penguin.

Little, R. (1970). 'Buddy relations and combat performance', in O. Gursky and G. Miller (eds.), *The Sociology of Organizations*. New York: Free Press, pp. 361–76.

McGinn, Bernard (1991). *The Foundations of Mysticism: Origins to the Fifth Century. The Presence of God: A History of Western Christian Mysticism* (Vol. 1). London: SCM Press.

Pahl, Ray (2000). *On Friendship*. Cambridge: Polity Press.

SEVEN

The Legend of Cú Chulainn: Exploring Organization Theory's Heroic Odyssey

Donncha Kavanagh and Majella O'Leary

We've become enamoured of a heroic view of management—even in government—the knight on a white charger, the manager who's going to come in and fix everything—and what you get is not management, but hubris.

Henry Mintzberg, *Guardian*, 26 January 2003

The Cú Chulainn Legend

IRELAND'S vernacular literature, the oldest in Western Europe, is divided into four cycles of prose sagas. One of these—the Ulster cycle—relates the stories of the heroes associated with Conchobar Mac Nessa, king of Ulaid (Ulster). These stories are mythological although they may be based partly on events that happened in Ireland around 500 BCE. The greatest hero of the Ulster Cycle is a warrior named Cú Chulainn (pronounced *coo culen*) and many of the stories recount his exploits. Cú Chulainn was born to live a heroic life and is often compared to Achilles or Hercules: he is invincible, although fated to a short life with lasting glory. His father was a god, Lugh, while his mother was a mortal woman called Deichtine, a conjunction of the human and the superhuman that is found in many mythologies (for instances, see Chapter 5 by Grint and Chapter 11 by Winstanley).

Cú Chulainn plays a primary role in the *Táin Bó Cuailnge* (the Cattle-Raid of Cooley), which is the foremost epic of the Ulster cycle. The story begins with 'pillow talk' between Queen Medb (pronounced 'Maeve') of Connacht and her husband Ailill who are arguing over who has the most possessions. Ailill eventually wins because Medb has no match for his magnificent White Bull. Medb, furious at losing, promptly sends a party, led by Mac Roth, to Cooley (in Ulster) to rent the famous Brown Bull for a year, and so win the argument. The owner of the Bull is agreeable until Mac Roth gets drunk and reveals that he would have taken the bull by force if terms had not been agreed. The deal breaks down and Medb goes to war to capture the Brown Bull of Cooley.

Medb gathers her army and marches towards Ulster. On the way, a sorceress appears and warns of impending defeat at the hand of Dearg Doom, Cú Chulainn, Ulster's champion. Medb ignores the warning, partly because the men of Ulster are suffering a weakness, due to a curse placed on them for the inhuman treatment of a pregnant woman. The only warrior exempt from the curse is Cú Chulainn because he is only seventeen years old. Cú Chulainn confronts and massacres Medb's advancing troops. Medb's army presses on, however, and the story recounts the constant battles with Cú Chulainn's. Medb eventually arrives in Cooley, lays waste to the area, and captures the Brown Bull. But the war with Cú Chulainn is taking its toll and they agree that her army will not advance as long as Cú Chulainn engages in single-handed combat with any Connacht champion.

Cú Chulainn beats each one in turn and soon no one challenges him. Medb deceitfully persuades Ferdia, Cú Chulainn's foster brother and close friend, to fight him. The two men fight for three days. At the end of each day they put away their weapons, hug and kiss, and send each other food and medicine. On the third day, Cú Chulainn kills Ferdia with his magical spear, the deadly Gae Bolga. In deep grief, he abandons the fight, allowing Medb's army to bring the Brown Bull back to Connacht. The Ulster army rallies and, joined by Cú Chulainn, gives chase. In the subsequent battle, they are victorious but Cú Chulainn spares Medb's life. During the battle, the Brown Bull meets and attacks the White Bull of Connacht. Both bulls devastate the country while they fight, with the Brown Bull emerging victorious—which meant that Medb won the argument—but fatally wounded. The armies consider destroying him, the cause of all their suffering, but they let him go back to Cooley where he dies. His body is dismembered and distributed around the country as a reminder of the folly of war. Peace is declared between Cú Chulainn and Medb, and for the next seven years there is no war between them.

In the war against Medb, Cú Chulainn had killed a warrior, Cailidin, whose wife subsequently gave birth to six children. Medb sent the children away to study magic and when they returned she sent them against Cú Chulainn. The sons of Cailidin had prepared three magic spears: the first of these killed Cú Chulainn's charioteer, the second wounded his great grey horse, and the third struck Cú Chulainn himself. Realising that death was near, Cú Chulainn tied himself to a pillar of stone so that he would die standing upright facing his enemies. Eventually he died but such was his fame that no one dared approach him. And so he remained for three days until one of Cailidin's daughters changed herself into a crow and landed on his shoulder and began to peck at his eyes. Then everyone knew that Cú Chulainn was dead.

The Context

The Cú Chulainn story is part of a collection of sagas that have been studied in depth for the tremendous insight they give into the life of the pre-Christian Celts.[49] These ancient stories have been highly influential, especially in the fields of literature and politics. In the early nineteenth century, they influenced the development of Romanticism following the publication of a series of poems about another mythical Celtic hero, Fionn Mac Cumhaill. In the early twentieth century, they formed an important part of the Irish literary revival and strongly influenced the development of Irish nationalism.

This raises a number of questions. First, can we—or maybe should we—say anything about a story that has been studied in depth by scholars of archaeology, history, geography, literature, Celtic studies, and anthropology? 'Yes', we answer, although we respect and are mindful of the rich and deep analysis in other fields. Second, is this ancient story about Cú Chulainn relevant to contemporary organization theory? Again we answer 'yes', if the story is used primarily as an interpretative lens to examine and reflect on the discourse of organization studies. As such, the story may be most useful in inspiring new perspectives and research agendas in our discipline rather than, for example, testing theory. We use the story as a 'deliberate disturber' to upset briefly our normal way of seeing things, although we are mindful of the dangers of over-interpretation.

At the outset, it is useful to ask what is distinctive about the Cú Chulainn story, especially when viewed from the field of organization studies. Most obviously it is a story about *heroes*. Our analysis, therefore, will focus on the interrelationship between the *hero* and the *organization*.

---

[49] The original *Táin* story can be found on the web, with a full English translation at http://vassun.vassar.edu/~sttaylor/Cooley. See Kinsella and Le Brocquy (1970) for another translation, discussion, and detailed maps. For a comprehensive editorial history of the *Táin* see O'Rahilly (1967). A classic analysis is provided, in German, by Thurneysen (1921) and also by Mallory (1992). For further interpretations of the *Táin* story, see Desmond (2002). For a general introduction to the Celts and Celtic mythology, see Chadwick and Cunliffe (1997).

Heroes and Anti-heroes

The Cú Chulainn story and other ancient Celtic stories (as well as the archaeological and anthropological evidence) strongly indicate that the hero was venerated and celebrated in Celtic society. In turn, the Celtic hero is but an instance of the heroic archetype that is found, according to Campbell (1949/1968), in the myths and stories of most if not all cultures (see de Vries 1963: 210–26, and Raglan 1936 for further description of the heroic archetype). According to this thesis, Cú Chulainn, Jesus, Hamlet, Luke Skywalker, Moses, Dante, and Krishna are all, to use Campbell's term, some of the 'thousand faces' of the heroic archetype. Yet, this concept of an archetype is of limited value, since it places all heroes into a single analytical category. We find it more useful, especially in the context of the hero in organizational studies, to distinguish four different types of heroes, which we will now discuss and compare: the Celtic hero, the Romantic hero, the neo-romantic hero, and the postmodern anti-hero.

The Celtic Hero

The primary concern of the Celtic hero literature is with heroic action; tribal warfare and individual prowess dominate the legends. Heroism, according to Becker (1974: 11), is 'first and foremost a reflex of the terror of death' and the hero is the individual who confronts and even transcends death. Death is neither feared nor avoided in Celtic society, and, similar to heroes in other cultures, the Celtic hero is the individual who could go into the spirit world, the world of the dead, and return alive. The Celtic hero is trained in various skills, such as shape-making, which renders him invincible. In addition, the Celtic hero, being superhuman, often undergoes a magico-religious experience on the battlefield. In Cú Chulainn's case it is accompanied by a temporary physical distortion (*riastradh*):

his body revolves within his skin, his hair stands up stiff with as it were a spark of fire on the tip of every strand, one eye becomes as small as the eye of a needle and the other monstrously large, his mouth is distended as far as his ears, and the 'warrior's light' arises from the crown of his head. By this startling transformation is his surge of martial vigour made manifest. (Mac Cana 1970: 105)

The Celtic hero is *born* a hero (typical of heroes in other cultures, Cú Chulainn's birth is marked by features such as incest and procreation by a god) and he is initiated into the heroic world through the performance of a series of great deeds. For example, Cú Chulainn (originally Setanta) was *named* a hero at just six years of age after being attacked by a fierce guard dog, which he killed by striking a ball into its mouth. After observing this extraordinary act, the druid Cathbhadh renamed him Cú Chulainn (hound of Culann), which it was thought would make a great warrior name. The Celtic hero chooses a *short life*—Cú Chulainn hears from Cathbhadh that if he takes up arms on a particular day he will be famous forever, though short-lived. Cú Chulainn thus chooses his destiny: 'Provided that my fame lives, I care not if I be on this earth but a single day' (Mac Cana 1970: 105). Although his life is short, the Celtic hero is *permanent*, so memorable is his performance in battle.

Despite his superhuman form, the Celtic hero is not without *frailties* and undergoes extreme suffering as a result of the human relationships that infringe on his role as a great warrior. A good example of this is Cú Chulainn's battle with his foster brother Ferdia. There is always a tension between the value of the human relationships and the need to be victorious in battle. But the human relationship rarely takes precedence and Cú Chulainn eventually dies alone. The Celtic hero is dangerously self-assured and many of his heroic acts are performed because of his confidence in his own ability—and immunity to the fear of death—rather than an attempt to prove his self-worth. Neither is he given to much subtlety. The combination of these attributes means that his responses are predictable and, as the Cú Chulainn story demonstrates, he is always liable to be outsmarted by less honourable and more cunning enemies.

In Celtic mythology, the *goddess* rather than the god is the ruler of the supernatural realm; the other-world is 'the Land of Women' and consequently the goddess often assumes a dominating role over the male hero. The Celtic hero thus is unusual in the extent to which he is influenced by the females in Celtic society and in particular the goddesses. Cú Chulainn and other warriors learn their special battle skills and ability to 'shape-make' from the goddesses and many of their heroic acts arise from challenges set for them by the females, and failure to meet the challenges results in punishment. For example, on one occasion Cú Chulainn is challenged by his wife Emer to capture two magic lake birds, which she wants for decoration, and his failure to do so results in a year of suffering from a 'sleeping sickness'. Cú Chulainn's greatest rival is Queen Medb who is a merciless commander-in-chief of the armies that she sends against Ulster—her very appearance deprived warriors of two-thirds of their valour. Medb is ruthless and unscrupulous; she even offers her daughter to any warrior who would fight Cú Chulainn. Even in the death of the hero, the goddess plays a significant role—Cú Chulainn is only assumed dead when he is visited by a goddess who takes the form of a crow and sits on his shoulder. The female in Celtic mythology is powerful and dangerous and the male hero cannot exist in her absence.

In the Cú Chulainn story and in other stories of the Celtic genre, boundaries are always fluid and ambiguous. Unlike the Greeks and Romans, the Celts did not functionally differentiate their pantheon and instead allowed fluid divisions between their gods. Cú Chulainn himself could outperform his peers in every sport, was a competent musician and lover, as well as being invincible on the battlefield. The human–inhuman boundary is also ambiguous in the

Celtic worldview. Most of the characters in the stories about Cú Chulainn are half-gods or demi-gods; they were either real people who were later attributed with god-like powers or they were gods who were given human frailties. According to the eminent French philologist Dumézil, the

(ancient) Irish live in a supernatural world. They do not oppose human and divine, and it is in fact difficult to disentangle the two. This penetration of nature by the supernatural is diametrically opposed to the Roman cosmovision. (Belier 1991: 50)

In addition, the boundaries between male and female are ambiguous, with the female taking on typically male tasks such as calling wars and training warriors as well as inflicting violence. Whilst the men in Celtic society are often noted for their physical beauty, the females are known for their dubious morals. Mac Cana (1970: 85) points out that some scathing comments have been made in relation to the morals of the female in ancient Irish mythology and Queen Medb, in particular. Medb's sexual capacity receives considerable emphasis in the literature; as well as being the lover of the prodigiously virile hero Ferghus mac Roich and others, she is said to have claimed that 'never was she without one man in the shadow of another'. The primordial violence of the Celtic goddess can be contrasted with the behaviour of the Roman and Greek goddesses, for example, the virgin goddess Minerva whose act of violence has been associated with defending the honour of her father and protecting against profanity (see Chapter 9 by Guerrier).

The Romantic Hero

Romanticism emerged in the early nineteenth century and, from the beginning, it drew inspiration from the heroic legends of Celtic folklore. In particular, MacPherson's reworkings of old Celtic stories anticipated and resonated with the Romantics' celebration of the fantastic and supernatural, with their nationalistic championing of native folklore and ballads, with their nostalgia for rural and pastoral ways of life, and with their veneration of the heroic individual. In this regard the concept of the Romantic hero was influenced by the earlier concept of the Celtic hero, although Romanticism also drew on other heroic traditions, such as the Homeric epics and the tales of the Anglo-Saxon hero, Beowulf.[50] Romanticism was opposed to (and a development on)

---

[50] The advent of the Romantic hero was also related to modernity's displacement of the Judaeo-Christian paradigm. Drawing on the writings of Otto Rank, Ernest Becker (1973: 159–75) asserts that the heroic role, previously taken by Christ, had to be filled by another to meet the human need for heroes: 'If he no longer had God, how was he to do this? One of the first ways that occurred to him, as Rank saw, was the "romantic solution": he fixed his urge to cosmic heroism onto *another person* in the form of a love object' (p. 160, original emphasis). This shift was given material expression during the French Revolution when reverence for secular heroes officially replaced the veneration of Catholic saints.

eighteenth-century rationalism and is best understood in this historical context. If Rationalists saw (and see) the modern subject as cognitive, unified, centred, rational, and objective, Romantics see the human subject as possessed by an unconscious, 'deep interior' and as axiomatically creative, charismatic, imaginative, unpredictable, and consequently beyond the compass of rational analysis. These attributes are not equally distributed across a population, and in rare cases we will find a genius, a hero, or a supernormal individual.

The Romantic hero is characterized by an exaltation of emotion over reason and a heightened sensitivity, which often results in illness. Thus, Beethoven, Schubert, Chopin, Shelley, Keats, among others, all suffered from serious health problems, which enhanced rather than diminished their heroic standing. This depiction of the melancholic Romantic hero is common in literary representations such as Goethe's *The Sufferings of Young Werther* (Goethe and Steinhauer 1970), a classic story of unhappy love and suicide where Werther, the Romantic hero, is driven to despair by rejection in love. The Romantic hero is differentiated here slightly from the Celtic hero who although capable of highly emotional relationships lacks this extreme sensitivity. For example, Cú Chulainn on a number of occasions risks his life for Emer but he does not agonize over their relationship and prefers to impress her instead with his acts of courage. Of course, the passion of the Romantic hero is not confined to a love-interest and often is related to a cause that he or she strongly believes in.

In the nineteenth century, the role of the Romantic hero was probably filled most completely by Napoleon, who typified the individual challenging the world and subduing it by his genius. Other examples of this Romantic vision of the 'superman'—the Romantic hero is normally, but not always, male—include Nietzsche's *übermensch*; Carlyle's (1841/1926) heroic model of social change; and the various works by Beethoven, Byron, Hazlitt, Tchaikovsky, and others that celebrated Napoleon. W. B. Yeats was also attracted to the heroic dimension of the Celtic legends and in the late nineteenth century published a series of plays based on the life of Cú Chulainn. This and other similar writings—for instance, Lady Gregory published a version of the *Táin Bó Cuailnge*—profoundly influenced Irish nationalists in the early twentieth century who saw heroic self-sacrifice as a cleansing and sanctifying act. In many respects, the Irish Rising of 1916—which saw a small, disorganized group of 'rebels' take on the might of the British Empire—was a working through of this idea as well as being a symbolic re-enactment of the ancient confrontation between the seventeen-year-old Cú Chulainn and the armies of Connacht. Significantly, a statue depicting the dying Cú Chulainn was subsequently erected in the General Post Office in Dublin, where the rising was proclaimed and headquartered. This tradition of the heroic blood-sacrifice is a continuing theme in Irish nationalist theology—for instance, the hunger strikes of the 1980s—and in revolutionary movements worldwide—for instance, the 11 September attacks and the suicide bombings in the Middle East (see Chapter 5 by Grint).

Like the Celtic hero, the Romantic hero is often to be found in war or dangerous adventure, battling about the fundamental issues of the human condition. But while the Celtic hero was invariably linked with violence, the Romantic hero often employs non-violent methods to achieve his or her aims. Thus, instances of the Romantic hero include not only violent men like Napoleon and Hitler, but also non-violent protagonists like Gandhi, Mother Theresa, Martin Luther King, and Nelson Mandela. While this might be an uncomfortable grouping of individuals who would typically be set apart from each other as 'saints' and 'sinners', they can all be classified as Romantic heroes in so far as they have all inspired a significant and dedicated following and they are all people of action, battling over the existential issues that the Romantics see as important: life, death, justice, nationhood, good, and evil. Following Hook's (1945: 107–27) distinction, they are *event-making* rather than *eventful* individuals. In other words, their mark on history is due to their outstanding capabilities and the ease with which they can generate and inspire to action a powerful followership, rather than a peculiar set of circumstances that they happened to be involved in. Romantic heroes change the world, upsetting the status quo through their presence and ability. And in the tradition of Cú Chulainn, this presence is typically short-lived. The classic examples are the romantic artists Shelly, Byron, and Schubert, who, like human meteors, burned quickly and died young.

Unlike the Celtic hero, the typical Romantic hero is not multi-talented. He or she cannot compose wonderful poetry, play the harp, win every chess game, *and* beat a thousand warriors in battle. Neither is he or she the progeny of the Gods in the manner of the Celtic hero. Yet, the notion of destiny does seem to apply: the idea of an individual being preordained for great things through at least being touched by God. This divine touch gives the Romantic hero extraordinary qualities and a charisma through which he or she dazzles the world, inspiring tremendous loyalty, admiration, and love. He or she is extraordinary, talented, and creative—a genius. This characteristic marks off the Romantic hero as someone who is different, even deviant; or mad, in the tradition of one of the first Romantic heroes, Lord Byron, for whom the phrase 'mad, bad, and dangerous to know' was coined. And while Romantic heroes may not have the theological lineage of the Celtic hero, they are still worshipped and therefore liable to lead their unquestioning followers into the abyss. The exemplary case is Adolf Hitler, although Saddam Hussein is a good contemporary example. This dark side to Romanticism was recognized as early as the mid-nineteenth century and its existence was precisely why Pragmatism came to supplant Romanticism (and Idealism, which Romanticism influenced) as the dominant philosophy of the late nineteenth century. Pragmatism has maintained its dominant position throughout the twentieth century and it routinely energizes itself to lance potentially dangerous Romantic heroes. As Hook (1945: 157) succinctly asserted: 'If the hero is defined as an event-making individual who redetermines the course of history, it follows at once that a democratic community must be eternally on guard against him'.

This critique of the Romantic hero provides the basis for the next two heroic archetypes, the neo-romantic hero and the postmodern anti-hero.

The Neo-romantic Hero

The long-standing argument against the Romantic belief in human imagination is that it is ill-advised because it invariably leads to violence and destruction. This argument was first formulated in the mid-nineteenth century after revolution engulfed Europe, but it became even more compelling when the dangers inherent in extreme forms of nationalism—an ideology that was indebted to Romanticism—became more visible. In particular, Romanticism was linked to the Holocaust, on the basis that the former not only willed heroic monsters like Hitler into existence, but also created an environment where nationalism could easily turn into fascism.

The Pragmatic critique of Romanticism is compelling: Romantics are good to have about the place, but they must be contained at the margins since they are too naive to be entrusted with anything of real import. If Carlyle's argument—that 'Universal History, the history of what man has accomplished in this world, is at bottom the History of the Great men who have worked here'—was widely accepted in the nineteenth century, it gained few adherents in the twentieth (see Hook 1945: 18). Typical is Hook's assertion that 'every *major* development in the historical process is determined by social and economic forces in which heroes and great men are a negligible factor' (Hook 1945: 81, original emphasis). Feminists added their voice by criticizing the idea of history as a process determined by great *men*.

On the other hand, the Romantic desire for heroes is a profound if not fundamental part of the human condition. As James put it, 'mankind's common instinct for reality...has always held the world to be essentially a theatre for heroism' (quoted in Becker 1973: 1). Becker traces this heroic instinct to our innate narcissism; to the individual's belief that he or she will not die; to the fact that the unconscious does not know death or time; and to disillusion with earlier mythical and religious hero-systems. Our thesis is that this dilemma was resolved through creating space for—and indeed constructing—the *neo-romantic hero*. Like the Romantic hero, the neo-romantic hero shares many of the Celtic hero's attributes: he (and increasingly she) is extraordinary, gifted, talented, and attractive. Like his or her Romantic equivalent, the neo-romantic hero is recognized as an exceptional individual, an extraordinary oddity. But there are important differences as well.

We can identify two types of neo-romantic hero, the *prosaic* and the *phenomenal*. The prosaic (or 'low') neo-romantic hero is neither an exceptional nor a remarkable person, and is certainly different from the romantic concept of the 'great man'. Rather, he or she is more akin to the tramps, thieves, prostitutes, orphans, and peasants that the Russian writer Maxim Gorky takes as his heroic type: 'ordinary' people who are nonetheless heroic in so far as their lives involve enormous struggles against overwhelming odds, 'the plain, everyday, earthy heroism wrought by gnarled working hands guiding a family through hunger and disease' (Becker 1973: 5). Likewise, Solzhenitsyn celebrates the 'small man', such as the victims/survivors of the Gulag, whose heroism is based on great suffering and endurance rather than on achievement.

In contrast, the phenomenal (or 'high') neo-romantic hero is seen as an exceptional, singular person in the romantic tradition. But there are important differences between this heroic archetype and the Romantic (and Celtic) hero. First, he or she is limited and is certainly not multi-talented like the Celtic hero. The neo-romantic hero is allowed, even expected, to manifest the deviant, dangerous, and mad attributes of the Romantic hero, but this deviance is managed by displacing, containing, and enabling the hero into 'safe' domains such as sport, music, film, and—importantly from an organizational context—business. Crucially, he or she is excluded from the more vital domains such as politics and military endeavours. Overall, therefore, the neo-romantic hero is *benign*. Of course there was a heroic aspect to sport and music going back at least to the Romans and Greeks, but what is notable is the degree to which these domains became a hugely important—if not the primary—stage for heroes from the late nineteenth century onwards.

In particular, it is interesting that neo-romantic heroes are to be found (or perhaps one should say created) in the world of commerce and administration. Prior to the late nineteenth century, administrators and those holding office in commercial business organizations were, in the main, seen as ordinary, even mundane. Remember, for instance, Napoleon's disparaging comment about the English being a 'nation of shopkeepers'. As part of the systematic suppression of Romantic heroes that started after the middle of the nineteenth century, the world of business was encouraged and enabled to produce neo-romantic heroes, be they entrepreneurs or, even more incredibly, managers. We say incredible because bureaucracy was traditionally seen as anathema to creativity, humanity, and irrationality, the most defining attributes of the Romantic hero.[51]

An early example of the neo-romantic hero was the industrialist Henry Ford, while more recent examples include Bill Gates, Steve Jobs, and David

---

[51] In Chapter 8, Peter Pelzer describes how Romantics (represented by the Flying Dutchman), who strive for values beyond materialism, are alienated and lost in the contemporary world of commerce.

Beckham.[52] In particular, Gates and Jobs fit Hook's category of 'eventful' rather than 'event-making' men since, as Cringely (1992) has shown in his book, *Accidental Empires*, their success can be largely attributed to chance and serendipity.

In many ways, the neo-romantic, phenomenal hero is best understood as a *manufactured* entity, a fabricated icon who, at the extreme, is famous for being famous, a temporary construction and product of the culture industries. Even where the neo-romantic hero is seen to have some talent—for example, in sport, music, acting, or writing—their status is still perceived to be more a matter of good fortune than anything else and there certainly is no belief in a super-human ancestry. This means that Hook's (1945: 108–9) distinction between the 'eventful man' and the 'event-making man' is less useful when applied to the neo-romantic hero, whose 'greatness' is as much a matter of being in the right place at the right time as it is a consequence of truly outstanding attributes. Thus, the neo-romantic's status is *transitory*, as he or she stands in the limelight for a relatively short period before being displaced by someone else.

If the phenomenal hero is a product of particular systems of power and influence, the prosaic hero is marginalized by the same systems. At times, the categories may seem corrupted—as in the classic 'rags-to-riches' stories—but such 'transgressions' are also axiomatic to the understanding of each arche-type; the exceptions that prove the rule, as it were.

The Postmodern Anti-hero

Our thesis thus far is that the neo-romantic hero came to prominence because of the dangers perceived to be inherent in the Romantic hero. However, a more radical move from the hero to the *anti-hero* is also evident.

An important critique of the hero can be found in the writings of Joyce and Beckett who were antagonistic to many aspects of the Celtic literary revival, especially to Yeats's heroic images. Beckett's antipathy to the ideology of hero-ism is vividly depicted in his play *Murphy*, where one of the characters tries to brain himself against the aforementioned statue of Cú Chulainn that was erected in Dublin's General Post Office to commemorate the Easter 1916 ris-ing. In place of Yeats' (Celtic) hero, both Beckett and Joyce centre their nar-ratives on the anti-hero, the exhausted (predominantly male) ego of twentieth-century Western man. Their writings and ideas have been influential

---

[52] ' "In those days, people looked to gods and heroes more than they do today, so we wondered who they might look up to in a modern sense. It had to be David Beckham... We made sure Nike, the Greek goddess of victory, wasn't there too. After all, David's with Adidas". Katherine Boyd, spokesperson for Stourhead, one of England's most spec-tacular landscaped gardens, on news that Becks is to be immortalised in the Pantheon, a classical building dedicated to deities and heroes'. *Sunday Tribune*, 28 July 2002.

throughout the twentieth century and today; even in popular culture, heroes are routinely presented in caricature or ironically. Not surprisingly, the anti-hero has come to play an increasingly central role in television programmes (e.g. *Seinfeld* and *Friends*), films (e.g. *American Beauty, Tigerland*, and Woody Allen's films), advertising (e.g. the Budweiser lizard and Wassup ads, a contemporary take on Beckett's *Waiting for Godot*), and in popular depictions of organizational life (e.g. *Dilbert* and *The Simpsons*). The anti-hero, in these popular representations, is not just ordinary but *unattractive*. In contrast to other heroes, the postmodern anti-hero is more of a celebrity rather than an achiever, an object of identification rather than a figure of awe, and a narcissist rather than a selfless campaigner.

We can usefully distinguish three similar but different types of antiheroes, three sides to the one anti-heroic coin as it were: the *apathetic*, the *cynic*, and the *egoist*. The apathetic anti-hero is not only unsuccessful and disinterested in becoming successful but despises the success of others and views him or herself as a victim of their success and profiteering. Whilst the Celtic hero is always on the move, and the Romantic hero is on a journey, the apathetic anti-hero stays put in the very place or position he or she complains about. In a sense then, this anti-hero is defined by and even enjoys his or her misery. The apathetic anti-hero is depicted in Tangherlini (2000), who presents the storytelling tactics of paramedics who tell *self-deprecatory* stories in order to counter the media representation of their profession as caring and dutiful.

The *cynical* anti-hero is rebellious (although often lazy), defies authority, and often resists change and sees himself or herself as the moral opposition to the profiteering ways of others. The cynics attribute a moral authority to their inaction, which distinguishes them from the apathetic anti-hero. The cynic often emerges after experiencing what he or she perceives as an injustice. This injustice corrodes trust and creates an atmosphere of cynicism from which the anti-hero emerges. Sloterdijk's description of the cynic is especially apt:

He shows contempt for fame, ridicules the architecture, refuses respect, parodies the stories of gods and heroes, eats raw meat and vegetables, lies in the sun, fools around with the whores and says to Alexander the Great that he should get out of his sun... (Sloterdijk 1988: 103–4)

The *egoistic* anti-hero takes on a darker character and this is the anti-hero that is routinely depicted in popular culture. One may usefully contrast the Romantic hero with the egoistic anti-hero. If the archetypical Romantic hero's actions are motivated and influenced by a higher nature, the egoist's actions are motivated by a lower, primordial attribute. This anti-hero is not seeking to reach a higher state of being and is certainly not interested in personal sacrifice, one of the hallmarks of Romantic heroes. Instead, the anti-hero manifests the selfish side of the ego, is unable to resist temptation, and engages in antisocial behaviour including bullying and tyranny. If the heroic journey is about transcendence, rebirth, and liberty, the selfish anti-hero's life is about greed, accumulation, control, and alienation. In place of the superhero there is the tyrant; in place of generosity, greed; in place of compassion, hatred; in place of paradise, hell. In some extreme cases the boundary between the egoistic anti-hero and the Romantic hero becomes blurred (e.g. the case of Hitler) except of course one pities the anti-hero for having such a pathetic existence but one never feels pity for the Romantic hero.

Discussion

We began this chapter with Henry Mintzberg's observation about how we have become enamoured of a heroic view of management. Quite clearly, there is a contemporary celebration of the business hero—routinely deified on the cover of business magazines—who is depicted as being able to reinvent, turn around, and generally transform organizations through his (rarely her) individual genius. Elsewhere, Mintzberg has elaborated on and criticized this heroic view of management (Mintzberg *et al.* 2002). One of our objectives has been to contribute to this discussion by mapping out an archaeology of this phenomenon. Our historical approach has enabled us to theorize why organizational heroes and anti-heroes have come to be and their links with heroes and anti-heroes in other domains and times.

Now, we can sketch out some interesting hypotheses and questions for organizational theorists. For instance, is there other evidence to support or counter our thesis that society now seeks and constructs its heroes in the world of business because it sees the heroic role as too risky for the political domain? Who are the heroes and anti-heroes in organizational life and how do they operate? How are these organizational entities constructed and destroyed? Which discourses are leveraged in these configuring processes? What different types of heroes/anti-heroes can be discerned and in which contexts do they flourish (i.e. what other organizational attributes might they be related to)?

Much of our chapter has focused on Romanticism, a movement and paradigm that has been largely overlooked by organization studies generally, and—most surprisingly—by its critical theory and postmodern streams. Gergen, for instance, in one of the field's rare references to Romanticism, notes that it is now a 'vocabulary in remission' (Gergen 1992: 210), while a supposedly encyclopaedic review of organization theory's historical development (Lynch and Dicker 1998) makes no reference whatsoever to the discipline's Romantic tradition. Yet, the Romantic philosophy of individualism—that opens the world to the individual and witnesses marvels unimagined before—is easily discernible in much of organization theory even if its roots in Romanticism and Celtic mythology are now obscured. For instance, theories based on fundamental human needs and much of the writing about leadership and entrepreneurship have been strongly influenced by Romanticism (Gergen 1992).

There are other interesting issues that our study has only touched upon. First, in contrast to the Celts' worldview where *space* and *location* are charged with significance, the discourse of organization theory is virtually de-spatialized. This raises the question of what a more 'spatialized' organization theory might look like and how it might differ from the current discourse. Second, the Celts' nonchalance towards categorical distinctions reminds us of the contemporary scepticism towards rigid boundaries in and between organizations, and the valorization of cross-functional teams, project teams, heterarchy, and other provisional forms of organizing. In turn, many of these ideas have drawn on postmodern discourse, which has been centrally concerned with deconstructing 'essentialist' philosophies that we have inherited from the Greco-Roman tradition. This suggests that there is much to be learned and relearned about organization and leadership through examining premodern modes of organizing that have largely been overlooked in the organization theory literature. Third, the character of Medb in the Táin story sensitizes us to the idea of female *deviancy*—whether and how female misbehaviour differs from the misbehaviour of male colleagues. Again this has not been explored in depth within organization studies; where women are mentioned, it is often as the victim of harassment or discrimination by male colleagues. Fourth, while violence is a central motif in the heroic narratives of Celtic culture—and we should note that violence is often inflicted on and by women—the organization studies literature has had surprisingly little to say on the topic, probably because of the premium its functionalist heritage puts on order and stability. Of course there are related sub-literatures within the field—on conflict, deviance, sabotage, and so forth—but very little has been written on the subject of violence per se. In particular, there is an absence of theory on the relationship between violence and organization.

Conclusion

Heroic myths and legends help us become more human, since they remind us that life should be lived with a sense of heroic adventure, that we should individually craft our own heroic journey rather than follow another's path (Campbell 1949/1968). More generally, myths, legends, and fairy tales help us make sense of the world. They endure because for some reason they are meaningful and unveil deep, often hidden, explanations for why things and actions are as they are (Bettelheim 1975). Myths and legends, such as the Cú Chulainn story, are no less compelling today, even for those of us who spend most of our lives in organizations or thinking about organizations.

References

Becker, E. (1973). *The Denial of Death.* New York: Free Press.

Belier, W. W. (1991). *Decayed Gods: Origin and Development of Georges Dumézil's 'Idéologie Tripartie'.* Leiden: E. J. Brill.

Bettelheim, B. (1975). *The Uses of Enchantment: The Meaning and Importance of Fairy Tales.* London: Penguin.

Campbell, J. (1949/1968). *The Hero with a Thousand Faces.* Princeton: Princeton University Press.

Carlyle, T. (1841/1926). *Heroes, Hero-worship and the Heroic in History.* Champaign, IL: Project Gutenberg.

Chadwick, N. K. and Cunliffe, B. W. (1997). *The Celts.* London: Penguin Books.

Cringely, R. X. (1992). *Accidental Empires: How the Boys of Silicon Valley Make their Millions, Battle Foreign Competition, and Still Can't Get a Date.* Reading, MA: Addison-Wesley.

de Vries, J. (1963). *Heroic Song and Heroic Legend.* London: Oxford University Press.

Desmond, J. (2002). 'An evaluation of Freudian theories of desire in relation to the premodern tale of the *Táin Bo Cuailnge'.* Unpublished Working Paper, Department of Management, University of St Andrews, Scotland.

Gergen, K. J. (1992). 'Organization theory in the postmodern era', in M. Reed and M. Hughes (eds.), *Rethinking Organizations.* London: Sage, pp. 207–26.

Goethe, J. W. V. and Steinhauer, H. (1970). *The Sufferings of Young Werther.* New York: Norton.

Hook, S. (1945). *The Hero in History: A Study in Limitation and Possibility.* London: Secker & Warburg.

Kinsella, T. and Le Brocquy, L. (1970). *The Táin.* Oxford: Oxford University Press.

Lynch, T. D. and Dicker, T. J. (eds.) (1998). *Handbook of Organization Theory and Management: The Philosophical Approach.* New York: Marcel Dekker.

Mac Cana, P. (1970). *Celtic Mythology.* Feltham: Newnes Books.

Mallory, J. P. (ed.) (1992). *Aspects of the Táin.* Belfast: December Publications.

Mintzberg, H., Simons, R., and Basu, K. (2002). 'Beyond selfishness'. *Sloan Management Review*, 44(1): 67–74.

O'Rahilly, C. (1967). *Táin bo Cuailnge from the Book of Leinster.* Dublin: Dias.

Raglan, L. (1936). *The Hero: A Study in Tradition, Myth, and Drama.* London: Methuen.

Sloterdijk, P. (1988). *Critique of Cynical Reason.* London: Verso.

Tangherlini, T. (2000). 'Heroes and lies: Storytelling tactics among paramedics'. *Folklore*, 111(1): 43–6.

Thurneysen, R. (1921). *Die Irische Helden—und Königsage bis zum Siebzehnten Jahrhundert.* Halle: Max Niemeyer.

III

THE TRAGIC NARRATIVES: POSTMODERNITY AND ITS DISCONTENTS

Introduction

THE common theme of the chapters in this section is *punishment*. When planning the book, I had not quite appreciated how central punishment is as a feature of the narrative tradition. It has played a major part in many of the narratives in this book so far (the fall of Adam and Eve, the destruction of Ulysses and his crew, the labours of Hercules, and so forth), but in the chapters that make up this section punishment comes centre-stage, overshadowing even heroism. The protagonists at the centre of these chapters are tragic heroes, heroes who have to pay dearly for their exploits and whose suffering inspires the classic Aristotelian mixture of pity and awe. Some narratives of suffering can serve as warnings, although all authors in this section choose to view them as capturing some profound discontent of our times, and hence summing up our contemporary experience. The harm is already done and we, like the Dutchman, like Prometheus bound, or like the poor Lydian girl Arachne, are trapped in the dreadful unfolding of consequences.

When talking about cultural discontents and fissure points, some readers of this book will wish to make a distinction between progress-believing modernity, with its predominantly upbeat though anxious and guilt-ridden outlook, and narcissistic postmodernity, with its gloomily hedonistic ethos and moral agnosticism if not nihilism. Not all chapters in this section subscribe to the view that there is a massive and irreversible discontinuity separating our times from the high-noon of modernity. And even among those that make a distinction, not all believe that the discontinuity is cultural or material—discontinuities, like other boundaries, can exist as mirages, themselves manifestations of deceptions and self-deceptions. In the subtitle of this section, therefore, readers should not see a *prise de position* on the now ebbing debates on postmodernity.

Peter Pelzer (Chapter 8) is inspired by the endless wanderings of the Flying Dutchman and his phantom ship through the high seas to search for the discontents of modernity. The origin of the story of the Dutchman's curse, we learn from Pelzer, lies in the early seventeenth century, a time when vast properties could be amassed by sea captains in their travels to the Dutch East-India; these merchants literally flew through the seas, transporting their cargoes to Western markets, under poor deck conditions for their crews. The hunger for sordid gain and its single-minded pursuit in the high seas brings about dehumanization, obsession, and ultimately death. The Dutchman's eternal travels allow Pelzer to develop a highly original argument for humanity's loss of eternal meanings and absolute values. What Pelzer argues is that, when meaning loses its anchors, sense-making (Weick 1995) becomes an inadequate and doomed surrogate. What a difference between Ulysses' brilliant journey of discovery (in Dante's version), driven by the thirst for knowledge, and the Dutchman's dark wanderings in a world of eternal darkness and permanent exile. And yet both voyages are voyages of freedom, with no final Ithaca in sight. The journey without destination then comes to be seen both as the curse and as the thrilling adventure of our time.

The story of Arachne (Greek for spider) and Minerva, as told by Ovid, enables Yvonne Guerrier (Chapter 9) to develop some deep insights into the price of female success in today's organizations. Arachne, a consummate weaver of poor origin, challenges the goddess Minerva to a weaving contest. From that moment on her tragic fate is sealed. What is interesting in the story, however, is that Arachne's tapestry in the contest is every bit as good as Minerva's, only it depicts scenes that are less flattering for the gods (abductions, rapes, punishments) than of the glorious narratives featuring in Minerva's own tapestry. The goddess's anger at Arachne and her subsequent transformation of Arachne into a spider reveals her own powerlessness when it comes to criticizing the divine male order. What infuriates Minerva is that the powerless and poor girl can say what she, the goddess, cannot. The difference between Minerva's position and that of the Celtic goddess, discussed by Kavanagh and O'Leary (Chapter 7), is telling; in the Celtic myth, the boundaries between human and divine and between male and female are a lot more fluid. Minerva's godly power, unlike that of her Celtic counterpart, is entirely contingent on representing the will of her father Zeus—this is the price Minerva has to pay in order to achieve power within this male-centred world, the price of breaking the glass ceiling.

The will of Zeus also plays a crucial part in the story that animates Chapter 10. Few heroes have exercised a fascination through the ages equal to that of Prometheus, the titan, who, defying the will of Zeus, stole fire and the arts and crafts of the gods and offered them to humanity. As the liberator of humanity from darkness, poverty, and ignorance, he paid a great price, nailed on Mount Caucasus and visited every day by an eagle (Zeus's emblematic bird), which tore at his liver. As is well-known, Karl Marx saw in Prometheus the story of human self-emancipation, but also the costs of that emancipation. Ulrich Gehmann develops this argument showing how Prometheus offered the promise of total human liberation through the medium of technology, a promise that has since the onset of civilization created bright hopes, but one which has ultimately generated profound discontents and disappointments of its own. Technology may have given people unprecedented powers and may be credited with numerous achievements. But has it made us happier? Has it offered solutions to poverty, ignorance, and violence? Above all, has it provided answers to the questions of meaning and value? The myth of technique, that technology provides the answers to everything, is one that we find difficult to give up. But the story of Prometheus goes beyond technique—since technique itself emerges as a deeper layered expression of a Logos of domination and exploitation. As one of humanity's most exclusively male-centred stories, it expresses a will to subdue everything in the construction of a new human biosphere: an entirely *man-made* artificial cosmos. This biosphere is no fiction but one which, according to Gehmann, we currently inhabit—our 'technical' civilization, our Caucasian rock-face, to which we seem to be firmly locked.

The story of Phaethon, the young boy who suffers from incredible anxieties about his parentage, offers Diana Winstanley (Chapter 11) an extraordinary starting point for a discourse not only into the problematic nature of contemporary identity-formation, but also (like Gehmann), into the pitfalls of our technological civilization. Phaethon, the son of Phoebus, the sun-god whom he had never met in person, persuades his father to allow him to ride the powerful chariot of the sun just for one day to prove his divine credentials. Tragically, Phaethon loses control of the immortal horses and, after wreaking much celestial and earthly havoc, is brought crashing down to earth by Zeus to prevent further damage. Winstanley's chapter looks at the great challenge of fashioning an identity, especially by those who grow in the shadow of eminent parents. Heroism becomes a path to identity, but one for which the young person is all too often ill-prepared and ill-equipped. The family tragedies that follow the demise of such desperate heroics are touchingly unravelled by Winstanley.

The crash of Phaethon to earth, with its powerful evocation of the Challenger and Columbia space-shuttle 'disasters', also allows Winstanley to develop an argument regarding technological hubris that closely parallels Gehmann's. The flight of Phaethon becomes a symbol of the exaggerated importance accorded to technology, the power to fly away into distant worlds, not so much for the sake of exploration as Gherardi might have argued, but rather for that of narcissistic self-admiration, almost as a photo-opportunity for glamour, power, and beauty. Winstanley's treatment of the myth, like several other accounts in this book, seeks to remind us that some of the most fecund voyages of discovery are to be undertaken a lot closer to home, and may be altogether interior journeys, something that remained forever beyond the grasp of young Phaethon.

The closing chapter of this section (Chapter 12) offers us another narrative prominently featuring the punishment of a young man by a deity: this time it is Demeter, that most unMinerva-like of ancient goddesses, the mother goddess of the Earth with its richness of crops, trees, and flowers. She visits a terrible revenge on Erysichthon who, in his youthful impetuosity, defiles her sacred grove. In spite of repeated warnings, Erysichthon, an over-eager disciple of Prometheus perhaps, sets out to cut the huge poplar tree that dominates Demeter's grove, in order to build a roof for his banqueting hall. The goddess's punishment is to condemn the foolish young man to eternal consumption, whereby the more he eats, the hungrier he gets. Like Phaethon, he leaves behind a grieving family and much sorrow. This story enables Heather Höpfl to develop a powerful critique of contemporary consumption as a curse, the product of an insatiable appetite, which consumes the consumer. The eternal torment of the hero is the tragic torment of the addict who can never overcome addiction, whose every effort to meet a desire augments the desire. In this way, Höpfl offers the indispensable corollary to Gehmann's and Winstanley's chapters (Chapters 10 and 11), by arguing that our Promethean civilization and its technological and production mega-structures are a violation of the maternal element, serving to make us fat, unhappy, and oblivious to the sorrows of those around us. Above all, they create needs that can never be fulfilled.

The chapters that make up this section have undoubtedly darker hues than the others in this book. Humanity's tragic predicament, they seem to underline, lies in a vicious circle of delusions and discontents, first clearly articulated by Freud in the two masterpieces of his old age, 'The future of an illusion' (Freud 1927) and 'Civilization and its discontents' (Freud 1930). Freud, it will be recalled, argued that while different cultures may be characterized by distinct illusions and diverse discontents, the tragedy of the human condition lies in the fact that illusions reinforce the discontents for which they purport to offer consolations. Freud would maintain his faith in Logos, not as instrumental reason but as a capacity for critical reflection, as offering the only hope of breaking out of the vicious circle. Unlike the other four chapters in this section, Höpfl's conclusion allows for a ray of hope that the vicious circle of blind production and addictive consumption could be unravelled, not through the espousal of novel illusions, but through the discovery of a wisdom that engages both intellect and emotion. This would turn back the clock—the Flying Dutchman would finally find rest in his harbour, Arachne would be recognized for the unparalleled mastery of her delicate arts and for her willingness to speak her mind, Prometheus would forever leave the Caucasus not through the intervention of a mythical Hercules but through an act of self-emancipation, Phaethon would stop worrying about his image, and Erysichthon would discover peace and happiness in Demeter's grove without ever thinking of cutting it down and turning it into something useful. What a thought!

References

Freud, S. (1927). 'The future of an illusion', in S. Freud (ed.), *Freud: Civilization, Society and Religion* (Vol. 12). Harmondsworth: Penguin.

Freud, S. (1930). 'Civilization and its discontents', in S. Freud (ed.), *Freud: Civilization, Society and Religion* (Vol. 12). Harmondsworth: Penguin.

Weick, K. E. (1995). *Sensemaking in Organizations*. London: Sage.

EIGHT

The Flying Dutchman and the Discontents of Modernity

Peter Pelzer

> One day the mariners' collective imagination perceives the spectre of the Flying Dutchman on the oceans of the new world: 'blood red the sails, black the mast'. Aimlessly, the helm damaged or washed away, and every now and then without a living crew, it haunts the floods—a gloomy memorial in an optimistic age—and it dooms those crossing its way with a curse of aimlessness and life-in-death.
>
> Frank 1995: 19

'YOU certainly know the fable of the Flying Dutchman' (Heine, 1831/1981). Heinrich Heine introduced his description of the legend with this categorical assertion to the reader, indicating that he could rely on the knowledge of his contemporaries. We still know the name, perhaps we also know of the Olympic discipline, the class of small fast sailing boats; perhaps we are members of KLM's frequent flyer programme of that name, perhaps we have even experienced the latest performance of Wagner's opera at our local opera house—but *do we still know about the Dutchman*? And does he have any significance for us?

There is no such thing as *the* legend of the Flying Dutchman. This is not surprising, considering the fact that it belonged to the oral tradition of sailors for several centuries before going inland: it served a different purpose for each different audience. As there were no written documents about his 'original' life at sea, the legend was open to interpretation and variation. The scientific attempts to save the primary *mythos*, and to investigate its starting point, came too late for us to be in any way certain, but they at least provided enough material for plausible reconstructions.

Nonetheless, in all its enigmatic variations, the Flying Dutchman is a symbol for a time in transition. It is of no surprise that this legend was so popular in the nineteenth century: it expressed the widely spread feeling of discontent towards the effects of enlightenment, discovery, scientific progress, industrialization—in short, towards modernity itself. The aim of what follows will be partly to reconstruct, partly to interpret, and partly also to ask why the Dutchman still has a message to deliver—that is, if he really does. I will start with a reconstruction, which, with all its transformations, is an exciting story in itself. The interpretation works on the assumption that the legend's success inland derives from its capturing the feelings of discontent bred by modernity. Almost two centuries later, and focusing on the theme of organization, the idea here is to have a look at sense-making processes in organizations, especially at how they are handled theoretically. The slant is that a broader meaning is still absent from such sense-making structures. The feeling of discontent against modernity invariably prevails. The last part of the chapter plays around with the legend in order to enquire about its lasting value.

The Many Layers of a Familiar (?) Legend

The question mark in the heading is placed very consciously: as with any oral tradition, we cannot be sure about the original version of the Flying Dutchman, and the versions available do not produce a coherent picture. The development of the myth, once it is transported inland from the sea, however, is remarkable. At first, it seems to have been a folk tale among crews of leading marine nations of the period. But what were its original contents? The shortest possible description of the legend is taken here from the motif-index of folk literature: 'A sea captain because of his wickedness sails his phantom ship eternally without coming to harbour' (Thompson 1966: E511). As we will see, this abridged version is correct, but also misleading in a crucial way—it presupposes a certain view of the world. But the basic constituents are present almost in their entirety:

• it is the story of a sea captain;
• there is a reason for the curse he bears, which is the leitmotif of the legend;
• the ship is not able to come to harbour;
• it is a phantom ship, that is, a ship sailing without a living crew;
• it is doomed to sail eternally.

This is the kernel, which remained stable once it was written down, despite the expansion of the story in later versions, for example, by Fitzball (1826), Heine (1831/1981), Marryat (1837/1896), Wagner (1841/1993), and others. Although the legend itself was several hundred years old by this time, the first written accounts date only as far back as the early nineteenth century. There are numerous versions available,[53] but the version of *Blackwood's Edinburgh Magazine* of 1821 seems to be the most influential one:

[53] Frank (1995) quotes five basic versions; Gerndt (1971) lists twenty-one pages of sources which significantly used the Flying Dutchman or phantom ships with the typical characteristics of the Flying Dutchman.

They give different reasons for it, but my story is this: She was an Amsterdam vessel, and sailed from that port seventy years ago. Her master's name was Vanderdecken. He was a staunch seaman, and would have his own way, in spite of the devil. For all that, never a sailor under him had reason to complain; though how it is on board with him now, nobody knows; the story is this, that in doubling the Cape, they were a long day trying to weather the Table Bay, which we saw this morning. However, the wind headed them, and went against them more and more, and Vanderdecken walked the deck, swearing against the wind. Just after sunset, a vessel spoke to him, asking if he did not mean to go into the Bay that night. Vanderdecken replied, 'May I be eternally d—d if I do, though I should beat about here till the Day of Judgment!' And to be sure Vanderdecken never did go into that bay; for it is believed that he continues to beat about in these seas still, and will do so long enough. This vessel is never seen but with foul weather along with her. (Blackwood 1821: 128)

In the following, even more detailed version, the legend's origin is situated at the beginning of the Dutch East-India activities, in the early seventeenth century. Again, the captain's name, though a different one, is provided, and the purpose and destination of the journey are very clearly described:

At the beginning of the seventeenth century, there lived an entrepreneurial sailor by the name of Barend Fokke, who always sailed with full sails, never minding about the wind and the weather. He had iron bars fastened on his masts to prevent them from being blown overboard by strong winds, and even in those days he made the crossing between Batavia and Holland in just ninety days, sailing to and fro over a period of eight months... Because of his extraordinary speed, he was regarded as a magician, as being in league with the devil. This belief was strengthened by his unusual height and strength, his terrifying countenance and rude manners, and his continuous swearing.

After he had left the port for the last time, and when nothing more had been heard of him, people assumed that he had fallen prey to the devil, who had condemned him to sail forever on his ship between the Cape of Good Hope and the south coast of America, without ever being allowed to drop anchor in a port as punishment for his sins. In the last century, nearly every sailor of the Indian Ocean was able to tell a story of this strange, errant ship. Many a sailor had been called at night by the bewitched Dutch ship, and had seen it clearly: the crew on board only consisted of the captain, the boatswain, the cook and a single seaman, all very, very old, and with long beards. Every single question that they were asked remained unanswered, resulting in the ship's disappearance. (Das Ausland 1841: 945–6)

One characteristic here is the clear documentary quality. It is accurate, as if it is about a real incident that living witnesses could have reported. We are given the name of the captain, the ship is located within space and time, his offence and penance are named, characteristics of the ship are given, and, furthermore, the consequences of meeting it are described. All in all, this is in remarkable contradiction with the obvious intent and effect of the legend: it is a rational description of a supernatural event.

Both documents give a further hint of the legend's origin. They place the story at the Cape of Good Hope, mentioning the strong winds coming down from the inland hills. The Cape of Good Hope was one of the landmarks of the age of discoveries: the way to India. And just as if there had been some distant memory of the ancient ban of sailing through the strait of Gibraltar, with the statue of Hercules forming a gate to prevent sailors from crossing it, this new ban seems to have become the next point where the unknown lies right around the corner. It is quite legitimate to place the origin of the legend of the Flying Dutchman within the framework of the voyages of the Portuguese, and especially those of Bartholomew Diaz and Vasco da Gama in the late fifteenth century (Flohr 1989: 26). Diaz gave up and made about turn on his first voyage; he was shipwrecked in a storm at the Cape when he tried the crossing for the second time. During his own, ultimately successful trip, it was reported that Vasco da Gama had had to face the same problems as Diaz at the Cape. He rejected the demands of his crew to seek the shelter of a port, and to give up the whole trip. When he noticed signs of a growing mutiny, he had both the ringleader and the helmsman put in chains, under orders to withstand the storm. It is even said that he let the rudder free, and that he threw the sea maps into the sea with the words: 'From now on you shall have no helmsman... God will be helmsman now. His Will be done! We are not returning to Portugal!' (Gerndt 1971: 166) This interpretation of da Gama's voyage is taken from an early source, a history book of 1551. Another source from 1927 proved that in 1551 the building of the saga was already in process: Vasco da Gama had faced neither storm nor mutiny on his journey. It is, nonetheless, a matter of fact that the weather conditions at the Cape may change suddenly and unpredictably, even within a relatively restricted area, and that this part of the sea is characterized by treacherous currents. Lack of knowledge about these conditions made it very hard for sailing ships to pass the Cape of Good Hope, and resulted in numerous disasters.

Portugal was succeeded by the Netherlands as the leading marine nation, from the beginning of the seventeenth century and onwards. The founding of the Dutch East-India Company was one of the most successful start-ups in history. With the invention of new types of ships, they gained an advantage in speed on their way to India. The transport of valuable goods and their trading in Europe made the Netherlands into a rich country and turned many sea captains wealthy. The attribute of 'flying' refers to the unprecedented speed with which these ships were sailing. This combination of astonishing speed, the self-interest of the captains, bad working conditions on the ships, low wages, and heavy losses of ships might well have been the ingredients for the further development of the legend. It must also be noted that phantom ships were not just the mere imaginings of superstitious crews. It is documented that in the mid-nineteenth century there were around 2500 annual losses (Flohr 1989: 48). Of these, some 200 were given up by their crews because of serious damage, like fire in the cargo hold or leakages. But wooden ships showed a surprising robustness, and often did not sink immediately. It has been speculated that in the northern Atlantic there were always an average of twenty wrecks drifting for a month or more (Flohr 1989: 51). The sight of a phantom ship was a common experience, and collisions with these wrecks were a well-known form of accident.

This sounds like a plausible reconstruction of the legend's emergence. But we have to note that this is only speculation from hindsight. There are no written documents about the sailors' beliefs for the time between 1500 and 1800. And even if such documents existed, they would only represent the author's interpretation. So we have to face the fact that everything we know about the legend of the Flying Dutchman is a construct made up by landlubbers, or at least with the taste of an inland audience in mind. The captains' names, Vanderdecken and Barent Fokke, might as well have remained undocumented, the abjuration of God cannot be proven, and the salvation motif was completely absent before the 1820s (Gerndt 1971). It cannot even be said whether the name 'the Flying Dutchman' refers to the captain's person, or to the ship itself. However, what can be said is that the legend has had at least a second life inland. It may well be that its importance in the nineteenth century outweighed its significance as a folk tale in the earlier centuries; yet for this role it needed several changes.

The Flying Dutchman as an Expression of Discontent

In the oral tradition of sailors, the legend served the purposes of faith, explanation, naming, or entertainment (Gerndt 1971). These can be seen as the usual functions of legends. Faced with overwhelming real conditions, sailors used sea legends in order to cope with and structure their world. Further even, the Flying Dutchman became a symbol of two eras meeting in transition. It is certainly not accidental that the story became a topic of broad cultural interest exactly at the beginning of the nineteenth century. By authenticating the legend within a different context, that is, by transporting it inland, its role and function also changed, each time in accordance with its author and audience. It crossed class borders and became part of the heritage of high culture. As Laroche (1993) points out, this wanderer between worlds is not merely the incarnation of a person damned; he is above all the sign and symbol of an emerging era, situated between utopian romantic social dreams, the restoration, the dawn of national states, and enlightened demystification. The legend served to articulate the discontents of this new era. Two aspects of this condition will be discussed here: the loss of an eternal meaning and the loss of humanity that accompanied the increasing appreciation of material wealth.

Life-in-death

As already argued, the Flying Dutchman is one of several motifs dealing with the discontents of modernity. Frank entitled his book on the Flying Dutchman *The Eternal Voyage* (1995), and added similar motifs from Dante's *Divine Comedy*, the story of the Wandering Jew, Coleridge's (1798/1993) 'The rime of the ancient mariner', and from the more recent accounts of expeditions to cold and icy parts of our planet. Poe's 'The narrative of Arthur Gordon Pym of Nantucket' (1838) and 'A descent into the maelstrom' (1841) are typical examples of this development. They demonstrate how discovery and destruction ultimately merge into one. Predictably, the narrator remains absolutely cool when faced with his own death, and he becomes the observer of the destruction of the ship and his companions. He is the scientific eye, and he is saved in order to report on the events, as well as discourage others. The voyage to the South Pole, and the various descriptions of a figure in the midst of the icy landscape, surrounded by its cold winds, pick up the motif of the winds that blow from the mountains of the Cape of Good Hope. Still later, the voyage is transformed into the eternal Winter Journey. The increasing unreality of the plot corresponds to a change in the motif: the voyage to the end of the world becomes an inner journey into the eternity of the human soul. I am very conscious of the fact that this is an almost desperate abbreviation of Frank's rich argument; yet the point I wish to make is that the saga of the Flying Dutchman is part of a tradition. Without doubt, it is absolutely necessary to construct a meaning in order to compensate for a loss: after the loss of the transcendental economy of salvation, eternity manifests itself only as the sting of a yearning that is woven in or driven into language, and as the eternity of being on a way that lacks an absolute destination (Frank 1995: 242). This pattern is the fundamental experience of the Flying Dutchman; however, the emancipation from God, which establishes men and women as free human beings, means at the same time the loss of a substantial identity: that of an unambiguous destination or meaning of life. This is the allegory of Coleridge's 'Life-in-death', the experience of an eternal loss, a nightmare which 'thicks man's blood with cold' (Coleridge 1798/1993). The Flying Dutchman is the expression of a collective imagination that is trying to cope with and to compensate for the pathogenic features of the processes of rationalization and modernization; with this background in mind, an examination of contemporary sense-making practices promises to yield valuable insights.

Karl Weick's (1995) book, *Sensemaking in Organizations*, provides an excellent introduction to the topic, and to the process of defining sense-making. Of Weick's seven characteristics of sense-making—it is identity forming, retrospective, and enactive of sensible environments, social, ongoing, focused on and by extracted cues, and driven by plausibility rather than accuracy—the enactment of sensible environments is of special interest here. There is no such thing as a given, fixed environment that exists in separation from those living in it. It is always a mutual process. People are part of their environment; they act in it, and they create the very materials that in turn become the constraints and opportunities they face. Despite the fact that we all too often forget our involvement, and only feel we are the victims of the environment called organization, this too is an ongoing process. The present is a moment within that process, and as such it is one single link in the endless chain of the interaction between individuals and their environments. Weick calls this the 'enactment of sensible environments' (Weick 1995: 30). Yet, despite the irrefutable validity of this perspective, it cannot be considered an a priori characteristic for sense-making. Weick acknowledges that people seem to need the idea that there is a world with predetermined features, or ready-made information, and calls this, quoting Varela, the Cartesian anxiety: '…either we have a fixed and stable foundation for knowledge, a point where knowledge starts, is grounded, and rests, or we cannot escape some sort of darkness, chaos, and confusion. Either there is an absolute ground or foundation or everything falls apart' (Weick 1995: 37).

Weick doesn't talk about the Flying Dutchman. Yet by means of the Cartesian anxiety he implicitly gives a description of our position in modernity, and also describes the discontents that go along with the awareness that there are no harbours where we can anchor our systems of meaning. Weick acknowledges that the same ingredients used for sense-making are also tools for epistemology and ontology. This comes quite close to the question of how we make sense of, or how we give meaning to, our lives, or of how meaning is given to our lives in general—although Weick does not pursue this line of thought.

In my view, Weick also provides an implicit critique of sense-making in organizations, when the latter is perceived as an exclusively rational endeavour. Enactive environments also contain conceptions of meaning; ideologies and religious beliefs clearly shape the way people make sense of what they perceive, if they perceive at all. The important philosophical questions which have to be posed before arguing about sense-making in organizations (even if this sounds a bit solemn, considering the rational structure of the organizations that we are envisioning at present) are the following: is there a general meaning of life, does the existence or absence of such meaning have an implication for the sense-making process, and how can we perceive sense in everyday life? How does this process shape sense-making in organizations and its own theory, if at all? Or is it again part of another old story: the scientist as an impartial observer?

One of the foremost ideas that have arisen in the past two centuries is the concept of the overall absence of any given meaning, after the deconstruction of systems of belief and/or superstition, and the construction, reconstruction, deconstruction, and destruction of ideologies. It is the sense that there is no given meaning to life in general. Whether we like it or not, the process that began with the Enlightenment is leading to the complete demystification and disenchantment (*Entzauberung*) of our world, and to the sense that humans are completely responsible for what they do, without any extramundane salvation or eternal reward. On the positive side, this means a greater freedom for the individual. As usual, however, there is a price to pay. Freud began to describe and to explain this process in his 'Civilization and its discontents' of 1930 (1997): every time we gain something, we also lose something. Modernity, or civilization, as Freud put it, is an order imposed on a naturally disorderly humanity; it is built upon the renunciation, suppression, or regulation of instinct, that is, human sexuality and aggressiveness. Primitive men and women were not faced with restrictions on their instincts, yet their security to enjoy their lack of inhibition was very limited. 'Civilized humans have exchanged a portion of their possibilities of happiness for a portion of security' (Freud 1997: 79). As civilization must concentrate all its efforts on tempering human aggressiveness, its primary founding principle is order (accompanied by other regulatory ideas such as cleanliness or beauty). Within modernity, this development reached its climax: it became an excess of order, which led in turn to a scarcity of freedom. Bauman follows and updates the argument, very consciously referring to Freud's title as he does so in his *Postmodernity and its Discontents* (Bauman 1997), in order to emphasize what has changed since Freud wrote his own book. The discontents of both modernity and postmodernity have the same roots, yet they presuppose a reversal between the former and the latter. Bauman summarizes:

Security from the triple threat hidden in the frail body, the untamed world and the aggressive neighbours, called for the sacrifice of freedom; first and foremost, the individual's freedom to seek pleasure. Within the framework of civilization bent on security, more freedom meant less discontent. Within the framework of a civilization that chose to limit freedom in the name of security, more order meant more discontents. (Bauman 1997: 2)

At the end of the last century, we witnessed and participated in a reversal of Freud's findings. The security granted by order, and delivered by the state, became unacceptable to a majority of voters, who elected instead those who announced a redirection of politics: they would now serve to free the individual from superfluous rules and regulations. Individual freedom is the principal rule that guides decisions nowadays. The words, however, that in exchange for gaining something, you lose something, still hold true: 'only the gains and losses changed places: postmodern men and women exchanged a portion of their possibilities of security for a portion of happiness' (Bauman 1997: 3). At the same time, this also calls for responsibility regarding the creation of one's own meaning, or for the conscious acceptance of the meanings offered by culture; clearly, it can also mean an unconscious, stupid adoption of other people's meanings; yet that still does not alter the need for decisions in a world that lacks certainties.

Most importantly, humans are the only creatures who possess an awareness of their own mortality. Life is overshadowed by this certainty: in order to survive, humans must deceive themselves. Since humans know that they will die, they are constantly busy with giving shape to their lives, with giving sense to it. They are in search of a life that defers death to oblivion, and is not crushed by senselessness; a life that fills the threatening nothingness, and fills the void with meaning. This is a carefully concealed reality: namely, that almost everything we do serves the highest of purposes, which is to render possible a meaningful life that actually has no meaning at all (Bauman 1994: 17). Whereas Bauman sees the possibility of a purposeful life as a grandiose human achievement, Sofsky cannot draw any positive conclusion from such an analysis: there is no concept capable of easing the pain, of banishing the fear of death. Trying to give sense to the senseless only leaves behind in the end the clear awareness of senselessness. Sofsky's (1996) is a categorically dark vision: his remarks on the fear of death are taken from his *Treatise on Violence* (*Traktat über die Gewalt*), where he analyses the inevitable violence inherent in culture: violence is simply the consequence of a culture that aims at transcending existence. Violence is endogenous to culture; the ground on which culture is built is soaked with the blood of humans. Culture is imposed violently and is violently kept; it offers, furthermore, the means for destruction (Sofsky 1996: 217). Organizations can transcend the individual, and they often outlast, that is, 'survive', those working for them. The fear of death is one consequence of the loss of eternity: if nothing exists beyond death, any quest for meaning must take place in this life. This is the world the Flying Dutchman lives in: eternal belief systems gone, the world stormy, the environment violent, and opportunities just for a happy few.

Filthy Lucre: Romantic Reformulations

Although all of the sources quoted above have fallen into oblivion, there is nonetheless one notable exception: Richard Wagner's opera is still played all around the world. Wagner is an outstanding example for the early romantic reaction to the changes stemming from modern progress. The libretto of his opera is based on a work by Heinrich Heine (1831/1981: 309–14); Heine's invention was the inclusion of a possibility of salvation for the cursed captain. Yet whereas Heine was very ironic regarding the possibilities of this happening, Wagner left out all the irony in dramatizing the work. He saw the Dutchman as an opportunity to stage his philosophical view of the world: this was to be his second opera, and the first to support his idea of salvation. The ideas used for the libretto, furthermore, match closely those of early Romanticism. It is not coincidental that the interest in the legend of the Flying Dutchman corresponds with the rise of early Romanticism. An early example was Coleridge's 'The rime of the ancient mariner' (1798/1993), which uses the motif of forsaken salvation and of eternal errantry as a consequence of a crime against nature. The mariner finally finds salvation once he acknowledges the divine order. The conditions were changed for the Dutchman in the versions of Heine and Wagner: he had to find a truthful woman. The Dutchman's only hope lies in love and constancy on land, in the world of human beings. However, and this is the great criticism propounded by the early Romantics and by Wagner himself, humankind has forever lost its capacity for love and constancy: 'Eternal love has vanished from the earth!' (Wagner 1841/1993). Daland is Wagner's example. He is immediately ready to promise his daughter's hand in exchange for 'filthy lucre'. 'This type of haggling reveals people's powerless nature, however well-intended they may be, before the all-pervasive power of money' (Schönfelder 1990: 38).

The first half of the nineteenth century saw the change from a manufacturing capitalism to an industrial one, and with this the turning of Daland's attitude into a law of universal behaviour: it was possible either to gain wealth or to belong to the dispossessed classes. The price that must be paid for wealth is the loss of freedom: dependent on earnings, profit, and wealth, the professional merchant is the least free of men (Schönfelder 1990: 46). As the Dutchman strives for values that go beyond the daily struggle for material profit, the modern world must remain inaccessible to him. He is doomed to sail forever, and in the figure of Senta, who was ready to devote herself to the Dutchman's salvation, Wagner only showed the improbable possibility of salvation: she is truthful not only till death but even unto death; when Senta finally jumped off the cliff into the sea, the spectral vessel sank and the Flying Dutchman found release. Wagner, however, does not use the Dutchman's fate of being homeless, exiled in a metaphorical way, in order to refer only to the fate of the individual: he had in mind humanity as a whole. His reproach is that the human race has brought about the fall of the earth and of humanity, without hope for salvation: hence the Dutchman personifies now the curse of a world-discovering rationalism, and this is in a specific way the curse of modern men and women who lose their humanity (Frank 1989: 82).

Playing with a Legend: Making Sense and Changing Meaning

The legend may well be seen as a reading of patterns in a world in transition. What had been granted before as truth was now being increasingly questioned, and the economic developments showed changes, at least in terms of distance and speed, that needed explanation. The figures who embodied these changes were the entrepreneurs involved, such as Barend Fokke or Vanderdecken. Development itself was perceived as wrong when judged against the basic belief in a God-given, natural order: the captain was punished because he had challenged that divine order. The universal meaning, that is, the system of religious faith, provided the form for the sense-making of the particular events. At the same time, the Flying Dutchman became a symbol for the state of modern men and women after the loss—namely, for their being lost within a life-in-death. Read positively, this meant that one now had the obligation and the chance to give meaning to one's own life.

Is there then a message that is still valid for us? Did the divine order of the mid-fifteenth century transform itself into the order needed nowadays for running large organizations, that is, into our textbook knowledge with its basic assumptions in rationality? Anybody cursing it would be doomed to eternal perdition. What would that mean in our times? Before laughing it off, and repudiating all possibility of relevance, we should hesitate a moment and consider an example such as Porsche, the well-known manufacturer of sports cars, and its CEO Wendelin Wedeking. Porsche is a shareholder company which used to be quoted in the MDAX, the German stock index for companies that are not quoted in the DAX30, the index reserved for the thirty companies with the highest market capitalization, but which fulfil all other formal requirements. Porsche's reputation and profitability are excellent beyond all doubt, and there are frequent information sessions organized for financial analysts, the media, and investors. Wedeking, however, refuses to give quarterly reports. His argument is that the quarterly figures do not give an adequate representation of the company's mid- and long-term development, and that, on the contrary, concentrating on these figures, as markets are increasingly doing, leads to a false evaluation of the company, and in turn to a focus on optimization and on short-term profitability, instead of on a stable development and profitability. Furthermore, this requires investments that can reduce quarterly results: he therefore refuses to announce them. As the publication of quarterly results, however, constitutes a new requirement by the German stock exchange for a company to be represented in the DAX indexes, the refusal has been followed by a ban from the index. In other words, Wedeking challenged the ruling class of the 'holy' financial markets and was punished. By the way, Porsche's products are about speed as well . . .

The saga of the Flying Dutchman today stands not only for the consequences of the absence of God, but also for the absence of any single interpretation of a text, of a single truth. Those who have noticed that the eternal orientation has disappeared, that the helm is broken or washed away, and who try to deal with the consequences of being responsible without being completely able to control what they are responsible for, still seem to be a minority. In his afterword entitled 'the last word—and it belongs to freedom' Bauman gives a description of the conflict:

If monotheism means unfreedom, freedom born of a polytheistic reality does not, contrary to its detractors, mean nihilism. To be free does not mean believing in nothing; what it does mean is believing in too many things—too many for the spiritual comfort of blind obedience; it means being aware that there are too many equally important or convincing beliefs for the assumption of a careless or nihilistic attitude to the task of responsible choice between them; and to know that no choice would save the chooser from the responsibility for its consequences—and that therefore having chosen does not mean having settled the matter of choice once and for all, nor the right to put one's conscience to rest. (Bauman 1997: 201–2)

In short: what do we do with our freedom? If there is an answer, then it is one for the here and now, and one whose validity must always be checked again and again. The topic of these few pages, however, was not to provide the answer to one of the most difficult questions one can ask. The topic was to keep alive consciousness about the openness of the question. Since the first appearance of the Dutchman on the oceans of the new world until today, the crew has expanded. Every decision taken on the Dutchman's spectral ship affects our lives as we are sharing his knowledge about the freedom of the individual and about the pleasure of being freed from too strong an order. And we all know that this gain is ambivalent, and that it is accompanied by a loss of security. It is the same story: challenging God meant a pact with the devil, doubting the validity of a grand narrative means the necessity of developing one's own reasonable standards for acting, and relying on oneself means even greater uncertainty.

As the examples of the Flying Dutchman and similar motifs show, it is necessary to compensate for the loss of eternity, of an absolute destination. Such compensation takes place in the daily functioning of our organizations when they try to give the impression of a quasi-eternal existence; where their products gain a quasi-religious status; where a cult is built around CEOs of large corporations; where their decisions and actions are directed at a time beyond their 'reign'; where the amount of money made is taken as a measure of a person's significance; where meaning is replaced by motivation, as Sievers (1994) has analysed, and where other surrogates like a vision or a mission statement pretend to be more than vaguely formulated declarations of intent; where contradictions between the everyday life of employees and organizational life are 'generously' overlooked; the list goes on.

All of this is more than just the result of our collective travelling into the cold. The rationalism of world discovery destroys the transcendent economy of salvation. The proclaimed death of God is an emancipation that is accompanied by a loss. The self-evident destination of life has disappeared forever, and with it the meaning of life as our ancestors knew it. The almost desperate attempts to avoid thinking of mortality in our organizations are an expression of the consciousness of this loss. Acknowledging mortality means facing the abyss, looking into the void without the relief of deferring our responsibility to heaven or to any other extramundane authority. By ignoring this, the scientist as an impartial observer, and the sense-making individual in an organization, are in the comfortable position of facing an environment that is given, and that does not require questioning. This, however, may render an analysis if not useless, then strangely abstract.

Regarding the struggle itself for immortality, the legend contains a great irony. Barend Fokke is described as an entrepreneur, a self-employed shipping agent and captain. In our terms, he wrote a remarkable success story: he is independent, he is the head of a small company, that is, the vessel, he must have earned a great deal of money compared to his competitors, and moreover he gained fame from the mythical quality of his way of doing business. He is then a figure of public notice who would have been a star in the media nowadays, and would have thus achieved what many managers strive for: to put their stamp on a development, on a company, even on an economic sector, to achieve something that people will not forget, gaining that fame which elevates them from the rest of the grey crowd; in short, what they strive for is immortality. Fokke achieved this, yet he did so in a double-edged way, which is not desirable at all. We still know him, at least by his nickname, but what a price he had to pay for his stardom! The notion of immortality is taken literally, and so turns out to be a curse rather than a reward.

Leaving the irony aside, it can be stated that 'the belief in a linear sequence between idea and reality, between thinking and acting, has been rightly, and entirely, destroyed. The rules of humanity and progress are no longer able to refer to metaphysical certainty or historical legitimacy. The open society increasingly draws its understanding from the negative maxim of a "nevermore"' (Herzinger 2001). Nevermore—and it is not Poe's raven that is quoted here; it is rather the tradition of Adorno's argument: we may not know what constitutes a human being and right action regarding human matters, yet we *can* know what he or she should not be, and which action regarding human matters is wrong; only by this definite and concrete knowledge does the Other, the positive, remain open for us (Adorno 1953: 456). We cannot avoid the discontents of modernity: on the contrary, the gain of freedom means taking greater risks and having a larger responsibility. Only when we accept this will we be able to give meaning to our lives and our organizations. Then the Flying Dutchman shall be in turn able to repair the rudder, come to a harbour, and leave it for another destination, should this one turn out to be the wrong one.

References

Adorno, Th. W. (1953). 'Individuum und Organisation', in R. Tiedermann (ed.) *Soziologische Schriften I*. Frankfurt/Main: Suhrkamp, pp. 440–56.

Bauman, Z. (1994). *Tod, Unsterblichkeit und andere Lebensstrategien*. Frankfurt/Main: Fischer Taschenbuch.

——(1997). *Postmodernity and its Discontents*. Cambridge: Polity Press.

Blackwood, author unspecified (1821). 'Vanderdecken's message home; or, the tenacity of natural affection'. *Blackwood's Edinburgh Magazine*, IX(L), 127–31. Edinburgh: William Blackwood and London: T. Cadwell and W. Davies, Strand.

Coleridge, S. T. (1798/1993). *Selected Poems*. New York: Bloomsbury Poetry Classics, St Martin's Press.

Das Ausland, author unspecified (1841). 'Über den Ursprung der Sage von dem fliegenden Holländer, oder Gespensterschiff, Das Ausland, ein Tagblatt für Kunde des geistigen und sittlichen Lebens der Völker'. Nr. 237, 25 (August), 945–6.

Fitzball, E. (n.d.): *The Flying Dutchman; or, the Phantom Ship. A Nautical Drama.* London: Cumberland. (Translated and printed in Laroche, B. (1993). *Der fliegende Holländer, Wirkung und Wandlung eines Motivs.* Frankfurt/Main: Peter Lang, pp. 85–160 (first staged in 1826)).

Flohr, D. (1989). *Wer war der fliegende Holländer, auf den Spuren einer Sage.* Rostock: VEB Hinstorff.

Frank, M. (1989). *Kaltes Herz, unendliche Fahrt, neue Mythologie.* Frankfurt/Main: Suhrkamp.

——(1995). *Die unendliche Fahrt, Die Geschichte des fliegenden Holländers und verwandter Motive.* Leipzig: Reclam.

Freud, S. (1997). *Das Unbehagen in der Kultur.* Frankfurt/Main: S. Fischer.

Gerndt, H. (1971). *Fliegender Holländer und Klabautermann.* Göttingen: Otto Schwarz & Co.

Heine, H. (1831/1981). 'Aus den Memoiren des Herrn von Schnabelewobski', in *Heinrich Heine: Werke in fünf Bänden* (Band 2). Berlin/Weimar: Aufbau Verlag, pp. 281–339. Translated in English (1906). *The Works of Heinrich Heine.* London: E. P. Dutton and Company.

Herzinger, R. (2001). *Republik ohne Mitte.* Berlin: Siedler.

Laroche, B: (1993). *Der fliegende Holländer, Wirkung und Wandlung eines Motivs.* Frankfurt/Main: Peter Lang.

Marryat, F. (1837/1896). *The Phantom Ship.* London: J. M. Dent and Co.

Poe, E. A. (1838/1979). *Das gesamte Werk in zehn Bänden.* Olten: Manfred Pawlak.

Schönfelder, G. (1990). 'Damnation and salvation as underlying philosophical concepts in Wagner's artistic oevre', in W. Wagner (ed.) *Der fliegende Holländer, Programmheft 1, Bayreuther Festspiele.* Bayreuth: Bayreuther Festspiele GmbH.

Sievers, B. (1994). 'Motivation as a surrogate for meaning', in *Work, Death, and Life Itself.* Berlin: De Gruyter, pp. 1–46.

Sofsky, W. (1996). *Traktat über die Gewalt.* Frankfurt/Main: S. Fischer.

Thompson, S. (1966). *Motif-index of Folk Literature.* Bloomington and London University of Indiana Press.

Wagner, R. (1841/1993). *The Flying Dutchman, Romantic Opera in Three Acts.* Libretto quoted from CD, Naxos Opera Classics, HNH International Ltd.

Weick, K. (1995). *Sensemaking in Organizations.* Thousand Oaks, CA: Sage Publications.

NINE

Arachne and Minerva: Women, Power, and Realization

Yvonne Guerrier

The Story

Arachne was a young Lydian girl from a poor background who had incredible skill as a weaver. Her talent had made her famous. Even the nymphs and the naiads loved to come down not just to admire her finished cloths but also to watch her deft and light movements as she wove. It was clear to all that her talents must have come from Minerva, the goddess of weaving. But Arachne denied this, offended by the suggestion that she was taught by anyone, even a goddess. 'I challenge Minerva to a weaving contest,' she cried. 'If she wins she can do what she likes with me.'

WHEN Minerva heard Arachne's words, she transformed herself into an old woman and tried to persuade Arachne to back down, admit the goddess's supremacy, and beg for forgiveness. But Arachne rudely brushed off her warnings. 'Doesn't Minerva dare to come in person to compete with me?' 'She has come' replied the goddess throwing off her disguise.

The goddess and the girl rolled up their sleeves and began weaving. Minerva's tapestry showed her own victory over Neptune in the contest for the naming of Athens. She depicted all twelve Olympian gods seated on their thrones in full majesty gazing in awe at the olive tree, her gift to the city, which had sprung from the land where she had placed her spear. In each corner of the tapestry, as a warning to Arachne, she illustrated the punishments that had been meted out to human beings who had dared to challenge the gods.

Arachne's tapestry followed a different theme. It showed how the gods had abducted and deceived mortal women. It showed the many ways in which Jupiter had disguised himself to trick and seduce Europa, Leda, Antiope, and

Proserpine. It showed the disguises and seductions of the other gods: of Neptune, Phoebus, Bacchus, and Saturn. The tapestry was woven with such skill, you would have thought you were watching the events themselves.

> "And neither the goddess
> Nor jealousy itself
> Could find a stitch in the entire work
> That was not perfection. Arachne's triumph
> Was unbearable"
>
> (Ovid, *Metamorphoses*, translated by Ted Hughes)

In a jealous rage, Minerva ripped Arachne's tapestry from its frame and tore it to shreds. Then she hit Arachne three or four times across the face with her shuttle. Arachne could not live with such shame and, still defiant, she made a noose to hang herself. Seeing her jerking at the end of the rope, Minerva took pity and, rather than letting her die, transformed her into a spider.

> And so for ever
> She hangs from the thread that she spins
> Out of her belly.
>
> Or ceaselessly weaves it
> Into patterned webs
> On a loom of leaves and grasses –
> Her touches
> Deft and swift and light as when they were human.
>
> (Ovid, *Metamorphoses*, translated by Ted Hughes)

Ovid's telling of this story in 'The Metaphorphoses' still fascinates modern writers and artists. Ted Hughes chose to translate it as one of his 'Tales from Ovid'. A. S. Byatt chose to write about it in a recent selection of short stories inspired by Ovid. When Tate Modern opened in 2000, the Turbine Hall was dominated by one of Louise Bourgeois' gigantic sculptures of a spider, recalling Arachne's fate. But for the modern reader, the story is puzzling. Whom are we supposed to sympathize with? A modern retelling of this story would, almost certainly, unambiguously favour the underdog character (Arachne). In the film 'Working Girl', which has similar plot elements, it is the working class secretary (Melanie Griffiths) who ultimately triumphs over the upper class high-flying manager (Sigourney Weaver) who tries to take credit for her ideas. (Perhaps Arachne's problem was that she lacked a Harrison Ford). By contrast, the myth is bleaker, arguably more true to life, but more ambiguous. 'Did Arachne actually win the contest?' asks A. S. Byatt (2000). This is not the way in which myths work. Normally if there is a contest between a god and a mortal there is no doubt that the god will win. If Arachne won, why was she so cruelly punished by a goddess normally known for her cool and rational administration of justice rather than for her outbursts of jealous anger?

For earlier interpreters, the moral of the story was absolutely clear. It warned against the terrible consequences of hubris. Young women from poor backgrounds should not get ideas above their station or outside their gender. John Ruskin used this story in an address to a public audience at Woolwich in 1870 that included a large number of women who worked at the Woolwich Arsenal. Although at first, he argued, the story might seem to reflect badly on Minerva, her actions were just when you consider Arachne's crime, which was to weave pictures of 'base and abominable things' that would be 'a disgrace to the room of the simplest cottager' (Shearer 1996: 195). Women should weave pretty dresses to please their husbands when they come home from work, not pornographic tapestries!

Ovid himself does not seem to have seen the story in such dogmatic terms. The 'Metamorphoses' is, after all, packed full of those 'base and abominable' stories that Arachne wove into her tapestry and that the gods might prefer were not told. 'With which tapestry does his (Ovid's) text identify?' asks Italo Calvino (2000). He answers '. . . with neither of them. In the great array of myths, which constitute the whole poem, the myth of Pallas (Minerva) and Arachne seems to contain in turn two scaled-down selections in the tapestries, pointing in ideologically opposed directions: one to instil a sacred fear, the other inciting towards irreverence and moral relativity' (p. 28). 'Arachne and Minerva' is a story that explores responses to authority. What are the consequences of conforming or of subverting? Will the establishment always destroy those who attempt to directly subvert it? Do those whose role it is to defend the establishment have to destroy those who attempt to subvert it, whatever their private sympathies may be? Is order, even if flawed, preferable to the risk of disorder?

'Arachne and Minerva' is also a story about women within a male dominated world. The protagonists may be competing at a traditionally female activity (weaving) but the whole story is framed within a context of male power and authority. Minerva is a powerful goddess who is capable of winning a contest against one of the gods (Neptune), as her tapestry showed. But even she must answer to the authority of her father Jupiter. It is Jupiter's authority that Minerva is ultimately protecting and that Arachne is attempting to subvert. Arachne's jibes are, significantly, all against the behaviour of the male gods. There is no criticism of Minerva herself. (Although even Arachne might have recognized that that would have been asking for trouble).

Between these two protagonists, there are points of both similarity and contrast. Both are highly talented, famous, and independent. Both are operating outside the roles normally assigned to women in traditional societies. But the contrasts are also marked. There could hardly be a greater 'class' difference than between one of the most powerful of the Olympian deities and a poor foreign girl. Minerva is the insider with a powerful role within the 'establishment' and Arachne the outsider and the loner. Arachne has the brashness and arrogance of youth whilst Minerva, even though goddesses are strictly speaking ageless, seems to represent the wisdom (compromise) of experience.

Minerva

There are certain facts about the goddess Minerva that any early reader of Ovid would have inevitably known. Minerva is the Roman equivalent of the Greek goddess Pallas Athene. Pallas Athene is generally defined as the goddess of war and wisdom. She is courageous; she excels in battle because she is well grounded in tactics and strategies. She is the goddess who protects cities and harbours from hostile invasions. She is inventive; she taught human beings the civilizing arts and crafts of weaving, pottery, metallurgy, shipbuilding, and yoking oxen. Athene is the ever-near goddess who involves herself closely in the affairs of mortals, mentoring her favourites (like Odysseus). Her wisdom is directed to concrete, practical human affairs. Stein (1978), exploring Athene's relevance to people now, claims that she 'keeps us in the "real world"; she gives us the wherewithal to confront its problems, the joy of conquering ourselves, others, problems, and the sagacity and confidence to slay its dragons. She keeps us grounded in "real projects," out of idle and vain speculations' (p. 114). If one were to search for a deity of management, it would be difficult to envisage one whose attributes and qualities matched more closely of those we look for in contemporary managers, both male and female, than Athene/Minerva.

Nevertheless, Athene/Minerva has not been adopted by feminists as an unambiguously positive archetype. The paradox of Athene lies in her relationship with her father Zeus (the Greek equivalent of Jupiter) and to the story of her birth. According to the legend, Athene's mother was Metis, the goddess of wise-counsel. When Metis was pregnant, an oracle told Zeus that, if Metis had a male child, that child would depose Zeus. To prevent this from happening, Zeus swallowed Metis. But the child was a girl and when the time came for her to be born, Athene sprang fully armed and fully grown from her father's head.

For the classicist and colleague of Jung, Karl Kerenyi, what defines Athene is her closeness to her father. In anachronistic terms, Athene has very definitely broken through the 'glass-ceiling'. She is, argues Kerenyi (1978), the second most powerful deity amongst the Olympians, second only to Zeus, and (contrary to normal rules in patriarchal families) more powerful than her brothers. But she can seduce her father into protecting and supporting her only by identifying with him and by becoming, above all, a defender of the patriarchal order. The accusation is that the goddess born from her father's head has 'sold out' her female side. When Minerva/Athene chooses to side with her father's order rather than another woman and punish Arachne, she stands accused by feminists of being 'a woman but not a sister'.

The strategies that Minerva uses to maintain and exercise her power are strategies that women over the ages have used to gain a toehold into traditionally male bastions of power. A dynastic connection with a male leader helps. Many female global leaders have come into prominence because they have been seen as the natural successor, as wife or daughter, to a powerful man, for example, Indira Gandhi, Corazon Aquino, Benazir Bhutto, Violetta Chamorro and, although she has no formal leadership role, Aung San Suu Kyi (see Klenke 1999). If a direct dynastic connection does not exist, some type of emotional identification with the male is often established. Margaret Thatcher famously had no reference to her mother in her Who's Who entry whilst her admiration for her father, the mayor of Grantham, was extensively scrutinized. Marina Warner comments that she seemed 'like Athena, to be daughter only to the male, not to the female'. (1996: 53). Whatever their backgrounds and political persuasion, female global leaders in politics do not directly challenge the patriarchal nature of their societies, recognizing that that would amount to political suicide, and most (Ireland's Mary Robinson and Norway's Gro Harlem Brundtland are exceptions) studiously avoid being identified with feminist causes (Klenke 1999).

Image is everything. Minerva/Athene famously wore the aegis, which originally belonged to her father Zeus: 'her splendid cloak, the unfading ever-lasting aegis, from which a hundred golden tassels flutter, all beautifully made, each worth a hundred head of cattle' (Iliad book 2; see also Warner 1996: 106). The aegis and the helmet and armour with which she goes into battle help to distinguish her from the other goddesses. But she also makes use of feminine attributes; in her famous statue in Troy she was portrayed with a raised spear in her right hand and a distaff and spindle in her left. She was one of the original power dressers.

One of the 'authorities' on business image and dress style gave the following advice to women moving on to the board of companies:

If you are the first woman to be up for the appointment you'll need to look similar in tone and quality to the men... Smart suits, preferably with matching rather than contrasting skirts, are best. Fakes may have been fine until now but, for the boardroom, 'real' accessories are required. A good watch, quality earrings, brooches and chokers are what you need to smarten up your sober suits. For corporate events held in the evening choose appropriate styles... Many women destroy their corporate chances by not knowing how to dress outside the office; the more skin you show the more power you lose.... Have an attractive, not 'butch' hairstyle. Potential board partners don't want a male clone, they want a female partner. So hair, make-up, accessories and clothes, while appropriately restrained, should always be feminine. (Spillane 1991: 139–40).

It is easy to dismiss 1980s style gurus and power dressing. But their message for women seeking to get to the top is not so new. Clothes need to reinforce your power, to be obviously expensive, and to reflect your appreciation of good craftsmanship. There seems to be a need to armour the top part of your body with a suit jacket if not an aegis—but this can be quite flamboyant. (Women might be advised to wear a bright red jacket when, metaphorically, going into battle, for example, doing an important presentation.) You still need some feminine 'attributes' (Mrs Thatcher's infamous handbag, for example) but feminine does not mean sexy. The Minerva manager is well covered up.

It is an exceptionally difficult balancing act. On the one hand, the woman has to demonstrate her affinity with the male but without becoming 'masculine'. On the other, she needs to distinguish herself from other women, both from those who may be dismissed as 'just' wives and mothers, as well as those who have more radical objectives. On the aegis, Minerva wears the head of the Gorgon Medusa, the truly terrifying serpent-haired monster who turned all who saw her into stone and who Minerva helped Perseus kill. A Minerva cannot afford to be seen as a Medusa, a female archetype which is so scary that she might destroy (male) civilization. She must be on the side of those who would kill Medusa. But at the same time, she needs to demonstrate she has real power and wearing Medusa's head as a reminder of her monster slaying capacities is a way of emphasizing this. (For Margaret Thatcher, her opposition to the Greenham common women could serve a similar symbolic purpose).

But the other danger that Minerva managers face is that they may become perceived as women who just try fit in to a male world; who are the eternal seconds-in command, tolerated as long as they never aspire to the really top roles, and who are hence ultimately powerless, almost a joke. When Tony Blair was elected in 1992, there was a major increase in the number of women elected to Parliament in the Labour landslide. Many of these women had been carefully groomed to fit in with the image of new Labour (as had many of the men). But the press christened them 'Blair's babes', immediately undermining their power and status and relegating them to the role of the Prime Minister's 'groupies' perpetually in support.

I think we should be careful about defining the goddess Minerva/Athene herself as a 'Jupiter's babe'. Silvia Gherardi (1995), who uses the Greek goddesses as archetypes of female behaviour in organizations, comes close to this when she describes women in that world as

models of Athena-like, femaleness: women who take pride in their strategic talents and in their respected positions and in their respected positions as 'seconds-in-command'. Whether as 'the boss's indispensable secretary', as the exemplary pupil launched on a career by her mentor, as assistant to a manager more or less high in the hierarchy, these women speak with their master's voice (p. 75).

To compare this goddess to a secretary seems to me to underplay the power of this archetype and to overplay the extent to which being 'close to the father' means being the 'father's voice'. The myths surrounding Athene do not always show her doing exactly what her father wants; for example, it was she who helped Prometheus steal fire from the Olympians and bring it to earth, against the wishes of Zeus. Shearer (1996) argues that 'within the constraints of the new patriarchy, it is Athene who works constantly to redress the balance of power between Olympus and the human race, who champions human skill and understanding against the inexplicable ways of the gods' (p. 16).

A more appropriate current analogy might, therefore, be with the female human resource director who may attempt to use her power to mediate the actions of a male board whilst remaining loyal in general to the firm. This exploration of Minerva/Athene as an archetype raises questions about the consequences for women were they to use this strategy to achieve power. If the only way to get power in a male-dominated organization is to carefully manage your image and to discount any more radical objectives you may have, are you so constrained when you get into power that you cannot do anything? Is the female human resource director only used by the male board to manage redundancies in a slightly 'nicer' (because more feminine) way?

One aspect of their image that women managers are required to manage very carefully is their sexuality. One of the myths of modern work organizations is that they are both rational and desexualized (these two being in some way equivalent). Many writers have demonstrated the fallacy of this assumption and argued that it is more realistic to see organizations as having dominant sexual cultures that are hegemonically heterosexual; where sexuality is symbolized by the female body and by male desire (see Gherardi 1995; Hearn and Parkin 1995) precisely in the way this is done within Arachne's tapestry. Near the bottom of most corporations are those women whose roles require them to project a sexy personality: shop girls, waitresses, bar-maids, stewardesses, hostesses, receptionists, and secretaries. At the top, even in today's more politically correct culture, male sexual predatory behaviour can enhance power whilst a woman behaving in a similar way risks either losing her power as she becomes identified with the secretaries and hostesses or being demonized as a Medusa (like the Sharon Stone character in the film 'Basic Instinct') intent on the destruction of men (e.g. see, Konrad and Gutek 1986).

A study of a London city bank showed how the use of sexual language and metaphors posed problems for women managers.

Stocks are sexy or dogs, companies flirt with each other, touch up, get into bed with each other, etc., etc.,... No-one stops to examine the language, which is accepted without objection by both men and women ... In the bank, women had to laugh at men's sexist jokes but if they talked in a similar vein themselves it was considered distasteful (Rutherford 2001: 378).

Minerva is famously one of the virgin goddesses. Her virginity is not a moral choice but a practical one. A husband or child would create other allegiances and threaten her closeness with her father. There are obvious parallels with an English icon: Queen Elizabeth I. She was also born of a famous father, Henry VIII, who had destroyed her mother, Anne Boleyn. She too was very careful of the image that she projected and was known for her magnificent clothes. She too made skilful use of both male and female imagery in relation to herself: for example, in the speech 'I know I have the body of a weak and feeble woman, but I have the heart and stomach of a king, and of a king of England too'. She too remained unmarried, predominantly because of dynastic reasons; any marriage would have weakened her power, which was fragile enough at the beginning of her reign.

The recent film 'Elizabeth' focuses on the early years of the queen's reign. At the end, we see Elizabeth, having resigned herself to remaining unmarried, becoming the Virgin Queen. Her hair is shorn and covered with an elaborate wig. Her face is plastered with heavy white make-up. She is dressed in a magnificent but heavy and restrictive white gown. The image is one of renunciation and regret. Elizabeth, whom we have seen as an intelligent, emotional, sexually active, and vulnerable young woman, is giving up on much of what she is and what she may privately want, so as to become what is necessary in order to protect her power and her country. (Bauman, commenting on this same scene in the film, relates it to the way in which, in contemporary society, individual identity is achieved through a universal dependence on shopping for the products that can make us individual. When Elizabeth, he comments, decides to change her personality, she does it by 'changing her hair-style, covering her face with a thick layer of craftsman-made paints and donning craftsman-made head jewellery'. (2000: 84): the ultimate make-over. 'You gain independence by surrender', he claims)

The notion that leaders need to renounce or repress certain aspects of their personality in order to be effective is neither a specifically modern nor a gendered concern. It was, after all, the focus of Shakespeare's exploration of Prince Hal in 'Henry IV'. But this interpretation of Elizabeth touches on a very contemporary concern: that of authenticity, our right to be who we are.

For me, the puzzle of the Minerva/Arachne story is why is Minerva so angry. She is not just angry. She is specifically described by Ovid as jealous of Arachne. Robert Graves (1955) comments that her contest with Arachne was the only time the goddess showed 'petulant jealousy'; that is, this anger was out of character. Minerva is described as struggling and failing to find a single stitch out of place in Arachne's tapestry, but as a goddess her tapestry would have been stitch perfect as well. Obviously the jealousy and the anger were not just associated with its technical skill; it was what Arachne wove that gave her the edge over Minerva.

Gherardi goes on with an explanation that is not so different from Ruskin's (although her sympathies clearly lie elsewhere). 'Athena...was not enraged because of the impudence of Arachne's challenge, but because she brought the perfidious behaviour of her father into the public domain',(1995: 75) The goddess who is so close to her father is doing his dirty work and defending his honour.

But I am not convinced this is all it is about. It is worth looking again at the descriptions of the tapestries. Minerva's tapestry is ordered, hierarchical, and symmetrical. It is the view of the Olympians as seen by someone who is part of the power structure; all is fair, all is transparent, and all is in its place. By contrast, Arachne's tapestry is the view of the outsider. It shows the world as change and flux rather than as order and continuity. As A. S. Byatt points out, when Ovid describes Arachne's tapestry his writing 'is full of glee and movement, wickedness and writhing'. (2000: 141)

But how can Minerva compete against that? Arachne has woven the equivalent of the office gossip (in a company which has some pretty juicy gossip) while she has woven the equivalent of the company report or mission statement. Arachne simply has the better, more exciting stories. Is Minerva jealous because Arachne has told the stories that Minerva, because of her position, could not? Is she angry because Arachne undermines, not just Jupiter's, but her own view of the world as one where those at the top, the gods, have all the gifts, the skills, the knowledge, and the insight, and have every right to demand respect and gratitude from mortals?

A. S. Byatt, in her essay about this story, describes Velasquez's painting that illustrates it: 'Las Hilanderas'. 'On the left...is a somewhat doll-like female figure, wearing a large helmet and a buckler...raising a naked arm, in menace or remonstration', (p. 135). Velasquez, like Ovid, seems to have had sympathy with Arachne and the power-dressed goddess is reduced to an over-styled puppet.

Arachne

Anni Albers was a weaver who started her career at the Bauhaus but whose work was, for most of her fifty-one years of marriage, overshadowed by that of her husband, the artist Josef Albers. Late in her life she experimented with lithography and in 1968 she gave up her loom. She confessed that 'when the work is made with threads, it's considered a craft; when it's made on paper, it's considered art... The multiplication and exactness of the print process of printmaking allows for broader exhibition and ownership of work. As a result, recognition comes more easily and happily, the longed-for pat on the shoulder'. (Interview with Anni Albers by Polsky 1985, quoted in Schoeser 2002)

Textile art is women's art and there is a long tradition of it being used to subvert and criticize the existing order. On a recent trip to Chile, I came across some embroidered tapestries in a provincial museum. These had been worked by women during the Pinochet era to tell the story of those who had disappeared or been smuggled out of the country, both to bear witness to what was happening and to raise money for the cause. This is the way in which such women's art works. It is secretive, anonymous: something that slips in through the darkness to make a point quietly and furtively.

Textile art is also slow going. As Anni Albers pointed out, if you want to make a name for yourself in the art world it is much quicker and easier to make prints than weave tapestries. Ovid's description of Arachne and Minerva's contest rings false in this respect. However skilled and fast you are a major tapestry cannot be completed in a day or a week. Weavings are painstakingly built up loop by loop, colour by colour. As a spectator sport, one would have thought it has limited appeal.

However, there are plenty of modern examples of the artist as celebrity and as performer. The contest brings to my mind the films of Jackson Pollack dancing over his canvases or the films of Picasso drawing doves on glass. We are entranced not just by the finished products but also by the physicality and mystery of the process of creation, much as the nymphs and naiads were entranced by watching Arachne work.

Arachne demanded far more attention than Albers' longed-for pat on the back. It is difficult to think of a time other than the present when women have claimed this type of artistic celebrity, coming out into the light of day rather than lurking apologetically in the shadows. A current equivalent of Arachne might be a British artist like Tracey Emin, the working class girl from Margate, who exhibited her unmade bed for the Turner prize and who stitched on a tent the names of all the people she had made love to. In a different art form, we may draw analogies with Madonna, another female artist who explicitly constructed her persona as a celebrity and who pushed the limits of what a female pop singer could do. Whilst the Minerva woman consciously manages her sexuality, the Arachne woman 'talks dirty'.

Arachne's images are particularly subversive and arresting because we know they are woven by a woman. The same images made by a man might seem less problematic because they could be interpreted as an invitation to objectify the gods' female victims and simply enjoy the erotic images. (Western art from Titian through to Picasso is full of such invitations.) But because Arachne is inevitably identified with the gods' victims, indeed she became one of the gods' victims, it is not so clear what she is trying to say. Her images are seductive but, at the same time, uncomfortable.

Post-Freud, we have another set of expectations about artists that is relevant here. The art critic Robert Hughes, in a recent television programme on Goya, defined him as one of the first truly modern artists. In his later life Goya, Hughes commented, never 'self-censored': he drew and painted what he felt, regardless of whether it would be acceptable, and no matter the consequences. The following quote from a best-selling book on being creative gives the popular take on this notion: 'we will discover the nature of our particular genius when we stop trying to conform to our own or to other people's models and learn to be ourselves, and allow our natural channels to open'. (Shakti Gawain in Cameron 1994: 69). We seem to be moving to another comparison here—between the artifice of the Minerva archetype, continually self-censoring and impression managing, and the authenticity of the Arachne archetype, following her artistic soul whatever the consequences. In this reading, Arachne is subversive not as some prototypical shop-steward campaigning to stop the abuses of the gods but as a free-spirit who depicts the world as she sees it, injustice and all, without a thought to the consequences. (A cynic might say that she was aware that her lack of self-censorship would have consequences, that it would increase her fame.) She is truly a heroine of our time.

Arachne is also 'of our time' in her world view, as depicted in her tapestry. A. S. Byatt contrasts her tapestry with Minerva's which is 'divided into clear spaces, each with its content', rational, hierarchical, solid, and modernist. By contrast: 'There is more in Arachne's tapestry than there would be space for in any work of shuttle and wool, more forms, more human bodies, more rape, more birth, a plentitude of flux ... Arachne's tapestry is Ovid's poem, a rush of beings, a rush of animal, vegetable and mineral constantly coming into shape and constantly undone and re-forming'. (Byatt 2001: 141)

Bauman (2000) defines the beginning of the twenty-first century as a time of liquid modernity. The solid patterns, configurations, and givens of earlier modern life, work, the class system, the family, political institutions are melting. 'Fluid' modernity', says Bauman, 'is the epoch of disengagement, elusiveness, facile escape and hopeless chase. In "liquid" modernity, it is the most elusive, those free to move without notice, who rule'. (p. 120)

In the same way, Arachne's gods do not rule through their open and rational exercise of power, as in Minerva's world view, but secretly and subversively by their ability to shapeshift, now a swan, now an eagle, now a shower or gold, now a flame, and now a spotted snake. It is significant that Arachne, who is utterly, authentically, and uncompromisingly herself, even after her metamorphosis, portrays a world in which it is never clear who or what anything or anyone actually is. 'Finding one's true self' only becomes important in a world in which there is a choice of many different selves that one could potentially find.

Another quotation from Bauman could almost have been written with Arachne in mind. Liquid modernity, he argues, is 'an individualized, privatized version of modernity, with the burden of pattern-weaving and the responsibility for failure falling primarily on the individual's shoulders' (Bauman 2000: 7–8). Arachne, the supreme individualist whose work is to make the ultimate objects of desire, will not let anyone else take the credit for her success (even a goddess), will not let anyone else dissuade her from putting her skills to the test (even a goddess), presents her world view as she sees it without any thought to whom it might offend (even a goddess), and finally accepts the consequences of her failure.

What does it mean to be changed into a spider? As Marina Warner (2002) points out, there is a contradiction between the world in flux that Ovid presents and the way that, in stories like that of Arachne, the metamorphosis freezes and stabilizes. Arachne is trapped forever in the body of the spider. That is, perhaps, the most terrible part of her punishment: she has lost the possibility for further development and change. In every respect, it is the end of the story.

Many writers on women in management have discussed the ways in which token women in male organizations face the danger of being trapped in particular stereotyped roles: as mother, seductress, pet, or iron maiden (e.g. Kanter 1977). Stereotyping works in the same way as this type of metamorphosis: the stereotyped person is never allowed to develop, change, be unpredictable, and step out of the stock character that she or he has become. One of the 'rules' of Arachne's type of metamorphosis is that, like a stereotype, the person is changed into a being or object that somehow represents their essence: the story does not work if the metamorphosis is purely arbitrary. What is spider-like about Arachne? There are the obvious links: the weaver Arachne becomes the weaver spider—it may even be argued that Arachne becomes her own loom[54]—the hanged woman becomes the insect by hanging from a thread. But then there are the apparent transformations. The beautiful young Arachne becomes an ugly wizen creature 'all belly with a dot of a head'. But perhaps this is what she was all along: the young sorceress who can conjure images that look real was always a wizen old witch. I am reminded of that drawing, designed to demonstrate selective perception, which can be read both as a young woman in an elegant hat and as an ugly old woman.

> It is not enough to praise other people:
> what I want is to be praised myself

Within the story of Arachne and Minerva, the two protagonists simultane-ously mirror each other and contrast with each other. This story is introduced in Ovid when Minerva, who has been listening to the daughters of Minyas telling stories to each other as they worked at their looms in the service of the goddess, recalls the story of Arachne. 'It is not enough to praise other people', thinks the goddess as she listens to the weavers' tales of other gods and heroes, 'what I want is to be praised myself'. Likewise Arachne does not want Minerva to take the credit for her skills; she wants to be praised herself. The goddess and the woman take different paths to recognition. Minerva is an establishment figure who takes her power from her family connections and who carefully sustains an image to increase her power. Arachne is the outsider who dares to believe that her talents alone will bring her recognition and that she need only be herself. Arachne is the more obvious loser destroyed by Minerva acting on behalf of the Olympian establishment. But to contempor-ary eyes, Minerva is a victim herself to the extent that she has 'sold out' when she chooses to destroy a woman in order to defend the honour of the male gods.

A friend of mine commented, when discussing a consultancy contract, 'you need a "man in a suit" to front the bid and I can't do that'. She added 'although there are some women who can do "man in suit"'. I would argue that women cannot actually do man in suit; 'woman in suit' is a subtly differ-ent performance, as I hope my discussion of Minerva has illustrated. However, the notion of doing 'man or woman in suit' fits with academic notions that gender is something that we 'do' at work rather than an aspect of who we are and where, crudely, doing male is about doing dominance and doing female

[54] My thanks to Paula James for this observation.

is about doing difference, much as in Arachne's tapestry (West and Zimmerman 1987). The Minerva/woman in suit archetype is about finding a way of doing female in a way which also allows doing dominance and the consequences of this. (Of course, equally not all men are comfortable with doing man in suit or see it as the only way of doing male but that is another discussion.)

Whilst in a more certain age, Arachne could be written off as mad (Dante calls her 'mad' Arachne and has her story carved on the pavement of the terrace of the proud in Purgatory) for daring to set her images of the world in competition with Minerva's, now it is Minerva who seems, if not mad, at least deluded for portraying a world which is fair, rational, and well-governed, where people are punished or rewarded on their merits. Arachne's teeming and chaotic picture of mortals, unjustly suffering at the hands of shape-shifting gods, seems both more fun but also more realistic. Arachne is independent, rebellious, and an artist. But perhaps we should not forget that, beyond a brief moment of glory, Arachne changed nothing. The Olympians carried on ruling and she was left weaving her spider's webs forever in some dusty corner.

Minerva was reminded of the story of Arachne as she listened to the daughters of Minyas telling each other stories as they wove. Unlike Arachne, these sisters honoured Minerva through their slow and painstaking work. Unfortunately, they also dishonoured Bacchus whose festival they should have been celebrating. And so the god of wine turned their threads and tapestries into ivy and vines. The workaholic sisters who did not know how to party were turned into bats. Whilst you are remembering to honour the goddess of management, says Ovid, you should not forget to honour the god of consumption. Another set of parallels to our twenty-first century world? Another story for another time.

References

Bauman, Z. (2000). *Liquid Modernity*. Cambridge: Polity.

Byatt, A. S. (2001). 'Arachne', in *Ovid Metamorphosed*, P. Terry (ed.), London: Vintage.

Calvino, I. (2000). *Why read the classics?* London: Vintage.

Cameron, J. (1995). *The Artist's Way*. London: Pan.

Gherardi, S. (1995). *Gender, Symbolism and Organisational Cultures*. London: Sage.

Konrad, A. and Gutek, B. (1986). 'Impact of work experience on attitudes towards sexual harassment'. *Administrative Science Quarterly*, 3(3): 422–38.

Graves, R. (1955). *The Greek Myths, Vol 1*. London: Penguin.

Hearn, J. and Parkin, W. (1995). *'Sex' at 'Work': The Power and Paradox of Organisation Sexuality*. London: Prentice Hall.

Hughes, T. (1997). *Tales from Ovid*. London: Faber and Faber.

Kanter, R. (1977). *Men and Women in the Corporation*. New York: Basic Books.

Kerenyi, K. (1978). *Athene*. Woodstock, CT: Spring Publications.

Klenke, K. (1999). 'Women leaders and women managers in the global community', *Career Development International*, 4(3): 134–9.

Ovid (1955). *The Metamorphoses*, trans M.Innis. London: Penguin.

Rutherford, S. (2001). 'Organisational cultures, women managers and exclusion'. *Women in Management Review*, 16(8): 371–82.

Schoeser, M. (2002). 'Anni Albers'. *Crafts*, March/April: 20–1.

Shearer, A. (1996). *Athene: Image and Energy*. London: Viking.

Spillane, M. (1991). *The Complete Style Guide*. London: Piatkus.

Stein, M. (1978). 'Translator's Afterthoughts', in K. Kerenyi (ed.), *Athene*. Woodstock, CT: Spring Publications.

Tate Gallery (2000). *Louise Bourgeois* (exhibition catalogue). Tate: London.

Warner, M. (1996) *Monuments and Maidens*. London: Vintage.

——. (2002). *Fantastic Metamorphoses: Other Worlds*. Oxford: Oxford University Press.

West, C. and Zimmerman, D. (1987). 'Doing gender'. *Gender and Society*, 1: 125–42.

TEN

Prometheus Unleashed: The Quest for Knowledge and the Promise of Salvation Through Technique

Ulrich Gehmann

The Myth

Pᴿᴼᴹᴱᵀᴴᴱᵁˢ—isn't he a figure from Greek mythology, located in the remote past of an *illo tempore*, of a time-gone-by, with which we have nothing in common any more? What could such a figure have to do with our 'post-modern' times, times that we perceive as being completely demystified, soberly organized, and stripped of any mythic ingredients? Before answering this question, we should first look at the myth itself.

Prometheus the Titan was a rebel against the existing cosmic order, and, by virtue of this rebellion, the liberator of humanity. A mythic hero, he took pity of humans in their early days when they lived in darkness and fear. He sought, even to his own detriment, to improve their lot by stealing and offering them fire, as well as the arts and crafts of using it, something that had been expressly forbidden by Zeus himself. From that moment onwards, humans have been able to enjoy warmth, light, protection, as well all the numerous technological advances that they required in order to create culture and rise above the state of mere nature. But Prometheus was severely punished for disobeying the decree of Zeus. Chained forever on a desolate rock on distant Caucasus, his only contact with the world was the daily appearance of a wild eagle which tore at his liver. His torture was ended after thirty, or a thousand, or maybe thirty thousand years, by the hero Hercules who killed the bird and unchained the Titan. A tiny part of the chain, however, was forged into a ring which Prometheus would wear forever. This then is the common version of the myth, a version where Prometheus stands as a *positive*, noble, and heroic figure—a version in which we, as followers and heirs of a Promethean mythology, are inclined to believe.

Yet there are other versions—less optimistic, less clear, even contradictory, shedding a different light on both the mythic hero, as well as on his apparently beneficent humanity. Such versions preserve the original narrative core: humanity is still liberated, the old cosmic order is shattered, and the Titan is punished. Yet at what price? And what are the consequences of this 'liberation'? Every mythos, a myth researcher said, possesses 'a solidified narrative core with marginal capabilities for variations' (Blumenberg 1996: 40); in looking at the versions to come, we should keep this narrative core in mind.

There is another feature common to all versions, however, and that is the ontological state of the world from which the tale departs, a bleak world of competition and conflict. At its very dawn, long before the arrival of Western 'civilization', the world is portrayed as a highly competitive space, populated by three different major categories of rival beings: the Titans, its autochthonous first inhabitants, the newly arrived Olympian gods, who defeated them, one may say today, by means of a series of hostile takeovers, and, last but not least, the humans. This is the image of a world that reflects the cosmology of warfare—a place marked by constant struggle and by attempts to acquire or to hold onto power in order to survive. This is a highly insecure place to live in, neither peaceful nor harmonious. In some ways, it is a world not so very different from our current experiences, in which all is competition, conflict, and change, creating a sense that you have to be a winner in order to survive at all, and that survival can only be achieved at the expense of others, who must be subdued and made to obey your rules. It matters little who those 'others' are—other enterprises, other people, other cultures, or the bare physical or system-dynamic forces we have to overcome in order to reach our goals. As the poet put it: 'I must Create a System or be enslav'd by another Man's.' (William Blake, *Jerusalem*, 1815). Competition, conflict, and strife are the ontological constants that are well captured by the political thinker in the phrase *bellum omnium contra omnes*, a war of all against all (Hobbes, cited in Russell 1970: 192 f.). These constants are the tale's departure point, in all its versions, and, in my view, its prime motivation.

Of all Greek myths, the story of Prometheus stands out as the most male-centred story—all its central characters are male; power is the motive and the objective on their actions. Love only features fleetingly, when Prometheus takes pity on humanity in its state of abject misery and neediness. Nonetheless, this is by its very essence a story of male heroes, male gods, and male victims, in a world where female presence can hardly be imagined. If, on occasions, this text lapses into the old-fashioned use of 'Man' as a generic term for human, this is to highlight what is disturbing and problematic in the myth that challenges our contemporary sensitivities.

The story's protagonist is himself problematic, in his origin, his motives, and his actions. The origin of Prometheus is unclear, both as a name and as a figure. The name of Prometheus, like that of his Judaeo-Christian counterpart, Lucifer, could mean 'bearer of knowledge/light', but also 'one who can see in the future', one who has foresight and is capable of *anticipating* things to come (Blumenberg: 343). Some suppose that he was an old volcanic god, like Yahweh, an interesting parallel in our Greek and Judaeo-Christian cultural roots. The archetypical symbolism of fire shows that the capability for creation is inherently ambivalent, since it also entails destruction (Kerenyi 1981: 168). In the older versions of the tale, Prometheus is a Titan but of unclear parentage. His actions too are shrouded with ambiguity. In some versions, he acted like a Jahweh, creating all the plants, the animals, and also the humans. In others, he did nothing of the sort; on the contrary, at the world's beginning, the gods (who at that time included the Titans) were alone and they were *glad* of that; the human kind arrived only later, as an unwanted addendum in cosmic evolution. In still others, gods and people shared a common diverse origin, existing in parallel but without an inner connection between them—the three competing species portrayed above.

Beyond it all, Prometheus' character remains ambivalent, Janus-faced. In many versions, he, the 'caring' one (another meaning of his name), has an alter ego, a twin as old as himself, Epimetheus, 'the one who only learns in hindsight'. In a well-known version from Plato's *Protagoras*, Epimetheus is assigned the task of granting different gifts to the different species at the dawn of creation in order to enable them to survive and prosper. When he finally reaches humans, Epimetheus has exhausted his supply of offerings, and can give nothing to them, thus leaving them weak and unprotected. This fatal error *forces* Prometheus to steal the fire and the arts from the gods (for different versions, see Kerenyi: 168 ff.). For our purposes, it is interesting to see, first, that whatever he does, Prometheus is always accompanied by a shadow embodying his very opposite, his dark side which endangers all his plans; and second, that he steals not only fire, but also the 'arts'—what the Greeks called Techne, from which we derive our word for 'technique'. Technique, then, is that genuinely human capability to construct things in 'unnatural' ways, ranging from simple manufacturing processes to the most refined management techniques, in line with human goals (Mittelstraß 1981: 59 f.). In this way, the myth suggests that to become truly human it is not enough to be equipped with 'fire', the capacity to be creative or inventive; the practical know-how is essential too, as embodied in the arts of technique. And this again suggests that, in becoming truly human, we are irreversibly haunted by shadows: the capability to construct things in unnatural ways means not only shelter, cooked food, civilization, and culture, but also leaving behind irreversibly the natural cosmos—a state that we are experiencing today.

All versions of the story of Prometheus share an imagery of the early humans in their 'natural' state as being defective, poor, and disadvantaged creatures, who needed a second 'creation' in order to survive (Kerenyi: 169)—something that is offered to them by the Titan. Yet the real drama of those early humans, living in a hostile world without hope, love, or pity (that most Promethean of attitudes), is captured at its bleakest by Aeschylus, in his tragedy *Prometheus Bound*. For the species of Man, it would have been better not to have existed at all. This is not a hopelessness of subjective despair, but an objective result of the mythos. Man, a being who has to 'live in the dirt and eat his meal uncooked' is not simply much weaker than his divine competitors, but above all an 'akosmeton genos', an undecorated, unequipped species, with no genuine place in the world. An unloved species too: Zeus, the new CEO in charge, cannot stand those humans, and is confident that all of them will perish one day soon. In this version, Prometheus too has no high opinion of humans, his theft of fire being driven by his own political ambition. He needed humans for his plans, probably a *coup d' état* against the new divine order. He too was convinced of the objective worthlessness of humanity, however (equipped, as he is, with 'foresight'), he also knew that once mortals possessed fire, it could not be revoked by Zeus (Blumenberg: 331 ff.). In this variant, Prometheus proceeds like a marketing man, shrewd, clever, and convincing: he tells people nothing about their true fate—that their existence has no reason at all, that it lacks any meaning. Instead, he uses blindness, pretence, and illusory visions. Consciously, he is about to commit an error, an error of cosmic proportions: in passing fire down to humans, he is to provide them with 'blind hopes' (Aeschylus). These hopes will never be realized, yet they will nevertheless develop a momentum of their own. Thus, the Promethean act causes an irreversible change: the emergence of what we call culture. Prometheus raises the former ephemeral genus to the status of a world power that even Zeus will not be able to ignore, ever again. *This* was the Promethean offence against the cosmic order: to have made the best out of a bad thing, by transforming Man's objective worthlessness into a state of being capable of existing. And, since Man is still worthless in actual terms, this amounts to a feat of deception. It carries, however, its own serious consequences (Blumenberg: 338):

It is Prometheus who first made humans into real human beings...fire, as the force of creation and invention, is the premise for the transformation and improvement of all natural things. Culture is hence a means...of engendering autonomy. Through his gift of fire, Prometheus becomes the author of humanity, he gives it its *differentia specifica*—its distinctive features, something that will come up again in anthropological palaeontology.

The Promethean Promise

The mythological as well as the archaeological records are in agreement so far. Fire, the creative and inventive Logos, the application of technique, of those arts that the Titan had stolen, are the preconditions so that humans may become cultivated, 'civilized' animals, as opposed to just *animals*. This is the epitome of the Promethean promise: to liberate Man—once and for all. A Titanic ideal: total liberation. In the context of a modernist interpretation of the myth, we are now witnessing the results of this promise; we are living, moreover, in its aftermath, namely the liberation of humanity through technique. In short, we live in a Promethean world, a world inaugurated by rebellion, whose liberation comes from technique and whose mythology is a Promethean mythology, our 'on-going mythology' today (Gehmann: in preparation).

What was then the mythological programme offered by the Titan, those 'blind hopes' Aeschylus spoke of? In my reading, there are three core features to the myth: rebellion against a cosmic order, a supplanting of nature by culture, and the introduction of a mechanism of continuous transformation.

(1) Rebellion constitutes the starting point and the heart of the myth, and it is a feature that made it especially attractive to Marx, Nietzsche, and many creative minds of the Romantic Movement. It is a rebellion against any existing order which restricts the liberty of Man, and denies his wish to become fully self-determined; not only partially, or from time to time, but *fully*. If there are any constraints to your freedom (so the mythological maxim goes), rebel against them; destroy them, whenever and wherever you can. People must be self-determined (so states the Promethean ideal), not the slaves of some alien power of divine or earthly origin. This maxim easily turns into a myth of Creative Destruction (Schumpeter 1943: 83), the mythological and practical foundation of our economic order, the world of Capitalism we inhabit: all that is new calls for the destruction of all that is old, in a *constant* manner. The Titan's fire works in both ways: it creates and destroys, in order to forge a world that is artefact, a "second human nature", and, at the same time, a genuine place to live in.

(2) This constitutes the next feature of the Promethean promise: that people, in order to be *truly* free, have to construct a realm of their own, a 'second nature' once removed from the natural state of the world. This world is made in accordance with human will and conceptions, it is a world opposed to the primordial one of dirt and toil—a world without any deeper meaning at all. Culture versus Nature: an entirely 'man-made' cosmos which ensures freedom from the hardships, darkness, and meaninglessness of nature. It is indeed a promise of Titanic dimensions. No wonder that in the nineteenth century Prometheus became the symbol par excellence for freedom, both for those who viewed technology as the force of liberation, and for those who saw it as the force of oppression. Creative artists, driven by the romantic ideal of the self-destined individual, espoused the symbol of Prometheus, as did Nietzsche and Marx, for example, for both of whom Prometheus became the key hero, who 'stole new knowledge from the powerful, calling upon humanity to rebel and attain self-consciousness' (Ehrhardt and Reynolds 2000: 89). As major

Western projects which aimed at creating new artificial worlds that could house human freedom, Socialism and Capitalism shared this one idea in common: that Man himself is a Prometheus who can therefore achieve everything that he wants. We placed all our hopes firmly on this one belief, and it has engendered in turn the worlds we live in. This part of the promise came true, albeit not in the way we dreamed.

Imagine now what would happen if (1) and (2) were to combine. Since *every* existing world imposes constraints on the desire for unconstrained freedom, then, according to Promethean logic, every world 'as it is' has to obey the rule of creative destruction: it must be destroyed to give way to a more perfect, more free, yet also more artificial world. In Lenin's words, the better is the enemy of the good. *Progress* enters the Western world, and becomes its permanent resident, taking the form of the belief that we can get free through an uninterrupted sequence of 'improvements', brought about by continuous creative destruction.

(3) The third fundamental feature of the Promethean myth involves a logic of transformation as illustrated by a basic algorithm, $y = f(x)$, where a world, any world, can be constructed and transformed to serve our purposes, as a function of Man. Technique can transform any raw materials into the desired artefacts. This part too of the Promethean promise came true, and to an extent we never dreamed of. It turned into a reality of crushing dominance: *everything* can become functionalized, fragmented, and recreated again, in the interest of making us free, from creating simple machines to the genetic modification of human beings themselves. The transforming algorithm has universal applicability, since it is perfectly non-individual: it does not pause before individual concerns. For instance, it does not matter if some employees fear a new efficiency programme—they will be rationalized away, anyway. From the mythological perspective, their individuality does not count, it becomes annihilated by the $y = f(x)$ algorithm, which deals with relations of non-human entities—with technological relations between Mass and Power. The algorithm represents that second Promethean gift, those 'arts' which enable us to create new worlds.

The creation of such new worlds out of the old requires a particular form of logic, the logic of *the world as object*. Our surroundings, whether natural or artificial, even humans themselves, do not constitute living entities, with their own right of existence; they are instead just dead matter, raw materials to be used, worked on, transformed, or destroyed. Manipulation on a large scale requires the constant objectification of everything. Mass and Power are twins: the larger the masses (the 'objects') you command, the greater the power you possess. This simple technical relationship, founded on a basic algorithm of manipulation, becomes applicable everywhere, from 'natural' to social engineering.

The process of objectification is enhanced by a logic of analysis and dissolution. In order to be objectified, existing entities must be broken into their constituent fragments, making them *lifeless* and therefore *obedient* to your wishes. You can then rearrange these fragments in any way you like. This becomes even easier (more 'efficient', in modern diction) if the fragments are *uniform*. The more uniform they are, the more easily they can be controlled, which in turn will enhance the exercise of your power. This important relation between Mass and Power did not escape Lenin, Henry Ford, or today's corporate engineers of mergers and acquisitions.

The Outcomes

The Titan was right. He hadn't promised too much. Man, in 'his' Western form at least, was liberated from the cosmic order of hunger, cold, and darkness. The species remains, as at the beginning of the story, an a-cosmic genus, but one which has at last generated a distinct world of its own. The prospects of this world remain unclear, since, as opposed to his benefactor, this minor descendant is not endowed with foresight. Instead, like Epimetheus, Man can only learn in hindsight.

All the same, in the age of mass production, of unprecedented technical achievements and problems alike, of earthly paradises and hells, modern humans *are* free. As the eager descendants of the Titan, who will accept nothing less than total liberation, they have espoused what I wish to call the Myth of Modernity: namely, that 'all that *can* be done, has to be done', a myth which, when applied to any single person, means that 'anything one can become, one *must* become'. Now we are all free, living in an 'open' society, an 'open' cosmos, where we can pursue projects of self-liberation and self-actualization, entirely unconcerned about the projects of those living around us. This, in traditional terms, is to live in no cosmos at all.

This process develops its own system dynamics, which we are unable to control. Expressed in terms of the nature versus culture dialectics, this 'second' or new nature develops its own naturalness, which is as pitiless as the old one. The power of the masses that humans liberated in the course of their own self-emancipation have spectacular effects of their own, as the daily news about our growing tendencies towards the dissolution of our natural, social, and economical ecologies can bear witness. This is the new kind of dirt people have to face, the mountains of refuse which they themselves have created. I would now like to examine in greater detail the technical civilization we inhabit—this entanglement, which is the most prominent by-product of our Promethean emancipation.

As we have seen, the Promethean gifts comprised 'technology' in a literal and all-embracing sense: a technical Logos (instrumental reason/technocracy), which enables us to rule, to be the Promethean kings, and, in so doing, to emancipate ourselves. The first part of the promise was kept—technocracy rules. Liberation, however, has not been achieved and this is hardly surprising, given that the promise was for a *total* liberation, to be achieved by a very narrow set of means—technique. This leaves us with those 'blind hopes' that the tragic poet spoke of, where the solution to every problem appears to lie in *growth*—more technique, more artefacts, more products, and more problems too. This situation generates its own myth, the Myth of a Self-subsuming Technique, whose core narrative is that as humanity became civilized, it also became the victim of its own technical products, a Promethean slave. The tale becomes a literal bias, an assumption that characterizes our acts and our perceptions alike: namely, that it is our technique which is responsible for all the misery that we experience in our state of civilization. Since we must always be dependent on our technique (like the 'prosthetic gods' of Freud 1930), we are condemned to be powerless. This is what the myth proclaims, as a key component of our culture's body of knowledge. This, in turn, has led to a unique type of technical rationality (to use Max Weber's idea), representing an equally unique form of 'justice'. Since we are technology-bound and, hence, condemned to powerlessness, we must obey the programme; and we must do so completely. This programme is imposed on us by a kind of progress which we accept in its entirety, with its concomitant systemic entanglements—and we become its victims, in our Promethean, uncontrollable worlds. Within these worlds, each component is meticulously planned and created by human will; it is designed for a specific purpose, resulting in a spontaneous order of mechanized processes generated and kept running by mechanized individuals, 'humans' who obey exclusively to the powers of their own techniques.

What happened then to the myth of freedom, the original human dream of true autonomy, which was to be attained with the help of 'technical' Logos? A commentator (Guardini 1995: 53) observed:

People lack the will to belong to themselves, to their own Gestalt and way of life, or to create an environment which suits them perfectly, or even exclusively. Rather, they adopt ... the models of life imposed on them by rational planning and standardized machine-products, feeling in general terms secure that this is as it should be. Nor do they feel a desire to undertake their own initiatives; ... rather, they slot themselves in organizations which provide the model for the masses, and obey their programmes.

They emulate a modern-day Epimetheus who tries to become like his mightier brother, relying on the universal application of technique, a new form of $y = f(x)$ that embraces everything, and transforms everything. Thus, Logos turns into technocracy, its mythic roots being lost along the way, leaving an all-encompassing matrix where science, technique, industry, and society are irrevocably webbed together in a 'super-structure' (Rapp 1994: 82 ff.). 'Technique' itself turns into the collective term for the structure of the modern world as such, giving birth to a particular kind of logic, namely that humans are the powerless prisoners of their own self-created blueprints. Through the medium of technique, everything—culture, politics, and economy—melts together into an omnipresent system, a single, all-powerful conglomerate that incorporates or repels all alternatives. 'The productivity and growth potential of this system stabilize society, and keep the technological progress inside the frame of the existing power structures. Technological rationality thus became political rationality' (Marcuse, in Rapp 1994: 21).

This is indeed a rather resigned statement. No matter what we seek to undertake, 'the system' engulfs it all, or spits it all out, if it finds it alien to its chemistry. People are confronted with a regularity of facts that they themselves have created, and which now return to haunt them, in the form of psychological and social problems. These, in turn, call for still further technical solutions: 'People free themselves from the forces of nature by subjugating themselves again to the forces they have brought themselves into existence' (Schelsky 1961: 443).

Both statements show a Promethean *autopoeisis*—self-making, highlighting the tragic irony of history: in their efforts to free themselves, people have become nothing more than slaves—they have thus chained themselves onto a Caucasus of their very own making.

The myth of technocracy, namely that Technique Is Everything, is a myth which embodies more than simple subjugation. Dependence on a machine that promises us freedom, even as it denies it to us, is quite Janus-faced. We have already seen how the application of the maxim 'what can be done has to be done' leads to nothing but a nearly unrestricted loss of freedom. On the other hand, however, there still exists another belief in 'technique' as the epitome of the totalizing, yet unshattered mythic hope that, despite all individual differences, our Technique will eventually lead us to freedom. Our Promethean dream has thus not lost its force. It is still a widespread myth which equates progress with technology, one that is currently seeking to colonize the domain of natural reproduction with the possibility of artificial organisms and artificial humans capable of reproducing themselves—or indeed of machines creating new machines. This raises the Promethean myth of modernity to new levels, aiming to finally annihilate the old difference between Nature and Culture, by which token the existence of anything that is still opposed to people (= nature) and their world (= culture) would be thus eradicated. This then would be the ultimate aim of progress—that, in the end, there is only *one* world left, the human world, and no other.

And we *need* progress, for two principal reasons which are both separate and interlinked; I will refer to them in short as 'physical' and 'spiritual'. In the physical realm, we need progress for a very simple reason: we need to *grow* in order to *survive*. The reason is simple but pressing, since our economic system—the base of our material existence—has been explicitly designed for this purpose: Capitalism, this most successful product of a Promethean mythology of greed, relies on growth in order to survive at all. Growth constitutes its base, and without constant growth it would cease to exist—and with it, we would too, and absolutely. It is a very simple Promethean equation which has evolved into the sole guarantee for the life of an entire culture: growth = survival.

The other reason, the 'spiritual' one, is not as simple, yet it is equally pressing. The expansion of our technological knowledge has led to the loss of another kind of knowing, a knowing that I want to call a knowledge of orientation. This is quite unique to us as human beings (and is quite unlike the knowledge of all those wasps and ants building complex organizations). It is a knowledge which asks for the reasons why we are doing some things at all, and to what ends. For instance, why we are focusing upon technological progress, and *where* is this leading? Indeed, what is progress? It is progress away from where, and where to? According to the original plan (the Titanic promise) this was meant to create a paradise on earth, sheltering us from devastating threats. Yet, in its current realization, it has generated threats unprecedented in human history, exposing us to every type of instability on both the physical and the spiritual level; these are threats to the natural environment, the primary 'orientation crisis' of our times—our alienation of living as strangers in our own 'homes'. In any case, one constant remained: progress exists, and it is unstoppable. This leads to new questions, and to a wide range of new situations—in both actual as well as foreseeable future terms: what is happening to us, and, consequently, what *will* happen to us? What will be the outcomes of the new power relations of the masses we set free, those masses of impacts and problems resulting from our daily 'technical' operations, causing still further impacts and problems that will lead to further impacts, in endless sequence? How to liberate ourselves from the new chains of a Promethean causality?

Some Final Perspectives

It is the fate of every Prometheanism, a concerned critic argues, to experience a dialectical turn (Anders 1987: 24)—from a Promethean pride, which seeks to possess and control everything, to a Promethean shame, the sense of inferiority experienced by humans in front of their own creations. This is more than merely an attitude, but rather a general state of being: 'As the a-synchronicity of [present-day] people with the world of products daily increases, so does this gap become wider every day' (p. 16).

Here, too, progress is at work: the progress of the gap, generating its own entanglements. Is there a true Promethean liberation yet to come, to free us from the chains of causality which we have brought about ourselves? And is such liberation possible, in a world addicted to growth, a cosmos as closed as it can be, yet expanding at an accelerating speed? Would less be more? Can we stop the machinery, or decrease its velocity at least? It would require a reorientation, and perhaps a complete new beginning. At the present speed of machines, our fate is no longer in our own hands. The machine does what it wants, and not what we want it to do. It has developed its own 'regularity of facts' which must quite simply be followed. This reminds us of Zeus's early hope in the myth—that humanity would not endure in its present state, at least not as a humanity deserving its name. Nor, unlike the mythic story, is there a Hercules in sight to free us. We have to do it ourselves, and by ourselves alone. We are the ones responsible for what we have done, *we* are the ones responsible for the burdens of our freedom. There is neither an external force nor any mythic hero out there to save us. What remains is hope for true hope—this very last thing to slip out of Pandora's box.

References

Anders, G. (1987). Die Antiquiertheit des Menschen. Vol.1: Über die Seele im Zeitalter der zweiten industriellen Revolution. Vol.2: Über die Zerstörung des Lebens im Zeitalter der dritten industriellen Revolution. Munich: C.H. Beck [*Man's Antiquity. On the Human Soul in the Era of the 2nd Industrial Revolution* (Vol.1); and: *On the Destruction of Life in the Era of the 3rd Industrial Revolution*].

Blumenberg, H. (1996). Arbeit am Mythos. Frankfurt: Suhrkamp [*Work on Mythos*].

Ehrhardt, I. and Reynolds, S. (2000). Seelenreich. Munich/London/New York: Prestel [*Kingdom of Souls*].

Freud, S. (1930*a*). Civilization and its Discontents. *Freud: Civilization, Society and Religion*. Harmondsworth: Penguin. Vol. 12.

Frye, N. (1947). *Fearful Symmetry: A Study of William Blake*. Boston: Beacon Press.

Gehmann, U. (in preparation). Myth and Organization.

Guardini, R. (1995). Das Ende der Neuzeit. Die Macht. Mainz/Paderborn: Grünewald/Schöningh [*The End of Modernity: Power*].

Kerenyi, K. (1981). Die Mythologie der Griechen (2 Vol.). Munich: dtv [*The Mythology of the Greeks* Vol.1].

Mittelstraß, J. (1981). Das Wirken der Natur ['The Workings of Nature']. In F. Rapp, (ed.) Naturverständnis und Naturbeherrschung, pp. 36–69. Munich: Wilhelm Fink [*On the Understanding and Domination of Nature*].

Rapp, F. (1994). Die Dynamik der modernen Welt. Eine Einführung in die Technikphilosophie. Hamburg: Junius [*The Dynamics of the Modern World. An Introduction to the Philosophy of Technique*].

Russell, B. (1970). Denker des Abendlandes. Geschichte der Philosophie in Wort und Bild. Berne/Munich/Vienna: Scherz [*A History of Western Philosophy*].

Schelsky, H. (1961). Der Mensch in der wissenschaftlichen Zivilisation. Köln/Opladen: Westdeutscher Verlag [*Man within the Civilization of Science*].

Schumpeter, J. A. (1943). *Capitalism, Socialism, and Democracy*. London: Allen & Unwin.

ELEVEN

Phaethon: Seizing the Reins of Power

Diana Winstanley[55]

On what wings dare he aspire?
What the hand dare seize the fire?
(William Blake, 'The Tyger' from 'Songs of Experience'[56], 1789/1967: 42)

Reading Ovidly—Introducing Phaethon

THE story of Phaethon is both a personal, as well as an epic tale; in this chapter, I shall first present the version of Phaethon as told in Ovid's *Metamorphoses* (written c. 5 BCE), and then explore its relevance to our times. On the face of it, the story of Phaethon is about a young man goaded by his peers into trying to take hold of the reins of power. In an attempt to show everyone, not least himself, that he is the true son of the Sun God, he seeks to ride the brilliant chariot of his father across its daily, trail-blazing arc over the earth. Unable to control the wild horses that pull the chariot, he ends up ablaze and crashes down on the earth below, causing much damage, and finally dying in his father's great shadow. The value of a good story is above all its capacity for retake, and before Ovid, Euripides had already used the story of Phaethon in a tragic play, of which some fragments still remain (see Diggle 1970). Like many of Ovid's tales (Hughes 1997), the story of Phaethon lends itself to reflection on a variety of current concerns (Hofman and Lasdun

[55] Thanks are due to Dr Paula James, Senior Lecturer, Open University, Department of Classical Studies, who gave guidance on Ovid's narrative and poetic interpretation of the myth, as well as on current Ovidian scholarship.
[56] The Tyger appears in William Blake's 'Songs of Experience', the antithesis of his 'Songs of Innocence', where his feelings over the suffering of mankind and the corruption of innocence are aired.

1994); in this chapter, I offer a few contemporary retakes from the spheres of organization and of private life, demonstrating the versatility of the myth and highlighting its capacity to resonate with a contemporary audience.

Ovid is one of our greatest authors, a storyteller who writes of the ancient gods in ways which offer a deep insight into the human condition; his unique and sophisticated narrative skills have earned him the title of a 'modern' poet. In this chapter, I go further, arguing that he is also a postmodern poet—his greatest work, *Metamorphoses*, is about the fluidity of form and content, where not only people and landscapes are transformed, but the work itself shifts in ways that makes it impervious to fixed interpretations: Ovid is a protean poet par excellence.

The Story of Phaethon

The story of Phaethon is part of a fantastical panorama populated by heroes and Gods, monsters and nymphs, who encounter continual change and transformation as they stride and soar through the pages of Ovid's *Metamorphoses*. The very name Phaethon means 'the shining or beaming one', evoking the nature of his divine father, and at the same time tragically prefiguring his fiery fate. Ovid tells us that Phaethon is a young boy whose mother is Clymene, a sea nymph, and whose father is Phoebus,[57] the Sun God. The linking of 'son' and 'sun' is certainly an interesting modern homophone.[58] Clymene marries Merops, a mortal king who adopts Phaethon as his son. This makes Phaethon a mortal prince, and a mix of godly fire and water; in Ovid's version, he is also portrayed as a typically mixed-up teenager.

The story opens with two boys, Phaethon and Epaphus, playmates rivalling each other over the status of their parents. As far as we know, these two boys had not been linked before by any of the earlier tellers or illustrators of these myths, and their appearance, therefore, in this story is one of Ovid's first metamorphoses. Growing into manhood, and taking up an adult role in the world, is inexorably fraught with dangers; Phaethon and Epaphus, however, have even more reasons than most to be anxious, because their divine parentage adds genetic chaos into the already heady cocktail of adolescent

---

[57] The Sun God, Helios; originally, however, the Sun God was distinct from Phoebus and Apollo.

[58] The pun implied in the English translation through homophones would also have rung strong for Ovid's own readers: the son's name, Phaethon, was also a regular epithet of the Sun, his father, as, for example, in Vergil's *Aeneid* (5.105), where dawn is ushered by 'Phaethontis equi'—by the steeds of Phaethon, that is, Helios himself (from the Greek Phaos—Phôs, meaning 'Light'). The Sun-Phaethon, therefore, would also be here Phaethon-the-Son.

hormones: it makes their pubescent rites of passage even more difficult. Phaethon boasts that his father is the Sun God, Phoebus; Epaphus dismisses this claim as puffed up pride, and accuses Phaethon of creating an 'image of a false father' (*Tumidus genitoris imagine falsi*, 1.754). Phaethon goes 'crying' back to his mother for reassurance. She seeks to reassure him, but to no avail. He then enters the heavenly realm, and sets off for the nearby palace of the Sun God to ask for proof. This will give Phaethon the closure he needs regarding his own identity, as well as tremendous status in the eyes of others. Being an amazing weaver of tales, Ovid transforms in this way the ever-present sun into the always-absent father.

At the meeting of Phaethon and Phoebus, Phaethon stands in wonder at the magnificence of his father's palace; he is dazzled by the halo of sunbeams that crowns his father's head, and overawed by his chariot, inlaid with gold and jewels. Phoebus embraces his son warmly and proudly, and foolishly gives a promise of anything the boy might like, in order to help prove his identity. Once given, however, such promises cannot be broken. This proves to be the fateful gift, as the foolish Phaethon asks to be allowed, just for a day, to take his father's place on the chariot that hauls the Sun through the sky. As any father would, Phoebus begs his son to reconsider, but his pleas are in vain. Can we blame Phaethon for making such a demand on his father? By riding the chariot of the Sun he will be recognized by the world as his father's son; as the charioteer, he will be able to look down on all his classmates and cast off his own nagging anxieties. He will have the strength and power of a master of the universe.

Phaethon is only a teenager, and passing into the adult world is far harder than he can ever imagine. He attempts a truly heroic rite of passage—and fails to make the grade. He fails, because even as a temporary loan, he attempts to get his inheritance by wheedling out of an over-indulgent father a dangerous promise. He also fails because the offspring of immortal fathers cannot receive an inheritance from their parents who never die. Phaethon is thus one of Ovid's examples of the young and of those with delusions of grandeur, who attempt recklessly and fatally to short-circuit apprenticeship and the acquisition of skill—Icarus and Semele[59] being two others who, in seeking god-like stature, fall to earth or are burnt to ashes.

The Sun God next advises Phaethon how to steer his chariot, telling him of the wheel tracks in the sky that can provide a marker; clearly, the lad is not listening, and once he is careering through the sky, tackling the constellations, he takes leave of his senses. Not long into the fiery ride, Phaethon becomes all too witless to bring his workforce to order. The fact that he has no godly weight has already disturbed the horses' psychological equilibrium,

---

[59] Semele was a human mistress of Jove (Jupiter), who asks him to make love to her the way he does to his divine wife Juno; this act leads to her dying consumed by flames.

as well as the actual physical balance of the chariot: the unfamiliar driver lacks any authority, and the horses, unnerved by the mortal novice at the reins, career and gallop out of control across the universe, setting the earth ablaze and wreaking havoc in the heavens. Here Phaethon can be juxtaposed with Arachne (see Chapter 9); where Phaethon claims a role through kinship with a God, and loses it through lack of skill, Arachne claims a role through skill and mastery (at weaving), and loses it through challenging a God, and through refusing to acknowledge the debt to the one who is not just a goddess of weaving, but weaving itself.

Once Phaethon has dropped the reins, the horses run both free and fearful of their freedom. Phaethon himself is plunged into the darkness, blinded by the conflagration around him; what should have been a moment of exhilaration and intoxication becomes instead the start of his total annihilation. Phaethon's hands have dropped not just the horses' reins, but those of the narrative as well. From this moment on, Phaethon is caught up in the whirlwind of cosmic chaos, and the focal point of the story is no longer himself, but rather all that surrounds him.

Numberless myths of causation erupt around the planetary and earthly havoc that ensues. Ovid suggests this conflagration is the reason why Africans are black, as their blood was driven by the heat to the surface of their bodies; it is also the reason why Libya is a desert, and the myth suggests that the terrified Nile hid its head, so that even today its source remains unknown (see Wise 1976: 51). As the fate of the universe hangs in balance, Mother Earth calls upon Jupiter for assistance: he launches the lightning shaft that will destroy Phaethon, and send the Sun chariot reeling from the skies. Phaethon's final plummet back to earth gives him a moment of glory as a brief trailblazer, compared by Ovid to a comet. His embers plunge to the earth, and, around the stone marking his demise, his mother grieves, while his sisters, weeping in their sorrow, turn to trees; the amber itself that is formed by their tears will be used, in the distant future, as Roman wedding jewellery. Although Phaethon may have proved his divine ancestry, he remains mortal—and his human fallibility means he can never become a God like his father.

Phaethon Retakes: Rereading Ovidian Myths Today

A Personal Retake of Absence and Identification

There was something in the Phaethon story that resonated strongly with the author; my father was a politician, a Liberal MP and then life peer, as well as a TV presenter, TV doctor, and weekly columnist in the *Manchester Evening*

News. Every day before the six o'clock news and the Magic Roundabout, on his programme 'This is Your Right', his presence would beam through the television sets of friends and classmates, as well as my own. In Manchester, where I grew up, he was known by everyone, but not by me, although, like Phaethon, I basked in his reflected glory, enjoying and bragging about the connection. He made speeches that were recorded in Hansard; conducted hustings in draughty halls and entertained as an after dinner speaker, night after night; I can still remember my awe as he crowned a local beauty queen: both appeared dazzling from my position on the ground, and this reminded me of Phaethon's amazement at Phoebus's beaming crown. One of my few mementos of my father since his death is a video of the announcement of the voting in the first general election that he won as MP for Cheadle and Hazel Grove, in 1966. The video shows clearly the few minutes that were the happiest of his life. It is not often that a video captures such a moment, but his aura and delight beams through the footage, as he leans, amongst the excited clapping and cheers, to hug my mother. Like Phaethon, my experience of my father was of that of a beaming presence, omnipresent to everyone, but not present to me. In discussing this story with the editor, he reminded me of Leonardo de Vinci's comment that the sun can never see a shadow. If you are the sun, you are inevitably always in the sunshine, and maybe you cannot see what lurks in the shadows. Likewise, if you are the child of the sun, it can be hard to see yourself as a separate human being.

All children want to feel 'special', but this is much harder if the parent is revered on the public stage, and absent from home. What must it be like for other children of famous, 'god-like' parents—for Prince William, for example, walking in the shadow of a famous mother, Princess Diana, whose early and tragic death only elevated her further to almost immortal status; or for the sons of Tony Blair (and children of other prime ministers), as he is seen daily in handshakes with foreign dignitaries or grappling across the dispatch box of the Commons—is he still there to help with homework and play football? Growing up in the shadow of another can create a complex net of emotions, which can tangle up one's sense of identity and role.

Like many powerful magnates, Phoebus never seriously believed anyone other than himself could bring in the sun—not even Jupiter, the king of the gods. He is all-powerful and unique. If only Phaethon had followed in the footsteps of his mortal stepfather, Merops, he would have inherited a kingdom and been groomed in the arts of leadership. This is a key dilemma of adolescence—whether to follow fantastical dreams and whims, or take a more solid established path to adulthood. As a young adult, I tried to follow in my father's footsteps, studying politics at university and becoming chair of the students' union; I was well along the path to becoming an MP in his wake, then, when the ride began to feel bumpy, I suffered from debilitating asthma, tired from breathing air into this image of myself. Unlike Phaethon,

I voluntarily threw myself off the chariot: my descent was bruising, but only slightly so.

The desire to emulate famous, god-like fathers, and prove oneself through imitation, can paradoxically lead not to confirmation of identity and kinship, but to a doomed existence where one is a poor replica, a shadow of oneself. So, then, Phaethon's is the sad story of a child who yearns for his father, and seeks identification with him, but fails to construct a viable identity of his own (De Levita 1965: 76–95). Newbold (2001: 175) suggests that father identification is an essential part of our identity formation; but the absence of the father renders it impossible for Phaethon to shed his infantile ego-ideal and develop a more mature identity of his own, as separate from that of the ideal of the father. It is not easy for an ordinary mortal to create a mature identity through identification with a father who is a Sun God, who is omnipresent and absent at the same time; Phaethon failed in his attempt to become like his ego-ideal, while I abandoned mine when I found it to be unattainable.

One meaning of identity, discussed at length by de Levita (1965), is the social identity bestowed upon us by others, and this is the catalyst for Phaethon's journey. Our peers are our mirrors, acknowledging the sense of self that we project to them. When the image we have of ourselves, and wish others to have of us, becomes violently severed from the way others actually see us, there can be deep inner turmoil and crisis, particularly in those teenage years when our sense of self is so fragile that it cannot ward off the battering of peers. Fragmented and disjointed identities are the source and manifestation of many psychiatric disorders, such as, for example, borderline personality disorder. It is really no wonder that Phaethon splits in two, the fearless warrior on a mission to prove himself, and the fearful boy, anxious and afraid. Phaethon provides an almost archetypical example of someone who is in search of identity, with delusions of grandeur and aspirations to emulate a god-like state. He is part of an impressive and diverse company of mortals who appear in Ovid's text, and whose transformations, whether defence mechanisms, punishments, rewards, or spontaneous manifestations of an inner essence, can be detected in modern life as a feature of the human condition under social stress and personal crisis. *Fiducia Formae*—having faith in one's form or beauty, and being unassailable in terms of identity and shape— is shaken to the core by Ovid in every possible way. Changing identity, whether it is an assumed change, such as Phaethon's taking on his father's mantle, or a forced change, such as when Phaethon is destroyed by his grandiosity and his sisters are turned into trees, is an unsettling idea, developed in a myriad of ways by Ovid.

The story of Phaethon can be seen as that of an identity crisis played out at the physical and the psychological, the earthly and the god-like levels, using the device of uncertain parentage to light the fuse which sets the explosions in train. In facing their identity crises, Epaphus and Phaethon fit well into patterns of adolescent narcissism, manifested in 'self-absorption, delight in boasting and insult, sensitivity to shame and mockery, self-inflation, delusions of grandeur' (Newbold 2001: 175). As Newbold suggests, 'Most fantasies of power betray an underlying narcissism as they replace feelings of helplessness and separation with those of mastery and control' (p. 175). Phaethon's identity crisis exhibits itself in narcissism, and seeks resolution through merging with a father figure in order to assume mastery and control, and to gain the admiration of others. The greater the power of the father, the more helpless the child, and the stronger the fantasy of omnipotence becomes.

Rites of Passage and Contemporary Family Life

In contemplating my personal retake of the Phaethon story, I realised that there were other aspects of family life that it also reflected: beyond the identity crises of adolescence, and its delusions of grandeur, the story also comments more broadly on the social rites of passage into adulthood. In contemporary life, with the help of the media, we often find ourselves as voyeurs of the tragic and comic aspects of growing up. This theme is played out exhaustively in dramas, soap operas, and films (such as American Beauty, or The Graduate), where audiences are fascinated by the personal tragedies that can mark the transition through adolescence and middle age. Viewed from this angle, Phaethon's story highlights the confusion, bravado, and recklessness of male adolescence, and the rituals in which it seeks solace. Using the humorous style of an American high school heist, McHugh (1986) frames the story as a teenage son borrowing his father's Ferrari in order to take his girlfriend to a prom.

Here is an extract from the tale:

> "Phaethon, my son." Called the noble god in surprise.
> "Why do you come here to this lofty garage?
> What do you seek?...
> Answered this: "Dad, I've got a problem,
> And I really need your help. You see.
> There's this girl. I like her a lot. We're
> Going to the Prom together, if the Fates
> Be with me."...
> "Well Dad,
> It's like this, I told her my father was a god.
> She said that modern technology disproved
> The existence of all gods. She said she learned that fact
> In her Computer Math class. Now I'm beginning
> To believe it myself, and I'm the son of a God!
> Isn't there some way that I could prove our existence?"
> *(after some sighing and stalling)*
> ... The Sun God said "... If your girlfriend

Wants proof, she shall have it; ... Go on ask me anything."
'Phaethon got right to the point. "I need some wheels, Dad"
He said, looking fondly at the Sun God's Ferrari
Now gleaming from its recent waxing.
"I can't take my girl to the Prom unless I have a car.
Taking her in a god's Ferrari would be really cool." ...

Phaethon, the hot-headed boy struggling to be accepted by his peers, wants to be seen as 'cool', a James Dean of the skies. However, rather than assert his identity, as in the ancient heroic tradition, through a series of deeds that build his strength and character and win him the respect of others, he attempts, like many a rash adolescent, to do it with a single act of emulation and self-destruction—he crashes his dad's 'car'.

Branding the Image

It is telling then that the car industry has seen the marketing potential of branding a vehicle that can be associated with a spectacular teenage crash. Pelzer (2002) discusses the choice of Volkswagen to call their new car the 'Phaeton',[60] and asks why 'they chose the name of the first car crash victim in history'. Apparently, the Volkswagen speaker claimed the car had survived without damage despite the driver's demise. The branding of Phaeton, and the act of integrating the driver's name into the vehicle, begs comparison with the chariot of the sun, and can be seen as a symbol of mankind's aspiration to god-like status. The death of the driver does not so much suggest the failure of the vehicle, as it does its super-human power, which would take more than adolescent power to control. Cars and other fast machines have notoriously been extensions of the adult male ego, masculinity, power, and sexual prowess. Donald Campbell and his illustrious father Malcolm were between them 'the joint architects of 11 speed records on water as well 10 on land'. Tremayne (2003) tells the story of this fated son's emulation of the father. Donald grew up in his father's shadow, a hero of land speed records, a strict disciplinarian who sent his son to prep school at eight years, where the boy is said to have sold his father's autograph and 'basked in the reflected glory of having the fastest man on earth as a parent'. Donald grew up yearning to be like him, but also feeling that nothing he could do would ever be

---

[60] One might argue that already in the past 'Phaeton' was the name of a well-known, light, and sporty type of open four-wheeled carriage for two horses—yet the contradiction inherent in the mythological allusion remains ... 'Phaeton' (an alternative Latin form of the name and a long-established French spelling) is also considered easier to pronounce than 'Phaethon'.

quite good enough. In watching an early film, his widow commented 'There was this little boy, so proud of his father, and his father didn't even notice…', yet he worshipped him. Like Phaethon, no proof of his own capability was enough, and he took over Sir Malcolm's speedboat *Bluebird* after his father's death. It was in a later version Bluebird K7 that he attempted to break the 300 mph barrier in 1966 on Coniston Water. At a speed estimated at 328 mph, '*Bluebird* climbed inexorably into the sky before flipping back into the murky waters of the lake', (Tremayne 2003). Ironically, less than ten years later, I swam across Coniston Water above the wreck of Bluebird, in an attempt to impress my father who chugged alongside in his boat, on one of his few breaks from work…

Public Retakes—Space Travel, Consumption, and Spectacle

It is not just the car industry that sees the commercial opportunity of a spectacle; this contemporary 'retake' is conducted through the eyes of the ever-present media, where stories have many facets, exploited in the search for understanding, 'truth', and an audience. It is not just our personal, private, and family lives that come under scrutiny; the *camera oscura* also takes on the public realm and dissects it for private consumption.

Phaethon's conflagration in space evokes the treatment of a modern day spectacle by the mass media: there is fascination, dread, and awe at witnessing spectacles like airplanes being driven into buildings on 11 September 2001. In Glyn Maxwell's version of Phaethon (in Hofmann and Lasdun, 1994: 65–78), the story is told in a journalistic fashion, as a series of interview fragments with the drama's different characters brought together in the manner of an investigative documentary. Clymene, Phaethon, the horses, a spokesperson of the sun, a scientist, and the people of Africa, each have an entirely different take, and the reader is left to sift through the evidence and make sense of the fragments of the tale. This postmodern narrative tradition is one which echoes the playful contradictions and metamorphoses of Ovid, and shifts both perspective and storyteller for the sake of dramatic effect and voyeuristic entertainment.

Here are some extracts from Maxwell (1994: 65–78):

> Film of Epaphus
>
> Epaphus, his friend,
> Now drunk, shakes him and leers. Was this the time
> He told him his father wasn't his father really
> And Phaeton, stunned,
>
> Backed into space?
> No this time he grins….

Eous (one of the horses)

How did I know it was him?
> When we were torn through clouds and the East wind
I felt no weight on my back, heard no command,
And felt no pull, no hand,
No pilot. No escape now. Kingdom come.

Three images, that's all.
> One was his face, the boy, his face when he lost
The reins and then his footing—that was the last
We saw of him—he must
> Presumably have gone in a fireball—

A Scientist

Would he have suffered? Would he have suffered pain?
Would he have suffered? Lady let me explain.
He bore the worst
Of Heaven, curved
With Poison, Scorpio! ...

Clymene, his mother

Death was instantaneous,
Death is always instantaneous.
Loss was instantaneous.
Loss is always.

The strong visual image of Phaethon exploding in the skies readily evokes the Challenger shuttle disaster, and the more recent Columbia crash. Space flight has parallels with the Phaethon myth: human beings trying to extend beyond this world and into the heavens, in the pursuit of omnipotence and god-like aspirations. It is eerie how similar to Maxwell's (1994) perspectives on Phaethon have been reports of the Columbia space shuttle disaster in 2003, encompassing testimonies of NASA scientists and safety experts, and the tributes of politicians and relatives. Here are four quotations from the *Observer*, on the day after the disaster (1 February 2003):

The Correspondent:

The space shuttle Columbia erupted in flames yesterday as it re-entered the Earth's atmosphere at 12,000 miles per hour, killing all seven crew members and plunging America into mourning and despair.

President Bush:

These men and women assumed a great risk in the service of all humanity. These astronauts knew the dangers and faced them willingly knowing they had a high and noble purpose in life.

James Milford—a Barber and Resident of Nacogdoches:

It's all over Nacogdoches. There are several little pieces, some parts of machinery ... there's been lots of pieces about three feet wide.

Ron Dittemore, Head of the Shuttle Programme:

'We cannot discount that there might be a connection' (referring to an earlier incident which resulted in loosening of a heat resistant tile). An hour before the disaster, transmission of data from hydraulics sensors, sited on the left wing, stopped abruptly. ' It was as if someone had cut a wire'.

Our interest, capitalized on and nurtured by the media, can become voyeuristic and intrusive. An entire industry has developed around journalists and pundits, whose role is to interpret occurrences across the world or in space through the voices of whoever has an angle or story to give. The Challenger space shuttle disaster in 1986 spawned a host of investigations (the main one being the Rogers Commission 1986), books (e.g. see McDonnell 1987), book chapters (such as Feynman 1993), case studies (e.g. Morgan 1989), articles, videos, films, and documentaries (such as the BBC *Panorama* broadcast 'The Dream that Fell out of the Sky', 28 April 1986, and even as recently as 2000, the BBC2 programme 'Challenger'), broadcast on 23 January of that year. The common threads that seem to preoccupy accounts of space spectacles derive from a fascination, in contemporary times, to find out what happened, who or what was to blame, what pain has been caused, and how people have reacted to it, at the political or personal level. As well as seeking detail, there is a drive to seek meaning and make sense of it all.

In seeking the meaning of such events, Phaethon's story can be instructive. It is well-established that the Challenger's mission was not meant as a scientific breakthrough, but rather as the symbolic illustration of America's political and technological dominance over the skies, and a celebration of its multicultural make-up: this was a flight intended to impress the world with American superiority. The symbol conjured by the flight was that of 'prevailing over death through competence' (Schwartz 1988: 10). Yet, and while crowds watched the flight on the frosty morning of 28 January, 1986, seventy-three seconds after take-off the shuttle exploded—killing the five men and two women astronauts. Like Phaethon, the astronauts were blind to the incompetences that lay behind the mission; like Phoebus, however, there were also those who knew of the catalogue of shortcomings that lay behind the plan, yet felt powerless to stop this compulsion to fly. We may question how Phoebus could knowingly send his son on such an ill-fated mission, but the experience of the Challenger suggests that opposition can be futile in the face of an exigency to satisfy the demands of a stubborn superego.

The Challenger accident was subsequently found to be the result of the poor design of the O-rings, the rocket's safety seals on the field joints which circled the circumference of the spacecraft. These had been known to erode at low temperatures. Robert Boisjoly, an engineer, had declared in an letter earlier, to Robert Lund, Vice President of Engineering at Morton Thiokol, that 'it is my honest and very real fear that if we do not take immediate action to dedicate a team to solve the problem, with the field joint having the number one priority, then we stand in jeopardy of losing a fight along with all the launch pad facilities'. Later, Robert Lund was to recommend that no launch take place at temperatures of less than 53 °C, and on that chilly morning the temperature was around 28 °C. This information was available, the part had even been on the criticality list, and yet they still proceeded to fly.

The political and managerial will to proceed proved irresistible. One senior engineer at NASA exclaimed that under Lund's recommendation, 'we would be unable to launch until April!' There was a sense of urgency—the President, and NASA, needed, like Phaethon, to prove themselves immediately. The shuttle had cost the nation millions of dollars, $5 billion had been spent on a space shuttle programme which went back to the 1970s and to Richard Nixon's desire to woo the sunbelt's aerospace industries, a key heartland for the Republican vote, at a time when Vietnam and Watergate were eroding confidence in the American administration. Subsequently, President Reagan's 1982 policy consisted of two priorities—maintaining US leadership in space and expanding private-sector involvement and investment. At the time of the launch, President Reagan was relying on his talking directly with Christa McAuliffe, the teacher launched into space to give lessons from the skies, to boost his popularity. This, then, was part of the American Dream, turned into a narcissistic fantasy to match Phaethon's adolescent delusions of grandeur. The president and the space industry were both in need of reassurance.

Robert Boisjoly continued strenuously to voice his concerns. In his account to the Presidential Commission of Inquiry, he said: 'Mr Mason said we had to make a management decision. He turned to Bob Lund and asked him to take off his engineering hat and put on his management hat. From this point on, management formulated the points to base their decision on.'

From this point on, the flight was doomed; like Phaethon, they were not willing to let lack of technical competence, or the fear of failure, stand in their way. In the face of obsessive compulsion, technical incompetence as well as risks and fears can be overlooked. The experience of Challenger suggests that the fantasy of omnipotence in the skies, of power and mastery in times of national identity crisis and insecurity, can lead to almost anything.

Of course, there are key differences. NASA (the National Aeronautics and Space Administration) and all its subcontracting organizations are not the same as one boy. Real stories of space flight involve millions of hours of arduous labour, whereas a myth can dream up a palace, gods, and unbelievable flights and drama in seconds, without having to go through the arduous process of creation. However, marketing, advertising, and the media can blur the edges between reality and fiction, where the launch of space shuttles becomes a Disneyland-in-space (Schwartz 1988), and where even the branding of a new car becomes a heroic adventure. Myths such as Phaethon can offer a commentary on our times, but they can also be used to lure us with their glitter to consume, lock, stock, and barrel, the story, the image, and the product.

On its own, a technological disaster does not make as powerful a story as one which incorporates human suffering and the individual at its centre. Each story unfolds into another. In his television broadcast to the nation on 28 January 1986, Reagan alluded to someone else's aspirations in the skies, when he concluded his tribute to the Challenger crew with the words: 'We will never forget them this morning as they prepared for their journey and waved goodbye and slipped the surly bonds of earth to touch the face of God.' President Bush more recently made similar allusions in tribute to the Columbia crew. In researching Phaethon, this quotation drove me to seek out its origin. I was fascinated to discover another story which also seemed to capture some of Phaethon's spirit. Reagan was quoting 'High Flight', a sonnet written by John Gillespie Magee, a pilot with the Royal Canadian Air Force in the Second World War. Magee was killed at the age of nineteen, on 11 December 1941, during a training flight from the airfield near Scopwick, having come to Britain to fly in a Spitfire squadron (Rees 1992). In a letter to his parents, Magee says 'I am enclosing a verse I wrote the other day. It started at 30,000 feet and was finished soon after I landed'. The full text of the poem is:

> Oh! I have slipped the surly bonds of Earth
> And danced the skies on laughter-silvered wings;
> Sunward I've climbed and joined the tumbling mirth of sun-split clouds,
> And done a hundred things you have not dreamed of
> Wheeled and soared and swung
> High in the sunlit silence. Hov'ring there,
> I've chased the shouting wind along, and flung
> My eager craft through footless falls of air . . .
> Up, up the long, delirious, burning blue
> I've topped the wind-swept heights with easy grace
> Where never lark, nor ever eagle flew—
> And, while with silent lifting mind I've trod
> The high, untrespassed sanctity of space,
> Put out my hand and touched the face of God.

> ('High Flight' was published in 1943 in a volume called 'More Poems
> from the Forces', here transcribed by Rees from the original manuscript
> in the Library of Congress, and quoted by Rees 1992.)

Magee, like Phaethon, fell to and was buried on earth. Parts of his poem are engraved on his gravestone amid the military graves at Scopwick in Lincolnshire; he has been acclaimed as an early poet of the Second World War. In the same way that Nigel Rees talks of being drawn to visit Magee's grave, where even the petrol pump attendant at the service station was immediately able to size up his interest and direct him to the burial ground, so I, too, felt compelled to visit the Challenger Grave at the Arlington Cemetery in

Washington during a visit to the USA, where NASA and the White House can be viewed at a distance. The images of the explosion which filled the TV coverage, and the pictures taken whilst silently contemplating the grave, are still present with me today; like Phaethon's sisters, I felt rooted to the spot.

Concluding Comments

This journey through stories of Phaethon began with Ovid. Ovid's myths are about being playful with the banality of human existence, and his interests are human and contemporary:

Ovid takes mythology as a free space in which to play, in which to mock and extend, embrace, reject, invent and foreclose as he sees fit. He transposes it to the most familiar terms by removing that which is distant, divine, or supernatural and making the stories purely human and contemporary instead; his mythological world is very matter of fact. He turns mythology away from its concentration on the general and the generic, toward the illumination of unique moments in the life of the individual. (Solodow 1998: 75)

Ovid is prescient; the multi-dimensionality of stories, and the confusion between truth and fiction, fact and interpretation, is a current concern, but it is forestalled by Ovid, who enables the plasticity of his stories to celebrate metamorphosis and change. He baffles our senses as we soar from one level to the other, left reeling like Phaethon, like a fragment caught up in the chaos of the universe. His multi-dimensional approach to Phaethon, in his constant changing of register from distant to close, from the human to the supernatural, from exaggeration to understatement, underscores the plurality of ways in which a myth can be absorbed and interpreted. Ovid is an irreverent storyteller, something that keeps him apart from some of his more serious contemporaries such as Virgil, possibly a reason too for his exile from Rome by Augustus; he also knows how to tell a good story.

Ovid gives us just one author's perspective of Phaethon. The story of Phaethon had already been stolen by Ovid from others. Euripides had also written about this ancient myth and other authors had chosen different focal points—Heliades for example had concentrated on the story of Phaethon's sisters. Every writer taking up an ancient myth has their own tale to tell, their own angle of retake or deceit. It is not just authors and authorial intention, however, that breathe life into myths—the reader also has his or her own retake and motive. Barthes (1995: 127–9) has argued that: 'To give a text an Author is to impose a limit on that text, to furnish it with a final signified, to close the writing.'

Myths exist outside and beyond the author. But this does not mean that we have to go as far as Barthes, and kill the author, moving away from seeing 'him or her' as someone who nourishes a story or myth 'in the same relation of antecedence to his work as a father is to his child'. The handing down of a myth or a story from father to son, from mother to daughter, is an important part of its life; each telling and each reinterpretation creates the space for many more authors and readers.

We become attached to some myths, so that we may treat them as our personal property to mould to our will. But we cannot stop others from doing the same—no more than Ovid could stop Volkswagen from appropriating his Phaethon, or Euripides could stop Ovid, in turn, from doing the same. Nor can the families of the Challenger or Columbia victims prevent the stories of their children proliferating in the newspapers and media.

The power of a myth is to make thieves of us all; we may appropriate it in order to use it as our own lens. Myths, such as Phaethon's, can represent a number of different things to us, personal or social, entertainment or spectacle, product or branding, thrill or tragedy. Myths, more than any other type of story, expand beyond the boundaries of their authors: they are gifts from one generation to the next, and belong to us all.

References

Barthes, R. (1995). 'The Death of the Author', in S. Burke (ed.), *From Plato to the Post Modern*. Edinburgh: Edinburgh University Press. (Originally his preface to Brillat-Savarin's *The Physiology of Taste*, 1971).

Blake, W. (1789/1967). *Songs of Innocence and of Experience: Showing the Two Contrary States of the Human Soul*, a reproduction of the original. Oxford: Oxford University Press.

Diggle, J. (ed.) (1970). *Euripides Phaethon*. Cambridge: Cambridge University Press.

Feynman, R. (1993). *What Do You Care What Other People Think*. London: Harper Collins, Part 2.

Hofmann, M. and Lasdun, J. (1994). *After Ovid: New Metamorphoses*. London: Faber and Faber.

Hughes, T. (1997). *Tales from Ovid*. London: Faber and Faber.

Levita, D. J. de (1965). *The Concept of Identity*. New York: Basic Books. [Section 111 'Intermezzo—Phaethon'; 76–83.]

McDonnell (1987). *Challenger: A Major Malfunction*. New York: Simon and Schuster.

McHugh, P. (1986). 'Phaethon Goes Back to the Future', winner of Classical Association of New England Essay Contest, 1995, first published in *New England Classical Newsletter*.

Maxwell, G. (1994). 'Phaethon and the Chariot of the Sun—fragments of an Investigative documentary', in M. Hofmann and J. Lasdun (eds.), *After Ovid: New Metamorphoses*. London: Faber and Faber.

Morgan, G. (1989). 'The Challenger Disaster: A Case of Discouraged Feedback', in G. Morgan *Creative Organisation Theory*. London: Sage, 1–4.

Newbold, R. F. (2001). 'Narcissism and Leadership in Nonnus'. *Dionysiaca' Helios*, 28(2): 173–90.

Ovid (1987). *Metamorphoses*. (tr A. D. Melville) Oxford: Oxford University Press (with introduction and notes by E. J. Kenney).

Pelzer, P. (2002). 'Art for Management's Sake? A Doubt' unpublished paper.

Rees, N. (1992). 'High Flier' in *The "quote … unquote". Newsletter*, 1(2).

Rogers Commission (William P. Rogers, Chair) (1986). Report to the President by the Presidential Commission on the Space Shuttle Challenger Accident, US Printing Office, Washington, DC.

Solodow, J. B. (1988). *The World of Ovid's Metamorphoses*. Chapel Hill: University of North Carolina Press.

Schwartz, H. (1988). 'The Symbol of the Space Shuttle and the Degeneration of the American Dream'. *Journal of Organizational Change Management*, 1(2): 5–20.

Tremayne, D. (2003). *Donald Campbell: The man behind the mask*, Transworld; and quotes drawn from article of the same title by D. Tremayne, in *Classic and Sportscar Magazine*, 1997.

Wise, V. (1976–77) 'Flight Myths in Ovid's Metamorphosis: An interpretation of Phaethon and Daedalus'. *RAMUS*, 5–6: 44–57.

TWELVE

Demeter and the Curse of Consumption

Heather Höpfl

Lost Ideals

A T a time in history characterized by currents of apprehension, uncertainty, and anxiety about a future rendered precarious by terror; at a time of mediocrity paraded as high achievement, of avarice and an absence of compassion; at a time of forsaken idealism, of a failing imagination, and of work organizations regulated by feudal practices and medieval savagery; at such a time, it is not perhaps surprising to find that there is a renewed interest in the Greeks. Perhaps it is still possible to discover in Greek civilization some of the ideals of perfection which the modern era seems to lack, to rediscover aesthetic ideals of thinking, justice, and beauty, to rediscover meanings in myth and drama, music and dance, to find a system of philosophy which restores order to a disordered world; to find security in ideals of thought and form. In part, this backward look is towards a world of timeless absolutes, of immortal deities, and of clear archetypes: a world which can be interpreted by reference to archetypal principles. The Greek world is a world of geometry and mathematics, of lucid distinctions between light and darkness, love and hate, good and bad, and of clear moral and aesthetic values, where archetypal principles become personified in the deities who pronounce on and intervene in human activities (Tarnas 1991: 4). These deities play an important role in Greek thought, because they bring order and coherence to human destiny in a world in which the human world and the natural world are not conceived of as separate realms (Tarnas 1991: 17).

At the beginning of the twenty-first century, such apparent simplicities have considerable appeal: this is a time of excess. There is a preoccupation with production of all sorts, whether it be the production of abstract constructions or day-to-day objects—and the extent of such production is frenetic. Much of this production seems in some sense to be concerned with the desire to *define*, that is to say to *'finalize'* (L. [de]-finire, to finalize, to state exactly what a thing is) meaning. This is as true of the production of *theoria* as it is of the production of habits of mind, styles of living, and of those arte-facts which conspire in such constructions. Proliferating production is fre-quently justified on the grounds that it serves the interests of consumption, and, in the proliferation of excess, promises a liberating heterogeneity of choice and experience, of sublime objects and defining identities. The con-struction of sublime artefacts, objects of desire, personalities, 'life-styles', styles of interaction, ways of acting, ways of constructing identity, and so on becomes, however, an oppressive drudgery masquerading as an ever extend-ing choice—and choice itself becomes a bewildering illusion.

Of course, excessive production coexists with excessive consumption and, in the context of a concern with premodern narratives, the story of Demeter's terrible vengeance is salutary. Demeter is the goddess of vegetation and fertility, daughter of Cronos and Rhea; she is particularly thought of as the *Corn Mother*. In Italy she is associated with Ceres. Some have suggested that her name comes from the Cretan word *deai* meaning barley (Frazer 1925: 399), although this is regarded as etymologically dubious, or from dē, the ancient word for 'earth' (Hornblower and Spawforth 1998: 218), and, of course, from *meter* meaning mother. It is also said that her name means *Mother Earth* and that the Athenians referred to the dead as *Demeter's people* interred in the earth (Cotterell 2000: 34). In the *Iliad*, Homer refers to 'blonde Demeter' (*Il.* 5.500) to evoke the image of corn and barley.

Consumption and regurgitation have a role in many of the stories of Demeter. The story of Cronos devouring his children, because of a warning that he will be displaced by one of his sons, is well known. His youngest son Zeus is taken to Crete to be protected from his father, but Cronos swallows his other children, Poseidon, Hades, Hera, Hestia, and Demeter, together with a stone which Rhea wraps in bundling and pretends is Zeus. When Zeus comes of age, he forces his father to regurgitate the other children. Hence, the story of Demeter begins with consumption and disgorging. Even the familiar story of Demeter's daughter, Kore/Persephone, hinges on monitions about eating. Zeus, the father of Persephone, arranges for her to be the bride of his brother Hades, and for her to rule the underworld with him. However, Hades, impa-tient to establish this relationship, abducts Persephone and carries her away to the world of the dead. Forcibly removed from her own world, Persephone refuses to eat any food and pines for her release. Demeter is so distressed by the abduction of her daughter that she, too, loses interest in fertility and growth. As a result, the crops wither, animals do not reproduce, and all hope in the future is lost. In the face of such threatened famine, Zeus is forced to order Hades to release Persephone. However, Hades forces Persephone to eat a pomegranate seed (some say seven pomegranate seeds; Horowitz 1985: 35) and then, since she has eaten the food of the dead, she must spend a third of the year in the Underworld. It is Demeter's anger at the rape and abduction of her daughter Kore which brings sterility to the world.

The Lost Daughter

Before her abduction, Persephone has another name, Korē, meaning 'the girl', the daughter, and as such a girl, she is a deity of youth and joy, whereas as the wife of Hades, Persephone ('the source of wisdom') governs the fate of souls. Demeter also has the title Thesmophoros, which meant that she held a role as law giver. The Thesmophoria were an annual festival of Demeter that took place in the autumn, at the time of sowing. There was a festival, which was largely secret and in which participation was restricted to women. Persephone was honoured at her own festival, the Pherephattia, and, in Cyzicus, had the title of Soteira (saviour) in reference to her Return and to the saving of the world from famine. The relationship between Demeter and Persephone is so close that they are sometimes referred to as 'the Two Goddesses' and sometimes as 'the Demeters' (Dē mēteres) (Hornblower and Spawforth 1998: 218).

Indeed, another myth, the story of Tantalus, ruler of a kingdom in Asia Minor, provides evidence of the extent to which Demeter becomes distracted by her grief at being separated from Persephone. This story tells the grisly tale of how Tantalus cut up, stewed, and served his own son, Pelops, to the gods in order to test their omniscience. All the gods realised what had been done and recoiled in horror, except Demeter, who was so consumed with grief for her daughter that she did not notice and ate the flesh from the left shoulder. Later, when the gods restored Pelops to life, the piece of his shoulder which Demeter had eaten was missing and had to be replaced with a piece of ivory. Thus, Demeter is an icon of grief, an expression of the pain of loss and separation, and the initiates of the Mysteries of Eleusis had to demonstrate by imitation the grief felt by Demeter and Persephone at being separated (Freke and Gandy 2002: 138).

There are a number of themes here which are of interest: rape, abduction, loss, separation, return, and restoration. This chapter, however, directs its focus primarily at the theme of consumption: a father consuming his children for fear of being displaced by one of them; a mother so consumed with grief that she eats distractedly and consumes whatever is put before her; a daughter who pines and does not eat when forced into a union which is not of her choosing. However, the starting point for the discussion presented here begins with another violation—that of Demeter's sacred grove. It shows another face of Demeter's anger and another story of her revenge. It is an ancient story and yet it has immediate resonance with contemporary experience.

Violation

This account is based on the writings of the poet and grammarian Callimachus. He was the librarian of the Library of Alexandria and wrote in the third century BC. Ptolemy II appointed him as the librarian of the great library of Alexandria, and he held this post for more than twenty years. It is thought that he wrote approximately 800 books, including a catalogue of the works in the library. Callimachus is considered to be the founder of a critical approach to Greek literature, and many of his works demonstrate a sophisticated and elaborate structure. He seems to have been particularly concerned with the relationship between poetic form and content, and with the reconciliation of the intellectual content of the poem with its emotional consequence. There is an attempt, regarding the spirit of this chapter, to achieve a consonance in form and content, which is analogous to the stylistic intentions of Callimachus; in particular, there is an attempt to achieve a resonance between the intellectual content of the chapter and its emotional consequence; hence, the chapter seeks to set a tone that is in part heroic and in part vernacular.

The concern is first with his Hymn to Demeter, which invokes Demeter as a personification of the earth, as the goddess of plenty, as a figure of authority, and as an avenger of violations. It is also with the form of the poem and the intentions of the poet. In his commentary on 'The Hymn to Demeter', Hopkinson says of Callimachus that he 'guides us... into a subjective and highly literary story... (where) he lurks apart behind the insubstantial voice, and we are left with a poem *in vacuo*, a narrative whose obvious emotion and subjectivity have no definable referent. This is a disconcerting effect...' (Hopkinson 1984: 3). It suggests a structure which is haunted by subjectivity, of a presence carried by the text.

The Story

The story of the hymn runs as follows. In ancient times, the Pelasgians created a grove in honour of Demeter. The grove was so dense that an arrow could hardly penetrate its foliage. The grove was a *locus amoenus*, it was idyllic; yet, as Hopkinson comments, the scene 'is already undermined by a violence latent in the language and imagery' (Hopkinson 1984: 5), so that water 'boils up' from the ditches and the goddess is described as 'madly fond' of her grove. The peace of the grove is soon to be ruptured by the arrival of Erysichthon, and of twenty of his retainers, who rush into the grove and attack the largest tree, a huge poplar of supernatural size. Hearing the sounds of the axe and the shriek of the tree, Demeter disguises herself as her former priestess, Nicippe, and three times warns Erysichthon that he will incur the goddess's wrath if he continues. Erysichthon is not to be deterred and responds with a speech of 'verbal violence' (Hopkinson 1984: 7) in which he arrogantly explains that his purpose in taking the tree is to provide a roof for his banqueting-hall. Demeter is speechless with anger and assumes her own form. She towers to heaven and terrifies the servants who flee in dread. Her punishment is severe. She punishes him with a hunger that is wild and insatiable, which wracks his body with desire.

> At once she cast on him a dreadful hunger, burning and
> powerful, and he
> was tortured by the great disease. Poor wretch! Whatever
> he ate he desired as much again
>
> (Hymn to Demeter, 67–8)

She condemns him to consume and consume and consume; he can neither cease consuming nor be satisfied with his consumption; his mother and sisters, his old nurse and the serving-maids, all weep for him; his mother remembers him at the breast:

> 'His mother wept; and his two
> Sisters and the breast which had nursed him and the
> Many tends of slave-girls all uttered heavy groans'
>
> (*Hymn to Demeter*, 95–6)

His father shares his despair: the youth is doomed to endless consumption. Strangely, however, the story does not tell of Erysichthon's fate: the last section of the poem describes in detail the festival of the Thesmophoria, and a fertility ritual involving a sacred basket drawn on a cart by four white horses, followed by women who are barefoot and bareheaded; there is no resolution, no moral ending, no plea for mercy—there is only the curse.

Revenge

In terms of content, this is a story of vengeance: Demeter, the mother, Goddess of agriculture, fertility, and growth, takes revenge on the youth who violates her sacred grove, and condemns him to insatiable consumption. His punishment is that he will never be satisfied. He will consume endlessly, but never be replete. Worse, the more he eats the hungrier he will become, and eventually he will be reduced to eating trash and filth by the roadside. This is a terrifying metaphor of a relentless quest without satisfaction, of continual consumption, of hunger without relief. Clearly, there are innumerable ways in which this allegory might serve as a cautionary tale of contemporary life. One might draw ecological parallels as readily as individual ones. Perhaps the most important point in all this is the relationship between consumption and being consumed: one consumes and is consumed in the process. The relentless consumption of the youth consumes him. He is wasted by consumption and, of course, the story of Demeter herself and her grief for Persephone is one of being consumed by grief and destroyed by it, and, in her distraction, of consuming human flesh. It is apparent that consumption is a reflexive term which turns against itself: that which consumes is consumed. Clearly, there are many levels on which this correspondence works, but the point here is that the more frenetic the consumption, the greater the extent to which the consumer is consumed. Of course, this is quite obvious and evident in the behaviours and practices of modern life. This chapter seeks to illustrate some of the ways in which this process occurs, and ultimately to consider its significance for organizational life; first, however, it is necessary to give some attention to the originality of the work produced by Callimachus, which is quite unlike the conventional structures of his time.

Callimachus attempted to produce a new genre of poetic writing, in which intellect and emotion coexist and produce what Hopkinson has called 'a sophisticated dissonance' (Hopkinson 1984: 13). The order of the hymns is unusual, in that Callimachus presents a symmetrical arrangement of two short, two long, and two short poems. The first pair is masculine, the second pair mixed, and the third pair feminine. The short poems are mimetic, the long middle sections are epic, and the last two poems are written in a Doric dialect, which Hopkinson relates to their unheroic subject matter. However, he concedes that there may be no good reason, other than experimentation and a fondness for dialect, which prompts the 'feminine' poems to be written in this way. On the other hand, given that Callimachus is seeking to experiment with the relationship between the intellect and the effects of emotion, this movement could be a softening of the verse away from the epic style of the middle section, and into the feminine and vernacular closing poems.

In the following section, I have tried to follow Callimachus' example in using such 'sophisticated dissonance' in order to allow the intellect and emotion to coexist, first in the telling of six stories about consumption, and second in the tension which these stories create within the structure of the text as a whole. What follows, then, is a series of everyday observations which have a bearing on excess consumption, which are all based on experience, and which provide insight into the doubling effect of consuming, in which the consumer is 'him or herself' consumed.

The Stories

IABD Conference, 2001: The Holiday Inn, International Drive, Orlando, Florida

I came down in the lift with a huge man. His stomach was so big, that I had to stand to one side to avoid coming into contact with it. He was wearing shorts of such enormous size that they looked as if six people of average weight might fit into them. He was very sweaty and breathless. The act of carrying what must have been more than twice his optimal weight seemed a great burden. I saw him later outside Burger King; he had a huge bucket of what might have been chicken wings; these he rested under his arm, tucked in against his great stomach, and he consumed them with an almost mechanical movement. I was amazed by the size of many of the people on the street. Two women were eating gigantic hamburgers from great fists. One of the women was so large that her bottom half resembled a colossal parsnip: vast white hips tapering to tiny feet. I went into a sportswear shop across from the hotel. There I saw clothes large enough to sleep a troop of boy scouts. Outside, the victims of this terrible and relentless consumption continued to eat and to physically demonstrate their servitude to consumerism. Those enormous bodies testified to the inevitable logic of production. As I looked at those distended bodies, those gross excesses of flesh, I was profoundly saddened. It seemed to me that those massive bodies existed in order to validate excessive production, and that their destiny might be fulfilled by being made to sit open-mouthed at the end of the production line. This grotesque image has haunted me ever since. These people were not monsters driven by greed; they were the living demonstration of the success of production: consummate consumers.

Lancaster City Centre, Midnight

On Dalton Square, Queen Victoria gazes with condescension from her canopied pedestal as hordes of drunken young people swarm through the centre of the town. There is a police car parked at the corner of the square. In it two policemen sit watching and waiting for the disorder that will inevitably come as the night progresses. A stream of some ten or twelve drunken girls, all arm-in-arm, unsteadily meandered from one club to another: half dressed, stumbling, calling out vulgarities at passing men, 'on the pull', 'getting pissed', falling over, throwing up—a good night out. Young men in shirt-sleeves in sub-zero temperatures, singing football anthems or popular songs, go marauding through the streets of the old town: threatening other groups of men, propositioning groups of girls, urinating in the street, they are hell-bent on getting 'wasted'. The owner of a night-club speaking on Radio 4 says that he finds young women semi-clothed, passed out, having lost their handbags, their mobile phones, their virtue, lying on the floor of the women's toilets—wash-basins full of vomit. Women who boast they can drink several pints of lager and follow it up with ten or more shots. Men who find satisfaction in describing just how drunk they were, how many bottles they managed to put away, how much they had consumed.

Airline Cabin Crew

Well, it was very different before the culture change. We used to get fairly smashed at the end of a trip. Especially on long haul, of course. The room parties were famous. Some would say notorious. We used to take the unused miniatures from the flight and get a few bottles of cheap local booze. It was pretty amazing stuff. But, then, airlines were different in those days. You used to push aside the stresses of the job by drinking yourself insensible. Nowadays you have to be professional, and find your own way of dealing with it. Someone once said to me that airline cabin crew were like professional actors and that at the end of a show there is a fair amount of drinking and partying— that this was the way to find yourself again after having been someone else, that is, performing for other people. I suppose making yourself *available* to passengers is a bit like that. An actor once told me that at the end of a show you are physically exhausted but, at the same time, you are on a high, and that you have to drink to bring both states together; I must say that was certainly how I used to feel. Younger people don't seem to be as bothered about it as I was, but at times I think that is not such a good thing. Perhaps the company is everything to them and they don't see any other way—but I do not think so. Well, isn't that what they used to talk about in the culture change days—'winning the hearts and minds'? They do not draw the same line between work and life as we did, and I do not know which I think is worse: that we tried to keep a part of ourselves out of our work, or that the new crews do not seem to see a difference. I suppose it could be the way they protect themselves. If you put less in, you are less likely to be eaten alive by the job.

An Ill Wind

In the early 1990s, I was working with Stephen Linstead at Lancaster University on a management development programme for a major UK company. As part of the programme, we explored issues of emotional labour, and asked participants to provide examples drawn from their experiences of the workplace. One story concerned a newly appointed manager who was 'very full of himself'. This young man was apparently very quick to assume what he saw as the managerial role, and this had obvious consequences for his staff, who were expected to demonstrate appropriate deference to his self-importance. For about three weeks after his promotion, they reluctantly and grudgingly gave him the approbation he demanded of them, but then they began to formulate a plan for revenge. One afternoon, this pretentious and narcissistic new manager had an important meeting in his office: one of the company's senior managers was coming to hear his plans for the development of his area. He was not to be disturbed at any price. He would go down to the reception himself to greet his guest. Did they all realise how important this was for him? He planned the visit with meticulous care. Reports and graphics were prepared but he would present them. He did not want his staff to spoil his opportunity to make a big impression on the visitor, and he made this clear to them. He arrived in the morning, smartly dressed, a spring in his feet, a confident air. Unfortunately, what he could not have anticipated was that his staff, now thoroughly disaffected by his posturing, planned to bring him down. His glass-walled office beautifully ordered and polished, with fresh flowers on his desk, he responded to the call from the reception to greet his guest. However, while he was out of the office, his staff arranged for a colleague with an unenviable but practised capacity for expressing bodily wind to enter the office and emit a foul and obnoxious flatus. Then, the unsuspecting manager returned to his office, proudly opened his office door, and ushered in his guest to be greeted by the fetid smell his staff had left for him. The glass walls of the office made a theatre of this event, and as the new manager looked round at his colleagues, he was met by their various faces regarding him with a strange mixture of affected innocence, contempt, and satisfaction at achieving some degree of retaliation.

Air France Flight to Cape Town, 1994

It was the time of the atrocities in Rwanda and I was flying to Cape Town with a colleague. As is common with most airlines, the monitor screens gave us regular updates on our progress as we flew south across the African continent. The quality of service at that time was excellent and the crew kept the passengers provided with good quality food and drink. The lunch was smoked salmon and there were liberal servings of champagne. My colleague drank steadily and with enjoyment. The route map now showed that we were passing over Rwanda; 35,000 feet below us, people were being hacked to death with machetes, men were being rounded up and massacred, women and children were being brutally murdered, and we flew over drinking champagne and eating smoked salmon. As we passed through this vertically segmented space, as we moved from one centre of civilization to another in the security of the aeroplane, I felt like the angel of death flying over. At 35,000 feet champagne and smoked salmon and at ground level butchered human flesh.

Veni Creator Spiritus

Liverpool's Anglican Cathedral provided the venue for a rare performance of Mahler's Eighth Symphony, the 'Symphony of a Thousand'. The cathedral was packed to the doors. The choirs and orchestra took up a large section of the transept. The huge sandstone columns and high walls of the nave produced an extraordinary effect in the sound and especially in the choral pieces. It was as if the entire building vibrated like an enormous speaker, as if every molecule in one's body vibrated with the sound; it was as if the audience was dissolved in the sound, lost in the music. Veni, veni creator spiritus: the music calls forth the Holy Spirit. This is the symphony that Mahler wrote following a period of despair and an inability to compose: a time when he felt that he had lost his creative powers. It combines the old Latin hymn, the De Profundis, *Out of the Depths (I cry to thee)*, with extracts from Goethe's Faust:

> Alles Vergängliche
> Ist nur ein Gleichnis;
> Das Unzulängliche
> Hier wirds Ereignis;
> Das Unbeschreibliche,
> Hier ist's getan;
> Das Ewigweibliche
> Zieht uns hinan
>
> (Goethe, *Faust* Part II Lines 12104–end).

> All transient things
> are but a parable;
> the insufficient
> here becomes actuality;
> here the ineffable
> is achieved;
> the Eternal-Feminine
> draws us onwards.
>
> (Translation Luke, D. 1964 *Goethe, Selected Verse*,
> Harmondsworth: Penguin.)

Well, of course, not everyone might share my love of Mahler, nor my rapture about the performance, yet for me the evening was made unforgettable not by these things, but by the anonymous woman who sat directly behind me. She was obviously constrained by the length of the performance that inhibited her need to pass on her latest news to her companion. Consequently, very early in the performance, and in the first available quiet passage, she began: 'By the way, did I tell you that Nigel is working in Sydney now. Well, he's got a really good job with one of the big consulting firms. They are expecting to be there for at least three years. He might work in Hong Kong for part of the time but they will be based in Sydney. Fiona and the children have gone with him this time. Yes, they flew them all out Business Class. He is doing very well. They have an absolutely enormous harbour-view apartment and he is chauffeur-driven almost everywhere he goes. He says they do everything for him. They are paying the fees for the children to go to an international school... he's done so well for himself. We are very proud of him'. She rattled on and on, and, although common sense might say that I should have turned and asked her to shut up, it seemed to demand too much of me that I acknowledge her intrusion. After all, *Alles Vergängliche ist nur ein Gleichnis*—everything that passes is only an appearance—so both she and her Nigel and his success dissolved into mere appearance.

A Premodern Myth, Six Millennial Stories, and Some Organizational Implications

What is striking about the story of Demeter is the emphasis on consumption; this theme recurs and is replayed in a range of different ways in her mythology, in her acts, in her vengeance, and in her legacy. It is a story that has immediate resonance with contemporary issues. So, the myth presents familiar stories of violation, revenge, greed, and excess (excess which is insatiable), as well as of nausea, nausea to the point of exhaustion, of vomiting, and the voiding of self; stories of revenge and the desire for retribution, of separation and grief, and the pain of loss, and, quite differently, of the separation that brings isolation from the source of grief that assures comfort while others suffer: consolation and absence of consolation. It is about what it is to consume and to be consumed. In the stories presented in this chapter, there is an attempt to explore some of the contemporary echoes of the Demeter story. In this concluding section, the intention is to indicate some organizational parallels. The point of this is to elevate and to give presence to the everyday stories of organizations. These are readily available and do not require much more than a sensitive ear to access. The stories of the workplace are the stuff of everyday conversation, of gossip and rumour, of the heroic and the tragic, certainly about revenge and reversal. Canetti's 'sting' is an enduring topic of conversation in work organizations (Canetti 1987; Cooper 1990; Linstead 1994). Here the assertion is simply that many of the stories of the workplace, like Demeter's own, are stories that have some association with consumption. Individuals are consumed by their emotions, are consummate in their personal preoccupations, are prudent or prodigal consumers—of food, of material goods, of ideas and ideologies. Yet, as the story of Demeter's malediction on Erysichthon shows, consumption is not really the pleasure it appears to be, but rather a curse.

Ritzer's powerful McDonalization Thesis (1998), as he applies it to the perceived violation of French/European culture by EuroDisney (Ritzer 1998: 73), offers a ready example of the story of the violation of the Sacred Grove, the rape of the *locus amoenus*. Indeed, the presence of a McDonald's fast food outlet at the foot of the steps leading up to the Rialto Bridge in Venice could likewise be seen as a violation: a province, an area acquired by conquest. By the same token, the presence of McDonalds fast food outlets across the world offers a production line image of endless production and consumption, of not so much fast food as fake food. Erysichthon reduced to eating rubbish in the streets, obliged to consume and consume without end: double burgers, double–double chocolate cookies, large fries, a bucket of chicken, a family sized pizza, jumbo sausages, an extra large carton of popcorn. These are the material signs of a preoccupation with ingestion. Of course, there are other forms of consumption and ingestion in a throw-away society which requires people to be insatiable in order to continue to function: the newer model, the latest version, the cultivation of contempt for the past, and always the voracious drive for the new. Excessive consumption means there is too much to take in (L. con-sumere, to take in wholly, completely): one is consumed by consuming, nauseous, and heaving with excesses. Yet, there is a paradox. The very excess is not itself a fullness, but a vacuity. Ironically, Erysichthon's fate was to waste away, like a nineteenth century *consumptive*: the more he consumed, the less there was of him. The contemporary parallels are obvious. There exist many organizational stories which demonstrate the consumption of individuals by organizations, and of excessive intrusion into personal space, in expectations of behaviour, dress, commitment, performance. It is not the intention of this chapter to examine these further. The six short stories serve to demonstrate the perennial concern with narratives of consumption, and to alert the reader to both their ubiquitous nature and their power. So, just as Callimachus 'guides us...into a subjective and highly literary story...(where) he lurks apart behind' the text (Hopkinson 1984: 3), so too this chapter has also sought to offer, in the spirit of the book, a narrative which engages both the intellect and the emotion.

The final remarks in this chapter are concerned with the possibility of satisfaction and of an end to relentless consumption; the Hymn itself to Demeter offers no easy resolution and no remedy. In the mysteries of Eleusis, Demeter was represented by bread and Dionysus by wine, suggesting a mystical feast of God and Goddess, male and female, masculine and feminine; hence, one of the interpretations of the Demeter myths concerns the desire for the reunion of *consciousness* with *the psyche*. In other words, a reunion in which Psyche—Goddess, Daughter/Wisdom—are restored to Consciousness—God, Son/Logos (Freke and Gandy 2002: 198–209). The Eleusian Mysteries, then, suggest a way in which the insatiable curse of consumption might, at length, be satisfied; appropriately enough to the story of a vengeful goddess, this reunion involves the restoration of Wisdom, of *sophia*, to Consciousness, by means of the restoration of the Daughter and the return of the fertility of the Mother. Well, clearly this is easier said than done, but at heart it is simply a call for wisdom.

References

Canetti, E. (1987). *Crowds and Power*. London: Penguin.
Cooper, R. (1990). 'Canetti's Sting'. *SCOS Notework*; 9(2/3): 45–53.
Cotterell, A. (2000). *Classical Mythology, the Ancient Myths and Legends of Greece and Rome*. London: Hermes House.
Frazer, J. G. (1925). *The Golden Bough*. London: Macmillan.
Freke, T. and Gandy, P. (2002). *Jesus and the Goddess*. London: Thorsons.

Hoad, T. F. (1986). *The Concise Oxford Dictionary of English Etymology*. Oxford: Oxford University Press.

Höpfl, H. (2001). 'Of Mothers and Measures: The Mystery of the Assumption', in N. Lee and R. Monro, (eds.), *The Consumption of Mass*. Sociological Review Monograph Series. Oxford: Blackwell.

Hopkinson, N. (1984). *Callimachus, Hymn to Demeter*. Cambridge: Cambridge University Press.

Hornblower, S. and Spawforth, A. (1998). *The Oxford Companion to Classical Civilization*. Oxford: Oxford University Press.

Horowitz, A. (1985). *Myths and Legends*. New York: Kingfisher Books.

Linstead, S. L. (1994). 'The Sting of Organization: Command, Reciprocity and Change Management'. *Journal of Organizational Change Management*, 7, 5: 4–19.

Ritzer, G. (1998). *The McDonaldization Thesis*. London: Sage.

Robertson, N. (1984). 'The ritual background of the Erysichthon story'. *American Journal of Philology*, 105: 369–408.

Tarnas, R. (1991). *The Passion of the Western Mind*. London: Pimlico.

IV

THE REFLEXIVE NARRATIVES: EMOTION, IDENTITY, AND THE NATURE OF RELATIONS IN ORGANIZATIONS

Introduction

R EFLEXIVITY is one of those terms that easily degenerates into a cliché or a fad, indicating anything that distinguishes and privileges one from an unre-flexive other (Lynch 2000). All too often, it is simply used to indicate 'reflec-tive', someone who is capable of taking a step back from experience and casting a look at it with a degree of detachment. Most positivists would not flinch from such an view—the very term 'theory' comes from the Greek 'theoria', taking a distant view of a phenomenon or a situation. The reflexive narratives that lie at the heart of the two chapters in this section go beyond such simplicities. What they offer is an account of their authors' rediscovery of themselves as scholars and participants of organizations through the act of telling a story that alters them as tellers of the story. In this way, the telling of the story becomes part of the creation of a self-identity. This self-identity cannot be fixed in time, since with every new utterance, with every new interpretation that which is being interpreted has already changed. As Giddens eloquently describes it:

in the post-traditional order of modernity, against the backdrop of new forms of mediated experience, self-identity becomes a reflexively organised endeavour. The reflexive project of the self, which consists in the sustaining of coherent, yet continuously revised, biographical narratives, takes place in the context of multiple choice as filtered through abstract systems. (Giddens 1991: 5)

Both chapters in this section illustrate clearly the situation in which the writing of the chapter becomes itself part of an identity narrative, the story that provides the initial inspiration, undergoing numerous mutations and metamorphoses as it gradually takes hold of the author's identity. Giddens again:

A person's identity is not to be found in behaviour, nor—important though it is—in the reactions of others, but in the capacity to keep a particular narrative going. The individual's biography, if she is to maintain regular interaction with others in the day-to-day world, cannot be wholly fictive. It must continually integrate events which occur in the external world, and sort them into the ongoing 'story' about the self. (Giddens 1991: 54)

This, then, is the enterprise of both authors in this section—an enterprise that allows us to witness at close quarters the process of self-metamorphosis in the telling of a story that changes itself in the course of being told. The story itself in both cases meets urgent desires, not merely to construct a valid self-narrative but to discover a truth that has evaded the authors for a long time.

One may question whether such self-reflexive narratives may lapse into solipsism or self-deception, in the sense that Wilkomirski's and Menchú's narratives did (see Chapter 1). After all, the narratives in this section do (like those of Wilkomirski and Menchú) seek to provide their authors with a voice that had previously eluded them. It seems to me that what both authors have striven to show is that the stories themselves are ones that exist in many variants, negotiated by many participants and in constant flux; the authors have entered no narrative contract that they may then stand accused of having violated. This clearly sets their narratives apart from the hardened narratives of Wilkomirski and Menchú and makes them in a real sense 'storying narratives'. If self-deception is part of this storying, the authors do not seek to conceal it.

The story of the velveteen rabbit, a toy animal that only comes alive when the child who owns it develops a bond of love with it, is in sharp juxtaposition with the heroics of a Hercules or a Cú Chulainn. Indeed, the gentle irony of the rabbit's Odyssey will not escape the reader. And yet, this twentieth century children's story provides the impetus of deep self-questioning and eventual intellectual conversion for David Sims. The story's theme, that love brings to life or literally 'animates', is one that has been endlessly rehearsed by storytellers and artists; we have already encountered it in Chapter 6, as the Eros that animates David's reign. Sims, therefore, asks why the same may not be true of organizations, some of which generate extraordinary amounts of loyalty among their participants, while others languish as mere objects of instrumental usefulness and emotional indifference. The idea that organizations do not exist as independent objects is itself one with a long lineage and one that has become something of a velveteen rabbit in its own right, inspiring strong loyalty among a large group of theorists. In his chapter, Sims allows his love of organization to prevail over his love for the idea that organizations are 'merely' social constructions. Emotional as well as cognitive processes are involved in constructing a living organization.

Love, of course, is not an entirely benevolent emotion — hard acts have often been motivated by it. As Heather Höpfl (1992) and Howard Schwartz (1987) remind us in important articles, love for an organization can turn individuals into uncritical acolytes, capable of ruthless acts of injustice in its name. Sims is equally aware that love for an organization can itself be translated into neglect of one's family, one's friends, or oneself. One should not therefore jump into any easy conclusions about love helping to resolve all the problems and all the tensions; what is undeniable is that if many organizations are capable of generating passion in us, they cannot be treated purely as cognitive constructions.

The gaberlunzie is a fascinating Scottish folk character, the beggar who asks a farmer for a night's lodging only to disappear by the next morning, taking the farmer's daughter with him. In some variants, the gaberlunzie turns out to be a sexual predator, while in others he turns out to be a rich man travelling incognito who falls in love with the farmer's daughter and carries her away. This core ambiguity in the gaberlunzie character is drawn out to great effect in a narrative tour de force by Tony Watson (Chapter 14), who transposes the story to a gaberlunzie *girl*; she enters the life of a young man with folkloristic interests, drawing him out of his cosseted existence and eventually starting a music and publishing business with him. In a multi-layered narrative with numerous stories within stories, Watson depicts the constant transformation of the gaberlunzie story as it animates the relationship between the couple and becomes their organization's foundation myth. Once a person has been recognized as a gaberlunzie, reality can only be experienced through certain inevitable frames. 'Is he true or is he false?' 'Is it a garden path or the road to perdition?' 'Will their relation endure?' 'How can they reconcile love and business in their relationship?' And so forth.

Watson embodies the spirit of this book, in highlighting how an old ballad may not only enable the thoroughly modern characters of his story to make sense of their situation, but conditions their anxieties, hopes, and even feelings for each other. Like Winstanley (Chapter 11), Watson also shows the impossibility of guarding the story's text, protecting it from wrong-doers and clumsy spin-doctors. In an interesting twist in the tale, the couple at the centre of the story lose their story when the media appropriate it. They are confronted by troubles in a marriage, imminent business collapse, and a story that is no longer theirs to write or to complete. By inventing the gaberlunzie girl and telling her story, Watson, like Sims, like Case, and like Winstanley and maybe every author in this book, reinvents his own identity as a social theorist of organizations— he finally allows himself to create theory by writing fiction.

References

Giddens, A. (1991). *Modernity and Self-Identity: Self and Society in the Late Modern Age*. Stanford, CA.: Stanford University Press.

Höpfl, H. (1992). 'The Making of the Corporate Acolyte'. *Journal of Management Studies*, 29(1): 23–34.

Lynch, M. (2000). 'Against Reflexivity as an Academic Virtue and Source of Privileged Knowledge'. *Theory, Culture and Society*, 17(3): 26–54.

Schwartz, H. S. (1987). 'Anti-social actions of committed organizational participants: An existential psychoanalytic perspective'. *Organization Studies*, 8(4): 327–40.

THIRTEEN

The Velveteen Rabbit and Passionate Feelings for Organizations

David Sims

T HIS chapter is built around two stories. One is an old children's story about a velveteen rabbit, well known to many people, but one that I somehow missed in my childhood. The other is the story of how this children's story affected me when I came across it in my middle age. I heard it on a car radio while driving to my work at a university, and I immediately started to change my mind about some theoretical ideas that had been important to me for a long time. Years of theoretical arguments with others had strengthened my views in one direction; this children's story then produced a rapid, 'Damascus road' conversion: years of theoretical thinking were undermined by a rabbit.

Telling the Story

The Velveteen Rabbit (Williams 1922) is a story about a Boy who is given a velveteen rabbit for Christmas. He really likes his new Rabbit, but then he is given a lot of other new presents later in the day, and he forgets the Rabbit. Most of the other toys look down on the Rabbit, because they were more expensive, or because they represent something real, like a boat; none of them have ever heard of real rabbits. The Rabbit wonders about this idea of being real, and asks his friend the Skin Horse about it.

'What is REAL?' asked the Rabbit one day. ... 'Does it mean having things that buzz inside you and a stick-out handle?'

'Real isn't how you are made,' said the Skin Horse. 'It's a thing that happens to you. When a child loves you for a long, long time, not just to play with, but REALLY loves you, then you become Real.'

One evening, the Boy cannot find the china dog that he always sleeps with, so he is given the Velveteen Rabbit instead. Being velveteen, the Rabbit does comfort well. The child comes to love the rabbit more and more, and as he does so, the rabbit gradually comes to life. He is acknowledged by the Boy, the Skin Horse, and the other toys as being REAL.

The story goes on from there, as I shall explain later in the chapter, but this is where the version that I originally heard ended. This is as much of the story as we need to start talking about velveteen rabbits, reality, and organizations. It could have been another story; the Velveteen Rabbit is an archetypal story, and many other stories down the years have had a similar theme, and might have had a similar effect on my thinking. For example, a very similar moral is to be found in the film 'Toy Story'.

Meeting a Rabbit

I first heard this story a few years ago on my car radio on my way to work. I was listening to a general news-and-current-affairs programme from the BBC, in the middle of which there is a brief religious reflection. I have no idea who the speaker was (although I remember it as a woman's voice) or what point he or she was trying to make, but the story that was used was that of the Velveteen Rabbit. At the time, I was trying to make a difference as the Head of a Business School, and I had been thinking about organizations that I knew that seemed to me to perform persistently above or below my expectations, given their resources and opportunities. By the time I had reached my office, I was beginning to think about organizations as velveteen rabbits, coming to life when they were loved. By the following morning, I had become aware of several situations which were illuminated for me by thinking about whether there was anyone loving an organization or a part of it to life. I had also thought of several examples from my past experience that seemed to point in the same direction.

However, the idea that we might reasonably love our organizations, and that such love might be important for the way those organizations function, held problems of its own. Like many social scientists, I saw organizations as constructions: as having no reality of their own, other than being a mental construct projected for the sake of convenience onto a group of phenomena.

Academically, I had been brought up to believe in a dispassionate relationship with an organization. This relationship is based on the precept that organizations provide us with employment and security in return for our giving them our time, our skills, as well as our conformity to their demands ('organizational demands' also being a reifying concept, but one which has escaped censure). The view that we could, and indeed should, have dispassionate relations with our employing organization has been dominant over the last few decades, having been legitimized by Weber (Weber 1948) and the theorists of bureaucracy. Organizations have been dominated by a contractual view of the relationship between the member and the organization. The virtues of building a career by moving around, and by avoiding moral identification with your employer, have been emphasized, and at the theoretical level students have been given bad marks for personifying organizations. Even reification has been severely frowned upon, as lending the organization a spurious existence. Reification, it has been argued, can lead to muddled thinking and understanding about organizations. There is something almost quaint about loving your organization, something that suggests an innocent heroic identification with it, the moral counterpart of being treated paternalistically by the organization. It is reminiscent of old-fashioned children's stories, in which deeds of great heroism are carried out in the name of, say, defending your school.

I was trained to be wary of reification. Within such a framework, anyone who loves their organization is misguided, and may need help. At the same time, I saw organizations that drew love from some of their members, even when those participants had been taught that it was naughty to reify or personify organizations. Whatever the arguments, some people were willing to love their organization, and the organization seemed somehow to come to life in response to that love.

Led by a Rabbit

I acknowledge the power of this dilemma with some reluctance. I have spent some twenty-five years writing and thinking about organizations as individual and social constructions, and I am reluctant to have my mind changed by the resonances of a children's story. However, while I can still rehearse the arguments against reification, the idea that people can bring an organization to life by loving it convinces me far more. This idea has narrative truth and sense-making power. I give examples in this chapter of organizations being loved to life. I might not have recognized these before I was both liberated and captivated by the Velveteen Rabbit.

It is clear that many people have passionate feelings towards organizations, whether of love or hate. The more I thought about the Velveteen Rabbit, the more cases I could think of where it seemed to me that these feelings affect the effectiveness of the organization. Knowing in organizations is not dispassionate; people love and hate their organizations, and form 'meaningful long-term relationships' with them that are more reminiscent of their relationships with other people than of their relationships with things. In Bertrand Russell's terms, much organizational knowing is attained by acquaintance rather than by description alone (Russell 1946).

Dialogue with a Rabbit

As I thought more about the story of the Velveteen Rabbit, I found myself beginning to reconsider some of the prohibitions regarding personification. They seemed to me to date back to early studies in organization, which pointed out that organizations were not people, not having eyes, hands, brains, etc. It was therefore a category error to attribute personal characteristics to organizations, and it was likely to lead to conceptual confusion, otherwise known as woolly thinking. So both for the purpose of working in them, as well as for studying them, we have been through a long period where the orthodoxy about organizations is that they should not be seen as objects endowed with existence, and certainly not as persons. Having dialogued with the Velveteen Rabbit, I would now argue that the anti-personifying view is based on a model of organizations as mechanisms, which has been the sociological orthodoxy but which has never persuaded people not to treat organizations more like persons. The feelings of love, hate, or indifference that so many have felt for their organizations over time are soundly based on experience, and are not simply a category error.

To speak of organizations as if they were people has a long history. For example:

For just as the body is one and has many members, and all the members of the body, though many, are one body, so it is with Christ. For in the one Spirit we were all baptized into one body—Jews or Greeks, slaves or free—and we were all made to drink of one Spirit. Indeed, the body does not consist of one member but of many. If the foot were to say, 'Because I am not a hand, I do not belong to the body', that would not make it any less a part of the body. And if the ear were to say, 'Because I am not an eye, I do not belong to the body, that would not make it any less a part of the body. If the whole body were an eye, where would hearing be? If the whole body were hearing, where would the sense of smell be? (1 Corinthians 12: 12–16, NRSV).

St Paul is here engaged in a piece of personification. No doubt it was meant figuratively, but this image of the Church as a body has been a powerful one for two millennia, and has generated and sustained many narratives by means of which people have understood themselves and what they are doing within Western culture.

The mechanistic view of organizations was well exemplified by Mrs Thatcher's statement, when she was British Prime Minister, that 'there is no such thing as society'. In saying this, Mrs Thatcher may have unwittingly made many of us realise that there must be something wrong with the anti-personification rules. If there is no such thing as society, then to speak of improving society is nonsense. But if that really is nonsense, it would equally be nonsense to speak of making society worse, and yet we could see her doing it.

I suggest that the presumption against reification has persisted well after its intellectual justification has lost its power, even though it took a Velveteen Rabbit to point this out to me. Let us now consider some organizational examples of what happens when we listen to the practical theorizing of people who are not ashamed to have feelings towards their organizations, and who talk about the relationship between those feelings and the organization coming to life.

Rabbit Tales

The Rabbit Comes to Life

Even those who are sceptical about the importance of leadership will often acknowledge that the head of a primary or secondary school can be very influential over the quality of that school. In this section, I want to consider two cases of heads who are well known to their staff and their pupils for their extreme level of commitment to, and love for, their schools. Both are heads of UK comprehensive schools which had evolved from previously selective state schools. In both cases, at the time described, the heads had been in post for about eight to ten years. This is quite a long time for anyone to be doing any job, and already says something about the relationship between the person and the job. In both cases, the schools had been successful and highly thought of at the time the current head was appointed.

In the first case, Mrs Holden had come from being head of a less well-thought of school, which (it was said) she had improved greatly but not to anywhere near the standard of her new institution, which is a girls' comprehensive school. She said (quite frequently, with variations):

> I eat, drink and sleep this School. All the girls are uncut
> diamonds, just waiting to be polished.

This claim was universally accepted by both pupils and teachers. Whenever there was a school event, of whatever size, for example, a concert involving twelve sixth-formers performing pieces for their music exams, she would be there. Every girl in the school who was especially commended by a teacher would go and see Mrs Holden for personal congratulation. Every parent and child would be interviewed by her before arriving at the school. Of course, not all teachers or pupils liked her very hands-on style, but none of them seemed to have anything other than complete respect for her. She had a clear view of the purpose of the school, which was that it should be the best possible school for those who wanted to do well by their own efforts, regardless of their ability or background. When asked why her school's results were excellent, despite non-selective admission, she said that it was because only pupils who wanted to work hard went there; anyone else would be frightened off by her or by the school's reputation for success achieved through effort.

Her affection for the school seemed to be infectious. Pupils would come out with phrases which you would have thought had been made up expressly for the brochure; 'I really love this school'. Teachers would behave as if they loved it, showing affection and care to the pupils and loyalty and commitment of time to the school, well beyond the demands even of good professional standards. In the other case that I wish to discuss, Mr Beamish appeared to have an equal love for his school. Again, he would always be there, always involved, always expressing his respect and admiration for his pupils and staff. But it did not work the same way; with him, pupils and teachers did not seem to believe that his love was genuine. They regarded his commitment as cloyingly false, rather than as a genuine love of the school. Mrs Holden never said that she was attending everything in order to set a good example; she was there because she enjoyed it and because she expected to learn from it. Mr Beamish could not resist pointing out his commitment, and this made his enthusiasm less infectious.

In these cases, we see two institutions both running very well, but one significantly better than the other. We see those institutions being loved by their leaders, and this appearing in turn to be an important part of their success. We see one case where this love came across to others as being more for its own sake than the other, where it had more of a flavour of duty, and we become therefore aware that it is not only love that brings an organization to life, but also the style of that love.

Making Your own Loveable Rabbit

My next example of the implications of love for an organization comes from a small business which combines music, publishing, and stationery. Regular customers or old friends (not two distinct groups) of the owner/manager receive a regular newsletter from him about both sides of the business. In his May 2001 edition, he reflects on what he enjoys in his organization:

I am currently ten years into my second calling as a stationery tycoon and twenty five years into my first love—music publishing. And one thing never fails to bring out the very best of me—kicking sh*t out of the competition, especially if that competition is of the establishment persuasion... Come to either of my shops, by contrast, and you will encounter an individual who has a true *Passion* for Paper. Not only do I *personally* test every size, shade and texture of paper and card through my five Canon copiers before putting it on sale, but an informal panel of customers does tests for me on printers of all types. (Brunton 2001)

The evidence that this person not only has a 'passion for paper', but also loves the organization that he has set up, comes in the size of his monthly newsletter, and the attention that he lavishes on it. The May 2001 edition, quoted above, consisted of thirty-six A4 pages, and was a 'Double entendre special issue', with some eight pages of the same kind of material as in the above quotation, interspersed with specimens of the music he publishes or advertisements for the stationery that he sells. The difference between this and the other examples is that here the person has created the organization that is the object of his affection, and thus he might arguably be expected to have a different relationship with it. He has made his own Rabbit. He is crafting the object of his own affections, so it is not surprising that he loves it (although there are plenty of people who do not seem to love their own businesses).

Avoiding the responsibility of love

Brian had taken active part in building up a very successful department in a small University. After several years of service as a senior (though very young) professor, he left to take up a job in a larger University. There were several different versions of the story he could give (Linde 1993), including that his wife worked in the University he was now joining, that they could now walk to work together, and so on. Another version was that he had helped build his former department to be as good as it was going to get, and it was time to start again. However, one of his versions was that the main advantage of a large University was that you did not get to feel any kind of identification with it, or emotion for it. As he said:

It's wonderful. I just do my teaching and then I get back to my research. I'm not always worrying about how to make the University better, or the department better. There's no risk of falling in love! . . . The whole thing's bigger and older, and I just take it that it has grown up and does not need caring for any more.

He is extolling the benefits to the employee of not loving your organization. However, he is also acknowledging that he did love the previous one, and does not regret it. With his child-rearing metaphor, he has introduced the possibility of different kinds of relationship at different stages; to treat a teenage child as a baby is an inappropriate and harmful form of love, and may well express one's needs for domineering power rather than love. A loving relationship will change and develop over time, as indeed does the relationship between the Boy and the Velveteen Rabbit. It is also interesting that, whatever he says about the requirement to love the earlier, smaller University, he left it. So the love was not unqualified.

In most organizations, if we all worked simply in accordance with our contracts and our job descriptions, the institution would not be able to function at all. We depend on people serving in a way that is invisible to outsiders, or even many insiders, if the institution is to perform well. There used to be an appalling suggestion from trainers on stress management courses, to 'find ways of getting the monkey off your back onto other peoples' backs'. This is classic behaviour towards unloved colleagues in an unloved organization, and if there is much of it about, the organization and its members begin to suffer.

This is cynicism, the treatment of an organization as instrumental to our needs, without love. It kills Rabbits.

The Unloved Rabbit

The final example features an organization whose purpose is to organize and represent academics in its area of study. It has survived for twelve years, and has had alternate periods of growth and consolidation. It runs annual conferences with 400—500 participants, a journal, a newsletter, special interest groups, research training, and so on. Its finances are in good order; its governing Council meets regularly and constitutionally. There is nothing terribly wrong with it.

And yet, throughout its life, those involved have puzzled over why it has not been more successful. When they look at the performance of several other academic and professional organizations, they see many things that they can only covet for their own academy. The annual conference features relatively few original contributions from well-known names in the field; the journal is good but is not top-rated even by its contributors. The academic field that the academy represents is large and growing, and its potential membership is ten times its actual membership. The annual conference has often been organized with care and attention, and yet was still a disappointment to its organizers.

Several theories had grown up among members of the Council as to why the organization was not as successful as it might be. They would elect a new chair of Council and immediately start blaming the new person for the underperformance of the organization. Eventually this had happened too many times, and this explanation became ineffective through over-use. Then they would blame the competition from other academic organizations that dealt in the same field of enquiry, but this too proved unsatisfactory when it became apparent that the senior members of those academies had tried to be helpful and constructive, but had eventually given up in frustration.

I have had many discussions with senior members of this academy about the reason why it has never been as good as it might have been. There is no single explanation dominating the accounts of the members, but many would agree with the President when he said: 'There's nothing wrong with this organization. In principle it ought to work. But nobody seems to care about it, not as much as they do about their own universities, and it just never takes off'.

The organization's biggest problem is that plenty of people are prepared to devote a little time and energy to it, but no one loves it sufficiently for it to come to life. It remains doggedly velveteen; it never quite gets loved to life. All its senior members love their own institutions, and other smaller academic societies or invisible colleges, more than they love this academy. People are concerned about it, and they give some time and energy to it, but no one gives it the extra special touch of love.

Stuffed Rabbits

We have considered a number of case stories, and discussed how organizations seem sometimes to become real for people as a result of being loved. The relationship is a little more complicated than this, because you have to see some reality to an organization before you can start loving it. The Boy must have started thinking of the Velveteen Rabbit as real in order to start loving it. The relationship between being real and being loved is a spiral, not a line.

Recently, the role of 'champion' in an organization has evolved into the role of someone who is charged with loving a project or an activity to life. The champion's approach is quite different from an instrumental attitude, where people use organizations solely to satisfy their needs, or as part of a career, where they expect to move on when they have gained the experience they need in order to fit themselves for another role elsewhere.

The story of the Velveteen Rabbit goes on beyond the section I heard on the radio. Later in the story, the Rabbit gets left in a field, where it meets some real rabbits who try to play with it; they quickly become bored, because the Velveteen Rabbit cannot move, and then scornful, when they realise that this is because it has no back legs.

The reality of loved organizations may also be found wanting by those who love. They are often capable of making quite distancing, ironic comments about them. When people speak affectionately of their organizations, they often seem as fond of the parts that do not work as of the parts that do. Their organization's lack of back legs is almost accepted as part of its lovability.

Reality and unreality are not simply a binary distinction. Velveteen Rabbits and organizations are only ever partly real, and that is part of their charm. If the Boy had been given a real rabbit for Christmas, he would have been confronted with far more problems in caring for it, he would not have been able to take it to bed with him, and may well not have loved it as much. In the context, then, of the story, a real rabbit would not have been as real as the Velveteen one.

Rabbit Droppings

We have talked about loving something into reality. Hating into reality is also quite achievable, though I have seen more examples of this being done to a part of the organization rather than to the whole. People will speak with passion about their antipathy to the senior management team, or to the finance department, in a way which confers quite a solid reality on those entities.

Beyond love and hate, there are many different emotions with which we can relate to organizations, and these are best understood by thinking of the way we place ourselves in our stories of organizations. As I have said else-where, 'People understand themselves and what they are doing by creating a narrative in which they are actors, and writing themselves into it' (Sims 2001). Some of these narratives are stories of passion. In them, our actions can be understood in reference with our relationship to, and feelings for, the object of passion. Some of these stories may be developed with a tragic plot, in which the passion is seen as bound to go wrong right from the outset. Others have a comic plot, in which the passion takes place against a back-ground of chance events that seem to have no concern for, or relation with, the love in the foreground. Others have a romantic plot, where heroism may conquer all (C. Northrop Frye, as summarized in Hart 1994).

In some cases, the relationship with the rabbit may be extremely destruc-tive to the person. There are many people whose stories of their organizations include the most damaging behaviour on the organization's part. For exam-ple, it is not uncommon to hear people talk about the stress they feel as a result of their work, and to tell a story in which they are essentially victims of a sadistic and unfeeling organization. The cruelty that they ascribe in their story to the organization does not necessarily lessen the passion of their rela-tionship with it. Enormous commitment to an organization seems to be quite compatible with having the view that they are treating you abominably. *'Though he slay me, yet will I trust in him' (Job, 13: 15).*

Being Loved and Being Alive

Let us go back to the Velveteen Rabbit. Does it mean anything, in organiza-tional terms, to talk of coming alive when loved? We will take our four case stories in turn, in order to see what we can learn from them on this.

With the school, the head's interest in being part of all the stories in the school, along with her infectious telling of the story of the school to all audi-ences (with references to uncut diamonds, and the flavour of an immensely exciting process of development, by means of which people of real signifi-cance were being formed), led to all students and staff coming to accept that they were part of an exciting story, and duly acting out their part in that story. For example, the charitable fund for parental contributions to provide for extra equipment for the school was called 'The Women of Vision Trust'. Even in a cynical culture nobody laughed at this. Mrs Holden's storytelling was too convincing for that. Love was shown, in this case, through the telling of a story that brings your organization to life for everyone else as well.

The stationer was regarded by all who dealt with him as an eccentric. He was proud of doing his own thing, of being beholden to no one. He claimed to be the most politically incorrect man in England, and would offend every-body. Yet never would he say a word against his organization, nor did he let any part of his organization treat customers or other stakeholders with the rudeness that he was himself prepared to dish out cheerfully to all. Service quality was always exemplary. He was happy to be seen as eccentric and boorish, but the story of his organization was one of total professionalism. Loving his organization meant, for him, treating his organization with far more respect and seriousness than he was prepared to award to himself.

In the case of the university, the first university referred to seemed to have benefited from the love of many members. It was the newer of the two—there were still a few members of staff who had been around when it first received its charter, and a few locals who could remember when it was being built. The story of the university had been quite triumphant, rising from obscurity to high popularity in less than a generation. It was full of stories of people who had devoted themselves to its development. The university to which the professor moved, on the other hand, was relatively amorphous. Some of its history was enshrined in the names of those who had sponsored major buildings, but otherwise it seemed ahistorical. Brian did not feel the need to write himself into its story. Love, in this case, is wanting to write yourself into the beloved's story.

The academy is the perfect illustration of a total absence of the Velveteen Rabbit syndrome. Its lifelessness was hard to put into words. Its members should have been well placed to understand what was missing and to do something about it, but they somehow could not put their fingers on the problem. It was used instrumentally by many people for many purposes. I could not find anybody at all who had an altruistic or loving relationship with it. Interestingly, some of its subparts were quite different from this. Sometimes a conference, or a training event, or a special interest group would be organized with loving commitment, and would spring to life. However, what lived was always the part, in effect a separate organization, never the whole.

My Rabbit Right or Wrong

In the story of the Velveteen Rabbit, there were plenty of other toys that the Boy could have loved, but did not. His behaviour towards these toys is clearly discriminatory, and this was a form of discrimination which was self-reinforcing. As his commitment to the Rabbit grew, so the chances of any of the other toys gaining his attention decreased. My account of the Velveteen Rabbit so far has underemphasized the losers.

Mrs Holden would probably have objected to this; who could possibly lose from her devotion to her school? She had no other employer, and no other commitments to social or political organizations that would clash with it. However, we do not have any direct access to what Mr Holden or the Holden children thought about this. I have no reason to suppose that they were neglected, but it is hard to imagine that they did not lose out to the school, in terms of Mrs Holden's time and passion. They would have had good reason to feel jealous.

The stationer was prepared to be exceptionally rude and vindictive towards those who threatened his business. For example, if he felt that one of his publications had been given an unfair review, he would attack the reviewer, and probably the journal in which it had been published, in the next few issues of his newsletter. His forthright language and his love of double entendres would lead some magazines to reject his advertisements, and he would then mock them for their prudishness for some time. One of Brian's reasons for moving from the more loveable to the less loveable university was to increase his time with his family. No one ever damaged any other institution because of their love for the academy.

Love is not a zero sum game. It is possible that passion for an organization may not lead to carelessness about other parts of life, but it is also too optimistic to imagine that there are no losers from such a passion.

During the recent football World Cup, an England supporter caused considerable damage to a Belgian bar where he had been watching an England game on television. He was asked by a reporter why he had been so destructive. In tears, struggling to be articulate through emotion and alcohol, his answer was: 'I love my country. I love my country.' In some recent financial scandals, documents have been destroyed by people who loved their companies enough to cover up what had been going on. Street thuggery by nationalist groups is often justified by group members as being perpetrated out of love for their nation. If we love an organization, we may be prepared to do all sorts of things to protect it against threats. As Bailey (1977) put it:

...many would not be able to act with such passionate intensity if they did not also sincerely believe that they were fuelled on altruism. But the fact remains that even such people will encounter others whom they perceive as motivated by self-interest, who advocate opposing policies, and who therefore must be tripped up, knifed in the back, or in some other way disposed of so that the general good may be served. (p.xii)

The more we believe that the organization we love is for the good of human kind, the more violent we will be prepared to be to further its interests. Love can be dangerously blind.

Intertwining Stories

Our Rabbit has set us off on a journey in which I was persuaded by a story, and then found myself reconstructing my understanding of cases that I had already witnessed. I had to change my mind about the way I understood organizations, but there was still one more discovery for me to make in my interaction with the Rabbit.

I was struck in the narratives that I gave as 'Rabbit Tales' above, and in others that I have not selected for use in this chapter, by a common feature of love or other passion for an organization: people feel passionately about organizations if they see their own story and the organization's story as intertwined.

In the case of the school, the head shows her interest in the school by wanting to be part of all the stories. She frequently writes herself the smallest possible part in those stories—for example, by being a silent member of the audience at the back of events—but she is showing her love for the institution by not wanting to miss out on being part of even the smallest stories taking place within it.

For the stationer, he is creating a life-story that is both his own and his organization's. In contrast with the academy, the identification between the two stories seems almost total. This is the kind of person for whom you feel concerned if their business fails, or if they are made redundant. Their life-story and their work-story are so bound up that it is impossible to imagine the one without the other. Love does not permit you to keep a safe distance.

In the University story, the professor's narrative tells of how much more productive he is in his individual academic work when he is relieved of the love that he had had for his previous university. He has told a story in which that love had been costly, but his story also included the idea that the reason why his previous university had been so time-consuming was because he had made himself a central part of its story, serving on committees, being a part of the emotional fabric of the institution, and so on. His story and the organization's story had been thoroughly intertwined.

With the academy, what is missing is the coherent development of a story. Another way of looking at this would be to say that it lacks anyone who is prepared to get 'him or herself' involved in its story. Everyone is keeping their distance, as if from someone they do not trust and with whom they are not sure of the implications of associating. It is too small a part of the lives of all participants to be a major story for them. There is no passionate intertwining of stories.

The Velveteen Rabbit appeared briefly in the Boy's story on Christmas morning, and made a rapid exit. Then, when the china dog could not be found, the Velveteen Rabbit's story became fully intertwined with the Boy's own. Children make up stories about their toys. Becoming real, for a toy or an organization, only happens when you are really loved (or occasionally hated). And that happens when someone is prepared to intertwine their story with yours, to take you as a part of their story, and to see themselves as a part of your story. That is passion.

References

Bailey, F. G. (1977). *Strategems and spoils*. Oxford: Blackwell.

Brunton, B. (2001). *Oecumuse Superletter 1*. Ely: Oecumuse.

Hart, J. (1994). *Northrop Frye: The Theoretical Imagination*. London: Routledge.

Linde, C. (1993). *Life stories*. New York: Oxford University Press.

Russell, B. (1946). *The philosophy of Bertrand Russell*, P. A. Schilpp (ed.). Evanston, IL: Library of Living Philosophers.

Sims, D. (2001). *Death by chocolate: Comfort thinking and sublimated passion in organizations*. Paper presented at the 9th International Workshop on Managerial and Organizational Cognition, Paris.

Weber, M. (1948). In C. Wright Mills (ed.), *From Max Weber: Essays in Sociology*. London: Routledge.

Williams, M. (1922). *The Velveteen Rabbit, or How Toys Become Real*. London: Mammoth.

FOURTEEN

Shy William and the Gaberlunzie Girl

Tony Watson

A pawky auld carle cam owre the lea,
Wi' mony fine stories unto me,
Seeking oot for a charity -
'Will you lodge a beggar man'?

The nicht being cauld and somewhat wat,
It's down by the fire the auld carle sat,
The dochter's shoulder he began to clap,
And aye he ranted and sang.

He grew keen and she grew fain,
And little did the auld wife ken
The things the twa o' them were sayin',
Sae the auld wife feared nae hairm.

'Gin I was as black as I am white,
As the snaw that lies on yonder dyke,
I wad dress myself as beggar like
And awa' wi' you I'd gang.'

O lassie, dear lassie ye're far ower young
An' ye hinna the cant o' the beggar tongue
The nicht is caul' and the road is lang,
An' wi' me ye canna gang.

I'll bend my back and boo my knee,
I'll put a black patch on my e'e,
Sae like a beggar I will be
An' awa wi' you I'll gang.

So then the twa made up a plot
To rise twa oors afore the folk,
And softly did they slip the lock
An' owre the muir they ran.

An' in the morn the auld folk rose,
They sawna the beggar an' his clothes,

They sawna the beggar an' his clothes,
'But is any o' oor guid gear gane?'

'Syne naething's awa that we can learn,
The kye are to milk and the milk is to kirn;
Gae to the hoose, man, an' wauken the bairn,
And bid her come speedily ben.

He gaed to the room where his dochter lay,
The sheets were cauld, and she was away,
'Guidwife, guidwife' the auld man did say,
'She's awa' wi' the beggar man.'

Then some rode on horseback and some ran on foot,
A' but the auld wife, who wisna fit,
She hirpled aboot maist oot o' her wit,
'I'll ne'er lodge a beggar again.'

When three lang years were come and gane,
Back cam' the gaberlunzie again,
Sayin' "Auld guidwife for charity,
Wad you lodge a silly puir man?"

'An auld gaberlunzie I'll ne'er lodge again
I hadna a dochter but ane o' my ain,
An' awa' wi' a beggar man she's gane,
An' I dinna ken whence nor where.'

And either (i)

Auld wifie, oh wifie, what would ye gie,
To see your daughter back hame wi' ye,
Wi a bairn on her back and anither on her knee,
And anither comin' hame?

Or (ii)

'O yonder she's comin' owre the lea,
Wi' mony a fine tale unto thee,
Wi' a bonnie bairnie on ilka knee,
An' anither one comin' alang.

'O yonder she's comin' owre yon lea,
Wi' silks and satins doon to her knee.'
She held up her hands and she blest the oor,
That she followed a beggar man.

Synopsis: A beggar or gaberlunzie arrives and the door of a farmhouse asking for charity, and a night's lodging. He and the daughter of the house get involved with each other and plot to rise early in the morning to run away together. They do this and when the parents rise from their beds they find the man gone. No property is missing, but the daughter has disappeared. As a search for the young woman proceeds, her mother vows never to give lodging to a gaberlunzie again. But three years later the same man arrives with exactly such a request. Then, *in some versions of the ballad*, the beggar taunts the mother with images of her daughter living a beggar's life and producing baby after baby, *and in other versions*, it transpires that the beggar was no gaberlunzie at all but a rich man who is now returning with the daughter—his rich and happy wife—and their children.

William Lepple is the chairman of Gaberlunzie Books and Music, and he tells his story, one in which the ballads of the Gaberlunzie Man play a significant role. Here, though, there is no gaberlunzie man, but a gaberlunzie girl.

Let me tell you the story as best I can. It all began decades ago. And I must point out that we are dealing with territory where memory plays all sorts of tricks. It's not just my own memory that is involved here. I go over the story from time to time with some of the others involved—my wife especially. And our children, our friends, and people interested in the family business seem fascinated by our history. Every time we revisit the past some new reading seems to offer itself. We are still trying to make sense of it all. What we make of those events still has a bearing on our understanding of where we are now and, indeed, on our ideas about who we are.

It is impossible when telling the tale to forget certain continuities between our family history and some old Scottish folklore themes. My grandmother was the person responsible for bringing in this angle. It goes right back to the early stages of these events when I escaped up to Scotland for a weekend with her. 'Doesn't what you are telling me about remind you of the gaberlunzie man?', she asked me. At first I thought she was just trying to change the subject, having got tired of hearing about my fascination with the strange young woman who had recently turned up behind the counter of the stationary stores of the company where I was working as a rather unhappy training officer. I was spending my working life presenting staff courses on things like 'communication skills' and despairing of ever finding a way of making a living that would allow me to use my music degree or follow up my postgraduate dissertation on traditional folk song and music.

I found myself stopped in my tracks by my grandmother and her mention of the old song. She had listened to me going on about how this young woman was beautiful and seemed to have a deep self-confidence yet, at the same time, appeared to have little idea of how to do the simplest clerical tasks or to be able to find anything she was asked for from the shelves of the stores. She dressed in a dreadfully scruffy way, even for those days. And I admit that I used to wonder early on just how clean she was. She would say nothing of where she came from and she would not tell me where she lived. All she would say was she had to get away from where she was staying. Without really thinking about what I was doing, I said half jokingly that there was a spare room in my parents' house and that she could always become our lodger. It came as a bombshell to me when she said, 'Yes, that's what I'll do'. I could not get out of this—and my parents felt bound to go along with my spontaneous generosity. But they were not easy about it. And here was my grandmother reminding me of the tale of the gaberlunzie man. What might this mean?

A chapter of my undergraduate dissertation had examined the old Scottish folk ballad that related how the daughter of a farming family ran away with a beggar or gaberlunzie who had been given overnight lodging in the farm house. In modern terms, we might translate the line 'He grew keen and she grew fain' as 'they fell in love'. So was my grandmother, who had sung to me a version of the gaberlunzie song when I was doing my studies, pointing out to me that I was falling in love with the lodger in my parents' house? She would not say what she was getting at and left me to reflect, as I lay in bed that night, on just what I both felt *and knew* about our lodger. Yes, my feelings were powerful and it was true that I could not stop thinking about Jeannie. I had a strong sense that we were increasingly physically and emotionally drawn to each other. But who was she? Presumably my grandmother was noting the parallel between the song's gaberlunzie man and my gaberlunzie girl. She was unkempt and, early on anyway, bordering on the unwashed. Did this suggest that she had lived a fairly hard life up until now? Possibly. But the fact that she had difficulty even making a cup of tea for her workmates in the stores at work suggested that she might have lived a rather sheltered life. So here might be the other parallel between what was happening and the gaberlunzie songs—a parallel in the area of the gaberlunzies' mysterious origins.

In preparing my thesis chapter on the Scottish beggarman ballads, I observed that there were two gaberlunzies in the songs. First there was the gaberlunzie who was straightforwardly a beggar. He appeared in a proportion of the song variants collected in the second volume of the *Greig-Duncan Folk Song Collection* from Aberdeenshire and its vicinity and returns to the farmhouse after three years to taunt the girl's family with fact that she is sharing a beggar's life with him and their growing and burdensome family. Second, in the larger number of ballad variants, the lodger was not really a beggar at all. He was actually a rich man choosing to travel the country incognito. He might even have been a king. The great ballad collector and authority, Child, noted that the song was often 'attributed to our King James V the Fifth, who had the reputation of being fond of wandering about the country in disguises that enabled him to discover other people's faults and hide some of his own'.

In my dissertation I pointed to the existence of other songs and tales that followed the broad theme of a beggar turning out to be 'The Laird of Grant' or 'The brawest gentleman among them a''. But I made much of the footnote in Ord's *Bothy Songs and Ballads* to a version of the ballad with the 'rich laird' type of ending. The footnote recognizes the existence of 'several versions' of the ballad, but Ord says that the one printed is 'the most common in the bothies and farm kitchens in the North of Scotland'. This is why, he says, he has 'given it preference'. My argument was that there might well be a tendency (among performers and collectors alike) to 'give preference' to versions of stories—especially love stories—with happy endings. I argued that the greater popularity of one version of a tale, rather than another, can in no way be taken to indicate that this is either the more 'original' or the more 'authentic' version of the text. I theorized along the lines that folk ballads in the oral tradition were cultural artefacts with a flexibility that enabled the performer to 'flex' their storytelling in various ways, sometimes by altering words or emphases within stanzas, sometimes by adding in or leaving out stanzas. Thus we sometimes see the 'happy ending' of the beggar man songs sometimes left in and sometimes find it left out.

The supervisor of my dissertation called my analysis a 'postmodern' one and pointed to the parallel between the 'multiple choice endings' I was finding in the ballad record and the choice of endings offered in postmodern novels like Fowles' *The French Lieutenant's Woman*. If postmodernism is about coming to terms with the essential ambiguity and contingency of human life, then perhaps the 'pre-modern' oral ballad tradition was similarly at ease with the precariousness of existence. And I went on, in the conclusion of my dissertation, to argue that the fairly 'open texture' of the ballads left space for any given listener or reader to handle the ambiguity of the 'text' by choosing their own reading of any given set of words. A good example of this was the very line I came to discuss later with my grandmother. You could read the line 'He grew keen and she grew fain' to suggest that the beggar and the young woman 'fell in love' with each other. But you could equally read it to mean that they simply got sexually fascinated with each other. I illustrated this general point in my thesis by pointing to how the attribution of the gaberlunzie ballad to a Scottish king is interpreted differently by different collectors. Child, we saw, inferred the motive behind the legendary activities of King James to be one of discovering 'other people's faults' and hiding 'some of his own'. But Ord says that the song, when attributed to the king, 'is supposed to celebrate one of His majesty's own adventures in clandestine love-making'. Quite another matter!

All of these things from my scholarly past went through my mind as I lay in bed at my grandmother's house reflecting on the lodger in my parent's house. I'd written in my dissertation about the ambiguity of life and relationships as this was reflected in the ballad texts. My life, and one relationship in particular, was now the text I had to analyse. And it was full of ambiguities paralleling those in the gaberlunzie ballad. Was Jeannie a rich or privileged girl trying out working class life, or was she just a teenage 'lost soul' from a relatively ordinary background. Her speaking accent was rather indeterminate. The 'estuarine' use of glottal stops and twisted vowels could either have been something she grew up with or something she was affecting (like several of my middle-class student friends had). But, whoever she was, she wasn't 'slumming it' by lodging with my parents. Our house was a prosperous working-class council house, paralleling the relatively prosperous farming household in the ballad. But what if she were the daughter of a 'big hoose' or a castle, lodging for the moment in a council house? What might her motives for this be? And, most importantly, what might her motives be for getting emotionally, and perhaps soon sexually, involved with me? Was she on an adventure investigating human weakness, as Child inferred the mythical ballad-writing king was, or was she interested, as Ord says the legendary king was, in 'adventures in clandestine love-making'?

In spite of a sleepless night at my grandmother's, I returned south little clearer about what was happening. But on my first night back I was taken totally by surprise when Jeannie crept into my bed in the middle of the night. This event pushed all thought of textual ambiguities and Scottish folklore out of my mind. But the gaberlunzie stories came crashing back into my mind a couple of weeks later. It happened after I had recklessly asked her to marry me, on the way home from a party. She laughed at me. And then she started to cry. Only after the alternating tears and strange giggles had died down did she tell me that she had come to work at the factory after absconding from the Swiss 'finishing school' to which her wealthy parents had sent her. Her explanation for this was not terribly coherent. It started with an emphasis on a desire to 'get a life'. But at another point it became 'I realised I wanted a man'.

We did not sleep together the night of my proposal and Jeannie's 'confession'. And I found myself returning to my old scholarly interest in the ambiguity of texts as I lay alone in bed. The text I deconstructed, reconstructed, and deconstructed again was not a fusty old ballad this time. It was that simple line, 'I wanted a man'. Was this a statement of simple sexual desire—an expression of straightforward lust? Or was it that she was looking for 'the man of her life'. Or, yet again, was it just that she fancied getting married (a woman's 'man', in the Scottish usage I grew up with, was her husband). The ambiguities were very much like those of the gaberlunzie texts. One can read the ballad to suggest that the gaberlunzie travelled around in disguise simply to engage in 'clandestine love-making'. Alternatively, one can infer that he was going out in disguise (like the prince in Cinderella) to find a woman who would love him for 'who he was' as a person, as opposed 'what he was' as a king or a laird. Either of these things might apply to Jeannie. But I then realised that one did not have to make a simple either–or choice between these two possibilities. It was quite possible that the gaberlunzie, or Jeannie, was originally seeking sexual adventure and then, unexpectedly, fell in love with one of his/her seductees. I then came to recognize that what I wanted was for Jeannie to end up loving me, one way or the other.

I think it was Umberto Eco who pointed out that a postmodern man cannot speak straightforwardly to a woman about loving her. He is always conscious of all the texts, songs, and films that his words are echoing when he speaks. I agree with this now. But then I put aside the more reflective side of my old scholarly self and threw myself into the relationship with my gaberlunzie girl. Her father was the chairman of a large publishing company and he immediately took to me when Jeannie was eventually persuaded to return to the family fold—with me at her side. At the time I thought it was a wonderful piece of luck that her father liked me so much and I wondered whether it might be in part because he saw me as the son which, as yet, he did not have. Later, though, I came to wonder whether it meant that Jeannie might have been pressured by this development into accepting my second proposal of marriage. I will return to this point. For now, though, let me explain that before the wedding took place, Jeannie's father established Jeannie and me in a music publishing business of our own. After many hours of discussion and what, at various points, felt like vigorous interrogation, he put up the investment and used a range of his business contacts to help us. And he was most amused when I explained to him why I called the business Gaberlunzie Music. Jeannie was, at first, less amused. But I then noticed that at dinner parties, in talking to journalists, and at functions that she attended with me as the joint managing director of the firm, she would tell the tale of how we first met. In this she was always the 'gaberlunzie girl'. Early on, her story had me as a conquest that she had made: 'and then in that factory, I met the wonderful shy William, who has turned out to be this wonderful husband and business partner'. But as time went by I was increasingly portrayed as someone who had attached himself to her and could not then be shaken off: 'I was wondering why I had let myself become so involved with this shy and awkward school-teacher type when Daddy decided that William was very much like himself and would therefore turn out to be a successful business man, if we all helped and supported him'.

You will not be surprised to hear that my sensitivity to this shift of emphasis in my wife's public accounts of our romantic history put strains on our marriage, strains that clearly related to the ambiguity that had been there in our relationship from the start. But the tale of our personal relationship is also partly of the history of the Gaberlunzie business. And our personal difficulties put strains on the business too, because of our roles as joint managing directors. All my doubts about the ambiguities surrounding our first meeting came back and I found myself doubting whether I could trust her—in personal and business matters alike. She recognized this and grew increasingly remote in her manner towards me. I recognized that it would be wise for us to take a holiday and to go back over our whole history together. We might try to negotiate an agreed history of our relationship that could be told to others and could also frame the meaning of our marriage for ourselves. But before I got around to suggesting this, a crisis arose.

The crisis, which had implications equally for the marriage and the business, arose shortly after we had merged with a division of Jeannie's father's business to become *Gaberlunzie Music and Books*. This division specialized in books about music and Jeannie's father felt that it fitted better into the Gaberlunzie portfolio than into his own, mainly fiction-publishing, portfolio. The longstanding head of the division was retiring, so it was an opportune time for the merger to occur. So why was there a crisis? The problems first surfaced in the business part of our relationship, when it transpired that Jeannie had appointed a head of the new Gaberlunzie books division without consulting me. I was outraged about not being involved in such a significant appointment. I was then further appalled to discover that the man she had appointed was in my view rather young and, dare I say, 'unpolished', and was being given a massive promotion. But I was then devastated to learn, in the course of a blazing row with Jeannie, that she had been having a sexual affair with this man.

It was most unfortunate that the row between Jeannie and me happened in the lounge of a hotel where we had attended a dinner and a book prize ceremony. We had both had plenty to drink and a whole lot of people from the books business heard us shouting at each other and saw me walk out shouting 'I never want to see you again'. But, much worse, members of the press also witnessed the fracas. As well as unpleasant stories about our marriage appearing in the gossip parts of the trade press, rumours of a possible business break-up soon reached investors. Thus, Jeannie and I found ourselves facing both a possible divorce and the continuing shared responsibility for a business whose share price was crashing. What a mess!

This nightmare happened about ten years ago and I struggle to remember exactly what occurred. I do remember that I was serious about never wanting to see Jeannie again. My mind was now clear about the gaberlunzie character. The 'pawky auld carle' of centuries ago was a sexual predator. And so was the engaging escapee from finishing school that I had married. Maybe or maybe not the king/laird figure came to love and cherish the girl who fell for his charms. I had totally fallen for the charms of the Jeannie figure but she had certainly not come to love and cherish me. It was her father's identifying with me that pushed her into this disastrous marital and business partnership. And I was a fool, a mug, a shy scholarly working class boy seduced by a sexy adventurer and the promise of a wealthy lifestyle.

I thought that I had settled on this sad reading of the gaberlunzie tales and this bitter interpretation of my life and character. But I soon realised that I could not use such a pathetic narrative of betrayal as an excuse to give up. I could neither walk away from my responsibilities to the Gaberlunzie business nor walk away from Jeannie, at least from the Jeannie who was my co-managing director. She recognized this situation too and we went away for a weekend to talk everything over. Inevitably, the gaberlunzie story came into our discussions and we used it as a lever to prise open the mysteries of our meeting and early involvement.

In spite of the fact that Jeannie became pregnant with our first child that weekend, the occasion cannot be represented as a magic fairy-tale reconciliation after which we would walk away and 'live happily ever after'. Bitter things were said on both sides. But we agreed that we would give our main attention to the business. Only when we had got the share price fully restored would we return to the matter of our personal relationship. Whether we liked it or not, regaining confidence in the business would mean assuring everyone that the marriage was sound. This, in fact, worked out well and the business has gone from success to success since its near demise following Jeannie's affair and our subsequent public squabbling. However, the discovery of the pregnancy completely put paid to any thoughts of ending the marriage.

We still have our 'ups and downs' and still occasionally go back to do repair-work on the narrative of our life together. Inevitably, the gaberlunzie man and the gaberlunzie girl come into this. And our three children have all enjoyed the ballad as a bedtime story. However, they never know whether to believe Jeannie and me when we tell them how, after the first of our children was born and I asked whether she thought we'd have more children, she simply looked at me and quietly sang, 'Oh yonder she's comin' owre the lea, Wi' mony a fine tale unto thee, Wi' a bonnie bairnie on ilka knee, and anither one coming' alang'. Three bairnies it was to be.

Oh the Tales we Tell!

When we tell stories about our lives or about the work organizations with which we are involved we tell people a lot. But we hide a lot too. And the stories to which we listen also tell us a lot. But, by the same token, they too leave a lot hidden. But it is not only a matter of what is hidden in the story, it is a matter of what is left *open* for the listener to work upon (or play with, indeed). William Lepple was prompted by his grandmother to reread the ballad of the gaberlunzie man to help him make sense of current events in his life. He found a lot there to think about—as a result of both what the story did and did not say. As a student he had written about ambiguity and the 'openness' of texts in a scholarly way. Now he was experiencing that openness as a reminder about the openness or ambiguity of his own life situation and that of the Gaberlunzie Books and Music organization. The ambiguities both within and across versions of the gaberlunzie ballads merely made him more aware than he might otherwise have been of the mysteries surrounding the gaberlunzie girl who had come into his life and, also, of the personal and family relationships out of which the Gaberlunzie business emerged. He saw that the text that was his own life could be 'constructed and deconstructed' in the same way as the texts in the ballad books and folksong collections (Ord 1930; Child 1965; Shuldam-Shaw and Lyle 1983). The organization, too, is constructed and deconstructed for us in the story that William tells us and, of course, we do our own constructing and deconstructing of the organization as we actively read his account.

The multiple readings that can be made of texts are not only about events. They are also about the identities and 'moral characters' of the people in the stories. The gaberlunzie ballads provide different versions of who the beggar really was and different implicit judgements about his worthiness—they make different judgements about his 'moral' authenticity as well as about his authenticity, or otherwise, as a beggar. And William uses this 'openness' to probe the authenticity, in both senses, of Jeannie, the gaberlunzie girl. He does this early on as he is coming to terms with his growing interest in the young woman from the factory. But he does not so much come to a firm conclusion (at least about her 'motives') as suspend judgement as he allows himself to fall in love with her. But later on he returns to using the notion of textual openness to probe his circumstances when he discovers that Jeannie, his wife of some years, has been having an adulterous relationship. This time, William quickly comes to some very specific conclusions. There is no longer any ambiguity in the ballad: the beggar was a sexual adventurer, a rogue. There is no longer ambiguity about his wife: she has been a sexual adventurer all along. And this had profound implications for the organization as well as for the personal relationship between William and Jeannie. The reading that William was now making of his situation was one in which he was coming to terms with the danger that had been present all the time beneath the surface of the relatively happy events of his relationship with Jeannie and the success of their joint business activities.

Early in his story, William wonders about the significance of his grand-mother's reminding him of the gaberlunzie ballad. 'What might this mean?', he asked. One possibility is that his grandmother was drawing his attention to the old ballad to warn him of the possibility that he would be sailing into dangerous waters by embarking on a relationship with the mysterious young woman that he had been talking about. Storytelling generally can be under-stood as playing a role of handling the dangers of human existence. This was a theme I took up when warning that managers who attempt to manip-ulate the cultures of organizations are entering 'deep and dangerous waters' (Watson 2001). Following Berger's (1973) recognition that the 'socially estab-lished nomos' of human culture operates as a 'shield against terror', I argued that, in effect, we allow our culture to 'do our worrying for us' with regard to those sources of angst that could drive us to madness if we were denied a cul-tural shield. We 'talk to our culture' about our worries through 'looking at, reading about, engaging in stories in novels, newspapers, films, jokes and gos-sip—stories about love, death, hate, infidelity, illness, bliss' (Watson 2001: 21). There is a 'mythic' dimension to all these cultural products, and the way they function for us as adults is similar to the way fairy tales function for children (Propp 1968; Bettelheim 1976): 'Our anxieties are raised as the ogre storms from his castle, the murderer creeps up behind the victim, the adul-terous seducer slips in and out of the bedroom of the erstwhile faithful spouse' but 'order and calm is restored to our lives as the fairy tale ends with "and they all lived happily ever after"', the murder film comes to a close or we shut our newspaper and go to empty the dishwasher' (Watson 2001: 22). This 'closure' happens in many of the stories that we engage with.

Closure of the type we most clearly see in fairy tales does not of course hap-pen in the much messier lives of the readers or 'users' of stories—this perhaps being a key reason for people having to go on and on engaging with stories as they go through their lives. This is something of which William himself is apparently aware and which encourages him to be cautious about claiming a 'magic fairy-tale reconciliation' between himself and his wife. He talks of 'bitter things' that were said, tells us that the couple still have 'ups and downs', and reveals that the couple 'occasionally go back to do repair-work on the narrative of our life together'. And, yes, the gaberlunzie story is drawn upon as a resource when this is done. Both the dangers that the story forces them to contemplate and the closure or resolution that it offers are used by William and Jeannie to help them handle the dangers that still lurk in their lives, and help them adjust to the impossibility of a 'lived happily ever after' resolution in their 'real lives'.

In writing the above paragraph I have intertwined my own theorizing about storytelling and human culture with the theorizing of William Lepple. But who is William Lepple? He is a fictional character that I have made, if not 'made up'. He is not based on anyone I know. And whilst his life in no way parallels my own, especially with regard to his business life, his academic career, his love life, and his family relationships, he does share with me a fascination with Scottish folksong and having had a grandmother who grew up with and wanted to pass on a delight in songs and ballads like the gaberlunzie one. But where William is a businessman with a background in music and folkloristic studies, I am a sociologist who has at the centre of his research interests a concern with the interplay that occurs between the emergent biographies and identities of people managing organizations and the emergent strategies of the organizations that they both shape and are shaped by (Watson 2002, 2003). This was one of the themes of an ethnographic study of managers and managing in a large corporation (Watson 2001) and is central to a current ethnographic study of a smaller business organization. Partly because much of the research material that I have gathered in investigating these matters is too sensitive to be directly reported (Watson 1995), I have developed a hybrid form of research writing I call 'ethnographic fiction science' (Watson 2000, 2003) and, in the present piece, I have taken the next logical step of trying to engage with these same issues in a more-or-less straightforwardly fictional manner.

Although the narrative with which William Lepple presents us is very much a matter of stories, the piece as a whole is intended to explore the ways in which managers' and strategy-makers' working and non-working lives and identities relate to the way organizations are shaped, and vice versa. And there is also exploration of the more specific issue of how, in shaping both our lives and our business activities, we constantly tell and retell stories about ourselves and our enterprises. These stories are much more than reflections upon 'what really happened'. Stories obviously report events and characters. But they also help in the very *making* of those events and characters. One suspects that the telling and the retelling of stories about beggars who were really princes, lairds, and kings attempting to share some ordinary humanity with their subjects helped 'make' or legitimize authority relations in the societies in which they were current. And one would like to think that at least some of

the singers or storytellers who passed on versions of the ballad which portrayed the gaberlunzie as little more than a scheming beggar were displaying
a degree of political and social *resistance* by refusing to help humanize the
more privileged members in their societies.

The power that stories can take on in a modern organizational setting is very
effectively illustrated by the newspaper stories that came to be published as the
personal lives of the two key figures in the Gaberlunzie organization got into
difficulties. The marital problems of William and Jeannie were inevitably
going to create problems for the company of which they were joint managing
directors. But these problems were enormously exacerbated by the publishing
of stories that severely damaged investor confidence in the business. To what
extent, the reader speculates, was it the adulterous affair that threatened the
organization's survival, and to what extent was it the stories that were cir-
culated about it? Certainly, William and Jeannie saw the need to act in a way
that would enable them to rewrite the tales that were being told. It was vitally
important to produce a narrative that portrayed to the world both a happy
family and a healthy organization. They were greatly helped in this by the
contingency of the surprise pregnancy. And the appearance of this child, and
two subsequent children, links these events back to the gaberlunzie ballad for
William and Jeannie—and for us too.

The 'living presence' of the pre-modern gaberlunzie ballad in the fictional
modern Lepple family and the Gaberlunzie business helped shape a marriage,
a business, a near business failure, a business rebirth, and a family history
with which the fictional Lepple children are now growing up. The old ballads
dealt with the ambiguity of the human world, the contingency of that world,
and the precariousness of human existence. Contemporary stories necessarily
do the same, as postmodernist thinking reminds us. So perhaps we can think
of the old ballad makers as postmodernists *avant la lettre*. Oh the tales they
told!

References

Bettlehim, B. (1976). *On the Uses of Enchantment: The Meaning and Importance of
   Fairy Tales*. New York: Knopf.
Child, F. J. (1965). *The English and Scottish Popular Ballads*, 5 volumes. New York:
   Dover (originally 1882–98).
Ord, J. (1930). *Ord's Bothy Songs and Ballads*. Edinburgh: John Donald Publishing.
Propp, V. (1968). *Morphology of the Folk Tale*. Austin: University of Texas Press.
Shuldam-Shaw, P. and Lyle, E. B. (1983). *The Greig-Duncan Folk Song Collection,
   Volume 2*. Aberdeen: Aberdeen University Press.
Watson, T. J. (1995). 'Shaping the story: Rhetoric, persuasion and creative writing
   in organisational ethnography'. *Studies in Cultures, Organisations and Society*,
   1(2): 301–11.

——(2000), 'Ethnographic fiction science: Making sense of managerial work and organisational research processes with Caroline and Terry'. *Organisation*, 7(3): 513–34.

——(2001). originally 1994). *In Search of Management*. London: Thomson Learning.

——(2002). *Organising and Managing Work: Organisational, managerial and strategic behaviour in theory and practice*. Harlow: FT Prentice-Hall.

——(2003). 'Strategists and strategy-making: strategic exchange and the shaping of individual lives and organisational futures'. *Journal of Management Studies*, 30(3): pp 1305–23.

INDEX

accident 140, 183
achievement (*see also* heroism) 81ff, 125, 145
Achilles 116
adolescence 180f, 182
Adorno, T. 149
adventure 35, 129, 132, 187, 228
Aeschylus 168
Aesop 1
aesthetic knowledge 44
aggressiveness 144
Ailill 117
Albers, A. 159f
Albers, J. 159
Alexander the Great 127
al-Qaida 85f, 90ff, 95ff
    as leaderless group 92ff
anger 152, 158f, 194
antenarrative 2, 3
anti-hero 126ff
Aquino, C. 155
Arachne 131f, 134, 151–63, 179
Arafat, Y. 95
archetypes viii, 6, 119, 124, 156f, 160, 192
Archimedes 11
Aristotle 20, 112, 131
art
    and truth 17, 20
    women's 159
arts
    Promethean as technique 167ff, 170
    asceticism 71ff
assassins 90
asymmetric warfare 90
Athene (*see also* Minerva) 87, 154ff
audience 19, 177
Augustine 75
authenticity 158, 160, 231
author 189
authority 178, 233
    abuse of 110
    of experience 12, 22ff, 26ff
    of the expert 12, 26ff
    founded on friendship 112

male 153
    of the speaker 26ff
autopoeisis 173
Azzam, A. 92

Bali
    bomb attacks 96
ballads, Scottish 225ff
Barthes, R. 189
Baudrillard, J. 26, 97
Bauman, Z. 144f, 147f, 158, 161
Becker, E. 121fn
Beckett, S. 126f
Beckham, D. 125f
Beethoven, L. van 83, 122f
Beowulf 121
Bhutto, B, 155
bin Laden, O. 92ff, 95
Blair, T. 156, 180
Blake, W. 166
Blake, W. 176
Blumenberg, H. 167f
Boisjoly, R. 186f
Boje, D. xi, 2, 23, 49
Boleyn, A. 157
boundaries (*see also* stories and boundaries) 120, 121, 129, 131, 132
Bourdieu P. 41
Bourgeois, L. 152
bricolage 5
Brown, R. 34
Brundtland, G. H. 155
Buddha and Buddhism 54ff
bureaucracy 24, 125, 211
Burrell, G. 13, 60ff
Bush, G. W. 187
business (*see also* management)
    as arena for heroism 125
Byatt, A. S. 152, 158f, 161
Byron, Lord 123

Callimachus 194ff, 197, 203
Calori, R. ix, x
Campbell, D. 183
Campbell, J. 119, 129